UNITED APART

UNITED APART

Gender and the Rise of Craft Unionism

ILEEN A. DEVAULT

Cornell University Press

ITHACA AND LONDON

First published 2004 by Cornell University Press
First printing, Cornell Paperbacks, 2004

Printed in the United States of America

Library of Congress Cataloging-in-Publication Data
DeVault, Ileen A.
    United apart: gender and the rise of craft unionism / Ileen A. DeVault.
        p. cm.
    Includes bibliographical references and index.
    ISBN 0-8014-2768-1 (cloth : alk. paper)–ISBN 0-8014-8926-1 pbk.: alk. paper)
    1. Women labor union members—United States—History. 2. Sexism—United States—History.
3. Strikes and lockouts—United States—History. 4. Labor unions—United States—History.
5. Women employees—United States—History. I. Title.
    HD6079.2.U5D48 2004
    331.4'7'0973—dc22   2004001134

Cornell University Press strives to use environmentally responsible
suppliers and materials to the fullest extent possible in the publishing
of its books. Such materials include vegetable-based, low-VOC inks
and acid-free papers that are recycled, totally chlorine-free, or partly
composed of nonwood fibers. For further information, visit our website
at www.cornellpress.cornell.edu.

Cloth printing   10 9 8 7 6 5 4 3 2 1

Paperback printing   10 9 8 7 6 5 4 3 2 1

Contents

Illustrations

Acknowledgments

History is always both a solitary pursuit and one that lends itself to company along the way. Working on this project off and on for more than fifteen years, I have accumulated many debts of gratitude.

I have consistently received research support funds of various kinds from Cornell University's School of Industrial and Labor Relations (ILR), for which I am extremely grateful. A visiting scholarship for the 1993–94 year at the Institute of Research on Women at Rutgers University gave me an institutional home during my sabbatical leave. A fellowship with the New York Public Library Dorothy and Lewis B. Cullman Center for Scholars and Writers provided me with access to the Library's collections, an inspiring group of colleagues, and an office with a view of Fifth Avenue in which I wrote the bulk of the manuscript over the course of the 2000–2001 year. I will never be able to thank Peter Gay, the Library, the Cullmans, and the entire "second class" of Center scholars enough. Without that opportunity, I would still be toiling away on the draft of this book.

A number of librarians deserve special thanks here, including Barbara Morley, Patrizia Sione, and Richard Strassberg of the Kheel Center for Labor-Management Documentation and Archives at the ILR School's Catherwood Library. They are always friendly and always helpful. Catherwood's Helen Hamilton also spent years ordering newspapers for me on interlibrary loan. Martha Mayo at the University of Massachusetts at Lowell, Center for Lowell History, provided various types of assistance, as well as a fantastic Vietnamese lunch while I was in Lowell. Laura Linard and the staff at the Historical Collections Department of Baker Library at the Harvard Business School helped me access their wonderful records. Ruth Carr, chief librarian of the Irma and Paul Milstein Division of United States History, Local History, and Genealogy at the New York Public Library helped me locate three particular tenement buildings in the 1900 Federal Manuscript Census. My research trip to the New Bedford Whaling Museum to consult the Pierce Manufacturing Corporation records did not result in any useful information, but it did provide an afternoon's amusement for my family. Many archivists and librarians around the United States attempted to find materials for this project. Lisa Backman, manuscript specialist in the Western History Division of the Denver Public Library, sent me copies of items in her collection, as did Anne Salter of the Georgia Institute of Technology Library. Wright Langley of the Historic Florida Keys Preservation Board sent me a copy of

L. Glenn Westfall's book on Key West, and Tom Hambright of the Local and State History Department of the Monroe County May Hill Russell Library also sent bibliographical suggestions. Michael C. Lord, executive secretary of the Androscoggin Historical Society, searched valiantly for relevant information for me.

I would also like to thank Aad Blok, managing editor of the *International Review of Social History,* for allowing me to reprint parts of the article "Narratives Serially Constructed and Lived: Ethnicity in Cross-gender Strikes, 1887–1903," which I wrote for his journal. Similarly, sections of chapter 3 first appeared in " 'To Sit Among Men': Skill, Gender, and Craft Unionism in the Early American Federation of Labor," in *Labor Histories*, edited by Eric Arnesen, Julia Greene, and Bruce Laurie. I am grateful to the University of Illinois Press for its permission to reprint those sections here.

Many historians and others have shared their own research and knowledge with me over the years. This group includes but is not limited to Eric Arnesen, Ava Baron, Mary Blewett, Jeanne Boydston, Pat Cooper, Dana Frank, Lori Ginzberg, Julie Greene, Nancy Hewitt, Dan Letwin, Michael Lounsbury, Anne Mendelson, and Grace Pallidino. The informal "Lunch Bunch" of the ILR School, headed by George Boyer and including Sarosh Kuruvilla, the late Jim McPherson, Marty Wells, and Larry Williams, provided me with a few good research tips and lots of laughs, not to mention some serious conversations.

Over the years, the ILR School also provided me with a small army of research assistants, including Linda Bresson-Allard, Elizabeth Chimienti, Anne Farley, Joshua Fowler, Dan Goldhaber, Mary E. Graham, Annie Hsu, Hye-Young Kang, Chang-Kil Lee, Rebecca Michaels, Ann Oberfeld, Michael Roland, Hyea-Sook Ryoo, and Dara Silberstein. Tricia Rietz, then a graduate student at the University of Nebraska at Lincoln, did invaluable newspaper research for me in Omaha newspapers that were not available on interlibrary loan.

My sister, Marjorie DeVault, put me in touch with Joe Stoll, of the University of Syracuse Cartography Lab. With amazing good humor, Joe put up with poor photocopies and many changes to produce the maps in this book. Oya Rieger of Cornell University Library's Digital Library and Information Technologies staff provided considerable assistance with obtaining key illustrations. The Kheel Center's Barb Morley not only helped me track down illustrations from the Center's collections but also did a fantastic job helping me with digital reproductions from microfilm.

A number of friends and colleagues read all or parts of this manuscript in earlier forms. Mary Blewett, Jeanne Boydston, George Boyer, Marjorie DeVault, Lori Ginzberg, David Montgomery, and Nick Salvatore all read one or more chapters. Eric Arnesen, Susan Porter Benson, Eileen Boris, Pat Cooper, and Michael Lounsbury read the entire manuscript and contributed far more than two cents' worth. Students in my class titled "The History of

Women and Unions" during the spring 2003 semester also read the entire manuscript. Though I freely admit that I sometimes chose to ignore some advice, feedback, and suggestions, the encouragement I received from all these readers helped me make this a better book.

When I began writing my previous book, *Sons and Daughters of Labor*, Jackie Dodge had the thankless task of typing and retyping. Throughout this project, computers have always existed, and so no one person has had to type every word. Several, however, have provided administrative assistance, including Lori Ard, Brigid Beechler, and Jackie Dodge. Rhonda Clouse spent almost two years helping to insert editorial changes in the manuscript, typing in final footnotes, helping me with last-minute formatting problems, and generally dealing with my almost daily craziness. She is another person I will never be able to thank enough.

Peter Agree first signed this book with Cornell University Press back in 1991, taking the chance that I would come through on my vague proposal. Sheri Englund took over this project a few years ago. She has prodded and pushed and made sure that I would produce a book of which we can both be proud.

Finally, I want to acknowledge the contributions Diane Feldman and Sara DeVault-Feldman made to this book. Throughout the research, writing, and final preparation, Diane provided support and sustenance of many different types. I hope she knows how much I appreciate her presence in my life. And though I know that Sara would have preferred that I write a multivolume story about an ordinary young girl who discovers that she is really a wizard, the concept somehow seemed stale to me. Perhaps someday Sara will decide that labor history holds some interest for her and will read and appreciate this volume. Diane and Sara would both agree that I have sacrificed far too much "family time" for what they see as a fundamentally boring tome. Nonetheless, I thank them both for granting me the space and time to work on this project. I apologize for missing so many trips and activities (especially during Sara's kindergarten year, when I was in New York City), and I hope that eventually they will come to appreciate both my sacrifice and theirs. I never would have finished this book without their support and love. This book is dedicated to Diane and Sara, with love.

Introduction

It appears that [John] Highland and a companion visited Wood's warehouse, and . . . peered into the windows and tried to induce some of the girls who were assorting tobacco to join the strikers.
—*Wisconsin Tobacco Reporter*, February 27, 1891

One of the men pickets, "Sam" Feldman, was arrested for speaking to a young woman who he thought was going to take the place of a striker. . . .
"Girls, let's chip in one cent each to pay Sam's fine," cried Miss Drubin, climbing on a table and waving her hat around her head.
The suggestion was taken up with enthusiasm and Sam's hat was passed around by Miss Gussie Cohen. When it came back it contained 350 pennies, which were turned over to Sam, who spent the extra 50 cents in buying ice cream soda for the girl pickets.
—*New York Tribune*, August 5, 1900

"Everything is good natured, and that's what I like," said John C. Kness at the close of a meeting of the weavers held in Loomfixers' hall.
Mr. Kness had taken his violin to the meeting, and at its close he had started up a lively dance air, and another weaver had seated himself at the piano and played the accompaniment.
The incident brought a crowd of men and women of the union about the platform.
—*Lowell Courier-Citizen*, April 1, 1903

The small incidents described above capture brief moments within larger strike situations. While these might seem to hold little historical significance, they actually can begin to uncover the worlds in which workers' lives and experiences unfolded. In times and places when women and men held jobs strictly segregated by sex, such moments of camaraderie among men and women in strike situations seem quite unlikely. Yet, at the turn of the twentieth century, when both the labor market as a whole and individual jobs at the workplace were segregated by sex, it became clear to workers in certain industries that their jobs were so intertwined with and dependent on others that any sort of strike or other job action would fail without the support of co-workers who held different jobs and were of a different gender. Such strikes of men and women together form the basis for this book. In every

1

case, both the larger narrative of the strike and the small incidents of the strike can provide the historian with important insights into not only the outcome of the strike, but also the daily interactions of co-workers at work, at home, and in the union halls.

In 1991, Ava Baron credited historians working to create "a gendered labor history" with "seek[ing] to understand how gender operates, and the ways it has shaped and been shaped by economic institutions and relationships." The present book carries that project forward, "exploring the ways in which gender bias is structured into the fabric of unionism."[1] A close look at what I call "cross-gender" strikes—strikes in which both women and men participated—can uncover interactions among male and female co-workers that would normally remain hidden to the historian. Mirroring the sexual division of labor within each industry, these cross-gender strikes furnish snapshots of both cooperation between the sexes and the many fractures that existed just below the surface of such cooperation. In the heightened tensions of a strike, when workers have put their livelihoods on the line, incipient tensions among workers often come to light. While these tensions could revolve around issues of race, ethnicity, religion, age, or any number of other issues, as well as issues of gender, the emphasis here highlights gender as a category of analysis. Nongender issues necessarily complicate an analysis made on the basis of gender. The ways in which all these possible categories interact, intersect, and reinforce or undercut one another are crucial to uncovering the various possible dynamics of the strikes and workplaces under consideration.

The forty strikes that form the basis of this book took place in four broad industries: the boot and shoe industry, the clothing industry, the textile industry, and the tobacco industry. Over the decades between 1880 and 1910, women made up between 11 percent and 80 percent of all workers in those industries (see table 1). At the same time, the women in these industries made up between 73 percent and 86 percent of all female manufacturing workers (see table 2). Although failure might arise from any number of factors, the success of a strike depended on cooperation among its participants, both male and female. In fact, between 1887 and 1905, women constituted more than one-quarter (26 percent) of the almost 173,000 strikers in these four industries. Women made up close to half of all strikers in the textile industry and more than half of those in the chewing and smoking tobacco segment of the tobacco industry[2] (see table 3).

From Auburn, Maine, to Los Angeles, from Oregon City to Key West, Florida, the locations of the strikes in this book crisscross the United States.

1. Ava Baron, "Gender and Labor History: Learning from the Past, Looking to the Future," in *Work Engendered: Toward a New History of American Labor*, ed. Ava Baron (Ithaca: Cornell University Press, 1990), pp. 20, 13.

2. U.S. Bureau of Labor, *Twenty-first Annual Report, 1906: Strikes and Lockouts* (Washington, D.C.: Government Printing Office, 1907), pp. 90–91.

Table 1. Women as percentage of workforce in selected industries, 1880-1910

Industry	1880	1890	1900	1910
Total manufactur-ing workforce	16.7	18.1	18.5	16.4
Boots & shoes	10.8	15.7	18.9	23.1
Clothing[a]	77.0	79.4	77.9	73.4
Textiles[b]	38.2	50.6	51.1	50.2
Tobacco	14.1	25.1	51.1	44.5

Source: U.S. Department of Commerce, Bureau of the Census, *Population 1910: Occupation Statistics* (Washington, D.C.: Government Printing Office, 1914), table 15, pp. 55–56.
[a] Includes "dressmakers, milliners & seamstresses," "glove makers," "hat & cap makers," "sewing machine operators," "shirt, cuff, & collar makers," and "tailors and tailoresses."
[b] Includes cotton mill, woolen mill, hosiery & knitting mill, silk mill, and "other textile mill" operatives.

Table 2. Women in selected industries as proportion of total female manufacturing workforce

Industry	1880	1890	1900	1910
Total manufactur-ing workforce (number)	631,034	1,027,928	1,312,668	1,772,095
Boots & shoes	3.3	3.3	3.0	3.4
Clothing[a]	56.1	58.1	53.1	45.5
Textiles[b]	25.2	21.2	20.5	20.3
Tobacco	1.7	2.7	3.3	4.0
All four industries	86.3	85.3	80.0	73.2

Source: U.S. Department of Commerce, Bureau of the Census, *Population 1910: Occupation Statistics* (Washington, D.C.: Government Printing Office, 1914), table 15, pp. 55–56.
[a] Includes "dressmakers, milliners & seamstresses," "glove makers," "hat & cap makers," "sewing machine operators," "shirt, cuff, & collar makers," and "tailors and tailoresses."
[b] Includes cotton mill, woolen mill, hosiery & knitting mill, silk mill, and "other textile mill" operatives.

Some of the nation's largest cities—such as New York, Chicago, and San Francisco—are represented, as are some of the smallest: Edgerton, Wisconsin, and Haw River, North Carolina. Some strike locations are in what constituted the nation's industrial heartland a century ago (New Bedford, Massachusetts; Detroit, Michigan), while others took place in the developing New South of the post–Civil War years, and still others in the states of the far West. I selected many atypical strikes precisely because they highlight variations in race and ethnicity as well as factors relating to the industrial geography of the United States.[3]

This book begins chronologically with the formation of the American Federation of Labor (AFL) in late 1886 and continues through the establishment of the Women's Trade Union League at the AFL convention of 1903.

3. For more discussion on the selection of the strike case studies, see appendix 1.

Table 3. Percentage of employees of each sex striking in four industries, 1887–1905

Industry	Percentage of women striking	Percentage of men striking
Boots & shoes	16.57	26.36
Clothing		
Men's	43.06	81.64
Women's	62.11	86.94
Textiles		
Cotton goods	27.59	29.72
Cotton & woolen goods	24.38	30.21
Woolen goods	18.07	18.72
Tobacco		
Chewing and smoking	48.55	36.46
Cigars & cigarettes	45.42	73.00

Source: U.S. Bureau of Labor, *Twenty-first Annual Report, 1906: Strikes and Lockouts* (Washington, D.C.: Government Printing Office, 1907), pp. 90–91.

Beyond the institutional importance of these years is their significance in strike history. The famed eight-hour-workday strikes of 1886 swept many workers out of their workshops and into the streets; more than 400,000 workers employed in some 10,000 establishments took strike action during that year. The next peak in strike activity took place in 1903, when at least 500,000 workers struck some 20,000 establishments across the nation.[4] Between these two years, workers all over the United States faced the massive economic depression of the 1890s, which shattered the faith many people had in capitalism and in the good intentions of their employers. The Knights of Labor withered away during that decade, while the unions of the AFL staggered under the adverse economic conditions but survived the downturn nonetheless. Before, during, and after the depression of the 1890s, the unions of the AFL, and workers in general, faced opportunities to define themselves and carve out new spaces for themselves in the coming century. This book examines how they would do this.

The roots of the AFL's fundamental attitudes toward women workers and union members are evident in the participation of women in strikes during these years. Examining the participation of women during these early years of the AFL provides insight into the militance of women and the attitude of the AFL toward women. But we also find, in these strikes—in their leadership, their results, and their aftermaths—larger gendered attitudes within the AFL. The AFL's experiences with female workers in its early years affected the organization's attitudes toward all workers in fundamental ways. One key point of inquiry in this book involves the ways in which the unions that made up the AFL came to encode gender into their very structures. In fact, I argue that the hallowed words "craft unionism" came to be read as "male" perhaps even more than they were read as "white." In all their variations, the strikes

4. U.S. Bureau of Labor, *Twenty-first Annual Report*, table 4, pp. 478–79.

described in this book, and the issues those strikes raised for the unions of the time, played a role in determining how the unions of the AFL continued to deal both with women workers and with others they deemed to be "less skilled" than their own members.

In many ways, this book might be seen as a most traditional labor history in that its fundamental topic is strikes and unions. Stories and analyses of strikes and unions have been central to the field of labor history since it began with the work of John R. Commons and his associates, Selig Perlman and Philip Taft.[5] In the 1960s the work of E. P. Thompson inspired a new generation of labor historians. Combined with the concurrent rise of social history, these historians became known as practitioners of what is still, thirty years later, called the "new" labor history.[6] In this new history, there was more attention to how the categories of social history overlapped with workers' experiences in the workplace. The result has been a rich history that examines the ways in which workers experienced divisions among themselves as much as they experienced moments of solidarity. Ethnicity, race, and gender all have become important categories of study.[7]

For some practitioners of the new labor history, life outside the workplace became just as important for determining how workers would react to their situations as life inside the workplace. The new labor history often moved so far from the field's original interest in workplace organizations (unions) and their activities (strikes) that it came to be called, more properly, working-class history. In this new history, while the workplace might loom in the background as the final determinant of membership in the working class,

5. See John R. Commons et al., *History of Labor in the United States*, 4 vols. (New York: Macmillan, 1935); Selig Perlman, *A History of Trade Unionism in the United States* (New York: A. M. Kelley, 1950).

6. See David Brody, *The Butcher Workmen: A Study of Unionization* (Cambridge: Harvard University Press, 1964); Herbert G. Gutman, *Work, Culture, and Society in Industrializing America* (New York: Vintage Books, 1977); David Montgomery, *The Fall of the House of Labor* (Cambridge: Cambridge University Press, 1987); Melvyn Dubofsky, *We Shall Be All: A History of the Industrial Workers of the World* (Chicago: Quadrangle Books, 1969).

7. On race, see, for example, Eric Arnesen, *Brotherhoods of Color: Black Railroad Workers and the Struggle for Equality* (Cambridge: Harvard University Press, 2001), and *Waterfront Workers of New Orleans: Race, Class, and Politics, 1863–1923* (Urbana: University of Illinois Press, 1994); Daniel Letwin, *The Challenge of Interracial Unionism: Alabama Coal Miners, 1878–1921* (Chapel Hill: University of North Carolina Press, 1998); Timothy J. Minchin, *Hiring the Black Worker: The Racial Integration of the Southern Textile Industry, 1960–1980* (Chapel Hill: University of North Carolina Press, 1999). For examples of the importance of ethnicity, see James Barrett, *Work and Community in the Jungle: Chicago's Packinghouse Workers, 1894–1922* (Urbana: University of Illinois Press, 1987); Cecelia Bucki, *Bridgeport's Socialist New Deal, 1915–36* (Urbana: University of Illinois Press, 2001); Gunther Peck, *Reinventing Free Labor: Padrones and Immigrant Workers in the North American West, 1880–1930* (Cambridge: Cambridge University Press, 2000). Gender as a category is discussed separately below.

actions in the community and neighborhood, as well as working-class culture, took on greater explanatory significance.[8]

While working-class history continues to provide important insights into workers' lives, some of us in the field of labor history have returned to take a new look at the development of unions and that ultimate expression of working-class consciousness, the strike. These "new institutionalists" of labor history seek to bring the insights about community, race, ethnicity, gender, and other categories examined by the new labor history and working-class history back into the consideration of workers' attempts at institution-building.[9] This book is part of this return to questions of workers' institutions.

At the same time, this book is also very much a part of what has come to be called women's labor history. In many ways, changes in that subfield have paralleled the changes in labor history. For women's labor history, developments in women's history complicated and enriched its trajectory. Even more than in labor history, feminist poststructuralism has encouraged women's labor historians to pay close attention to discourse, agency, and essentialism.[10] As in labor history, this has meant growing attention to questions of race and ethnicity and to their influence on women workers' experiences. Over the last decade and a half, the plethora of studies that examine the gendered dynamics of specific occupations, often in single locations, has inspired the more comparative work found in this book.[11] Such studies demonstrate the importance of the contingencies of individual locations and workplace situations for understanding both the actions of women workers and their interactions with male co-workers. While such contingencies remain important considerations, works on such specific circumstances have called for an attempt to bring them together. In this book, I argue that bringing together the various geographic and industrial contingencies provides us with insights not only into the mutual workplace experiences of both men and women

8. See my own *Sons and Daughters of Labor* (Ithaca: Cornell University Press, 1990) for one example of this. See also Roy Rosenzweig, *Eight Hours for What We Will: Workers and Leisure in an Industrial City, 1870–1920* (Cambridge: Cambridge University Press, 1983); Kathy Peiss, *Cheap Amusements: Working Women and Leisure in Turn-of-the-Century New York* (Philadelphia: Temple University Press, 1986).

9. See, for example, Julie Greene, *Pure and Simple Politics: The American Federation of Labor and Political Activism, 1881–1917* (Cambridge: Cambridge University Press, 1998); Daniel J. Clark, *Like Night and Day: Unionization in a Southern Mill Town* (Chapel Hill: University of North Carolina Press, 1997).

10. See Baron, "Gender and Labor History," for an excellent discussion of these developments.

11. Mary H. Blewett, *Men, Women, and Work: Class, Gender, and Protest* (Urbana: University of Illinois Press, 1988); Dorothy Sue Cobble, *Dishing It Out: Waitresses and Their Unions in the Twentieth Century* (Urbana: University of Illinois Press, 1991); Patricia A. Cooper, *Once a Cigar Maker: Men, Women, and Work Culture* (Urbana: University of Illinois Press, 1987); Nancy Hewitt, *Southern Discomfort: Women's Activism in Tampa, Florida, 1880s–1920s* (Urbana: University of Illinois Press, 2001); Dolores E. Janiewski, *Sisterhood Denied: Race, Gender, and Class in a New South Community* (Philadelphia: Temple University Press, 1985); Carole Turbin, *Working Women of Collar City: Gender, Class, and Community in Troy, 1864–1886* (Urbana: University of Illinois Press, 1992).

but also into the ways in which the leaders of the labor movement utilized those gendered experiences in their attempts at the turn of the twentieth century to bring together the first long-lasting national union movement.

While collecting materials for this book, I was also reading and thinking about how best to explain what I saw as the overlapping layers of workers' lives, layers identified by scholars as class, gender, race, and ethnicity, as well as other categories, such as age, religion, and family status. Then I chanced on Iris Young's use of Jean-Paul Sartre's concept of the "series."[12] Young puts it this way: "Gender, like class, is a vast, multifaceted, layered, complex, and overlapping set of structures and objects. Women are the individuals who are positioned as feminine by the activities surrounding those structures and objects."[13] Here, then, was a way to think about the means by which workers manifested their gender, race, ethnic, and class identities both simultaneously and serially, one after another. On a theoretical level, then, this book argues that workers' perceptions and actions are "serial" in two senses of that term. One is Sartre's philosophical sense of individuals' consciousness of belonging to such categories in effect waiting to be ignited by external events and then acted on by the individuals in question. The other is the more ordinary sense of events being serial, of their occurring one after another—in other words, the standard understanding of historical narrative. My goal is to examine simultaneously how these two senses of the word "serial" explicate the ways in which individuals achieve awareness of their identities as members of specific categories.

My interest in using Sartre's theory is not to trace each of his many steps through the strikes in this book. Rather, I use his notion of the "series" to think about the complexities of these workers' identities. I pay particular attention to moments in strikes when the actions of the workers reflect their recognition that they are members of a particular "series" or category. Thinking about workers' identifications in this serial way does away with questions of whether any one category of identity is dominant over the others. Instead, the use of Sartre's concept underscores that every individual at every moment holds within herself or himself a simultaneous range of possible identities. Which of these identities will enter the consciousness of this individual, and therefore inform his or her actions, at any particular point in time depends on each person's role in the ongoing historical narrative, or serial.[14]

12. Iris Young, "Gender as Seriality: Thinking about Women as a Social Collective," *Signs* 19 (1994): 713–38. See also Sonya Rose, "Class Formation and the Quintessential Worker," in *Reworking Class*, ed. John Hall (Ithaca: Cornell University Press, 1997), pp. 133–65.
13. Young, "Gender as Seriality," p. 728.
14. See my use of Sartre's concepts in "Narratives Serially Constructed and Lived: Ethnicity in Cross-Gender Strikes, 1887–1903," *International Review of Social History* 44, supplement (1999): 33–52.

The serial nature of the historical narrative—the fact that one event follows another—is also crucial in this book. It is only within the actual twists and turns of the historical narrative that we begin to understand the shifting contingencies of specific situations. In turn, these contingencies both endow historical actors with the power of agency and at times deprive them of it. As described in appendix 1, the research for this book was conducted as research into each of the individual strikes that form the case studies at the root of the book. Long before I wrote anything like a chapter, I wrote narratives of the forty strike case studies. These narratives appear, often in bits and pieces, in what follows. I have attempted to maintain a sense of their narrative quality, of their seriality, of the fact that in each case certain things happened before or after other things. The decisions that workers or employers made at any point, the actions that they took, affected the course of the strike narrative. Such decisions and actions, however, were never predetermined, but rather always existed both within and despite the material constraints of the situation. Some strike stories appear several times in this book. Each telling of the story brings out different issues and highlights the importance of different "serial" identities. This examination of the narrative seriality of the case studies provides a sort of standpoint epistemology version of historical narration: the point at which actors stand in the narrative determines both their reactions to events and the unfolding of those events. Chapter 1, for example, introduces quite fully the narrative stories of four of the strike case studies, but even those strikes reappear in other places in the book, examined from slightly different angles to make other points. In other words, the same narrative, the same train of events, does not so much look different from another standpoint as it makes us look differently at certain issues.

The narration of the four strikes in chapter 1 introduces the reader to factors that are relevant to the mobilization of workers in each of the four industries covered in this book: the sexual divisions of labor the workers experienced; the types of unions they confronted or created; the choices they had to make. The strike stories thus show how the various possible complexities operated in the interaction of historical narrative, contingency, material conditions, and the actions of individuals.

Chapter 2 examines the strikes carried out under the auspices of the Knights of Labor during its dying years. Historiography on gender and the Knights has generally argued that the Knights provided women workers with greater opportunities than they had experienced before or would experience immediately after the disappearance of the organization. The cross-gender strikes under consideration here, however, show that the Knights organization, at least in its crumbling days, displays a much more ambivalent set of options for women. Chapter 3 goes on to look at the nemesis of the Knights: the new and growing American Federation of Labor. Cross-gender strikes undertaken under the auspices of AFL member unions demonstrate the ways in which the AFL based its vaunted ideal of craft unionism on gendered definitions of skill.

Chapter 4 begins the exploration of how issues other than those related to union organization and structure operated in cross-gender strikes. It demonstrates the varied roles that ethnicity and race could play in cross-gender strikes. For many of these strikes, geographic location plays a crucial role in determining the influence of ethnicity. Accordingly, the chapter suggests the ways in which ethnicity was limited in its usefulness to leaders of the new Federation. Following on this theme of geography, chapter 5 illustrates the implications of cross-gender strikes taking place in the areas I identify as the industrial periphery of the United States. Such strikes, usually taking place far from the influence of established unions, made room for new roles for rank-and-file workers of both genders as well as for women workers in particular.

Cross-gender strikes in all four of the industries under consideration also demonstrate the power of "family," both real and imagined. Chapter 6 explores the various roles family ties might play in different strikes. Family roles might provide the basis for strike solidarity or suggest important strike survival strategies for workers. At times, family relationships spurred the recognition of strike issues; at other times, however, family networks might impede strike unity. Chapter 7 returns to organizational issues, as it examines attempts made to broaden the AFL's craft unionism. Sometimes these attempts expanded opportunities for women workers, but at other times they merely re-encoded gendered assumptions about male and female militance and the utility of the AFL's craft union model.

The book's conclusion, chapter 8, looks toward the opportunities that the Women's Trade Union League, founded at the AFL convention of 1903, provided for women workers. Though this organization could not overcome completely the gendered craft unionism embedded within the AFL, it did attempt to bring more women into the AFL and to broaden the influence of women within that organization.

The American Federation of Labor entered the twentieth century ensconced as the primary vehicle for the nation's organized workers. As such, the attitudes of the AFL toward women workers provided the basis for virtually all later attempts at organizing women. The cross-gender strikes that are the basis of this book illustrate both the ways in which men and women would move forward united and the ways in which they would remain apart. That both females and males could at times feel drawn together and at other times feel driven apart, and carry both those feelings into their actions and their organizations, is the ultimate lesson I hope this book conveys. That workers strove to unite in strike situations is an old lesson taught by labor history; that they often fragmented along lines of gender, race, ethnicity, or other categories is a lesson often hammered home by the new labor history. Both these tendencies are evident in the strikes discussed in this book, and the reverberations of those tendencies appear in the very structure of the unions that attempted to mold their members' fragmented experiences into a sense of national unity.

1　*Strike*

"This is to be a friendly, manly fight."
—*Boston Globe*, March 29, 1903

T he strike narratives in this chapter serve as introductions to the four industries covered in this book, their gendered divisions of labor, their unions, and the types of issues that might appear in their strikes. This is not to say that these four strikes are necessarily typical; indeed, like all the case studies in this work, these strikes highlight the nuances of particular circumstances. For two of the strikes, that of shoe workers in Chicago in 1892 and of Lowell textile workers in 1903, I narrate the events of the strike paying particular attention to certain contexts, such as the division of labor, industrial architecture, and urban geography. Seeking to probe the way in which a striker might have experienced the strike, I focus on individuals in the other two strikes, those of Baltimore garment workers in 1892 and New York City cigar makers in 1900. The strike stories narrated below thus show the operation of the complexities possible in the interaction of historical narrative, material conditions, and individuals' agency.

Clothing: Baltimore, 1892

Cilea Grott walked to work each morning through crowded streets filled with the smells and sounds of Baltimore's Jewish immigrant community.[1] She was one of the relatively lucky young women who worked in the city's coat-making industry, where she might earn as much as six or seven dollars a week, rather than in the lower-paid pants or vest portions of the garment industry, where she could earn only half as much. Leaving her friends at the sidewalk, she might have entered her workplace through a side entrance, climbing to the third floor past both living quarters and other workshops. In the shop itself, Cilea found heaps of cut coat pieces ready to be sewn together by male sewing machine operators and basters, probably including her boss himself. After the men completed the basic work of constructing the garment, Cilea and the other "girls" in the shop finished the piece with

---

1. Unless otherwise noted, the story of this strike comes from coverage in the *Baltimore Sun* [hereafter cited as *Sun*].

11

hand sewing. Clippings of fabric littered the floor. The coal stove used to heat the pressers' irons filled the room with heat by midday, making the temperature intolerable in the summertime. During peak season, up to six teams of workers, each consisting of a machine operator, a baster, and two finishers, along with a presser for every two teams, would be working in the shop. Twenty-five people, twelve of them young women like Cilea, worked in this 25-by-18-foot room. Singing or exchanging neighborhood gossip competed with the whirring of the sewing machines in the shop. If she was extremely lucky—and quick at her work—Cilea might have been able to see the sun through a window's dirty panes, or even at times feel a breeze in the spring. Working at least twelve-hour days, six days a week with only the Jewish sabbath off during the busy season, Cilea might have worked on at least sixty different coats in order to earn her weekly seven dollars in pay.[2]

Baltimore's sweatshop district was the setting in which Cilea Grott, and many other Baltimore garment workers, recognized and began to act based on what they had in common as garment workers. Though they worked, lived, and worshiped alongside their bosses in the cramped workshops, they still knew just who it was who set the "task" (the number of coats) assigned to a given pay level, deducted fines from their pay for broken needles or botched garments, and paid them only when he was paid by the wholesaler to whom he sold the coats. Cilea's co-workers had formed two local assemblies of the Knights of Labor in 1886: Local Assembly 6915 of tailors and Local Assembly 7120 of female sewing machine operators.[3] In fall 1891 an apparently more attractive union option appeared on the scene, and both Knights of Labor assemblies switched their allegiance to the newly organized United Garment Workers of America (UGW), which was affiliated with the American Federation of Labor (AFL). Baltimore's male garment workers made up UGW Local 26, while Local 33 was the women's local. By the following spring, Cilea Grott was serving as secretary of Local 33.

In early June 1892, Baltimore's labor newspaper, *The Critic*, published a series of exposés of the city's garment sweatshops. The paper scoffed at the pride local manufacturers had in their goods and decried local sweatshops as "dens and slop-shops as foul as any in the byways of New York."[4] In one article, subtitled "Is it a wonder these men and women strike?" the reporter described the shops as

---

2. This description of Cilea's workday draws from "Sweat Shops," in Maryland Bureau of Industrial Statistics, *Second Annual Report of the Bureau of Industrial Statistics of Maryland* (Baltimore: King Bros., 1894), pp. 80–114, particularly the description of Harris Cohen's shop on pp. 94–95.

3. See Jonathan Garlock, *Guide to the Local Assemblies of the Knights of Labor* (Westport, Conn.: Greenwood Press, 1982), p. 180.

4. *The Critic*, June 11, 1892, p. 1. Eric Arnesen brought this series of articles to my attention.

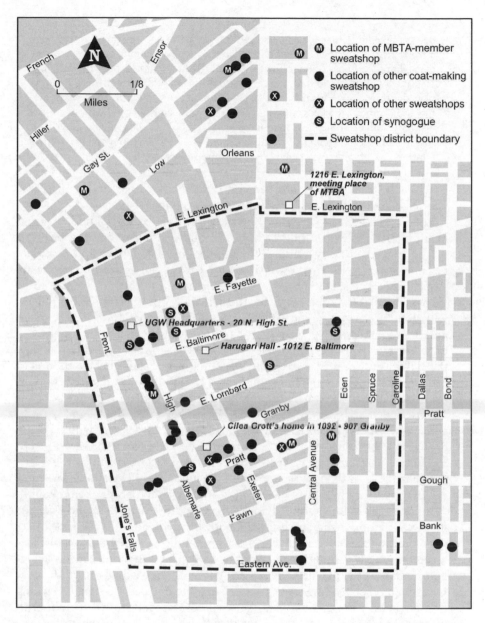

Sweatshop district, Baltimore, Maryland, c. 1892–95 (Syracuse University Cartography Laboratory).

disease-breeding pest-holes . . . as revolting as a Russian prison and very near as dirty. Miserable men and women filled the rooms, cringing and cowering at the sight of the "boss," trembling for fear of discharge, not daring to refuse any task put upon them, and afraid to even call their tongues their own. Born as near slaves as human beings can well be in this age and cowardly in the extreme, these miserable wretches toil from twelve to eighteen hours per day, in rooms not fit to stable a mule in, as near naked as decency will allow men and women to toil and sweat together, wearing out their lives for whatever the grumbling contractor who employs them chooses to pay.[5]

Yet, as the article's subtitle hinted, these "cowardly" and "miserable wretches" had already begun to take action to improve their lot.

Long hours at work and the uncertainty of pay led Cilea and her union brothers and sisters in spring 1892 to demand a uniform ten-hour day and a regular payday every Friday. When Cilea and her fellow union leaders began making these demands of their own bosses, only to be met by the argument that one small subcontractor alone could not afford to give in to such requests, they decided to make the demands more general. To help them with this, the general secretary of the national union, Charles Reichers, arrived in Baltimore in late June. Reichers's experience in organizing similar groups of workers in New York and elsewhere helped him move quickly to shape the Baltimore workers' movement, bringing order where before there had been virtually none. On Thursday, June 23, union leaders distributed their list of demands to the subcontractors who employed them. The new, expanded list of demands included five items. First, they called for a signed, yearly agreement, binding on both sides. Second, all workers employed would belong to the United Garment Workers. Third, the workday would be shortened to a standard ten-hour day. Fourth, workers would receive their pay every Friday. Finally, a "walking delegate" from the union would be allowed to enter each shop twice a month to ensure that union standards were being kept.

Initially, the unions received no response to their demands, and over the next week union members discussed both the demands and the lack of response from the contractors. The most vocal union members probably harassed their bosses about the demands as well. The demands seemed reasonable, and humane, to Cilea and her co-workers. They would afford the coat makers a modicum of the respect and leisure that had been so signally lacking in their lives. After the weekend, several contractors offered to talk with workers at the end of the week, but it did not take long for the activists to realize that the contractors planned to deliver the week's finished work to the wholesale houses and then lock out their employees. Members of both local unions voted to go on strike in support of the demands. They sent Secretary Reichers to the Baltimore Federation of Labor meeting on Wednes-

5. *The Critic*, June 18, 1892, p. 1.

day, June 29, where he informed the local federation that the two unions would strike the following day, "when the shops were full of work."[6]

Almost one thousand workers went on strike on June 30, crowding the streets around union headquarters on North High Street. The strikers had worked for at least thirty-four individual contractors, and the union was now asking that contractors put up a five-hundred-dollar bond to ensure that workers receive their pay. During the first few days of the strike, contractors panicked, interpreting workers' demands as requiring higher wages and complete abolition of piecework. Many claimed they could not sign a yearly agreement because they never knew if they would have consistent work throughout the year; others balked at the bond requirement, probably because they could not come up with the money.

Over the next several weeks, however, a number of contractors gave in to the workers' demands, signing the agreement and putting up the bond. By the end of the first full week of July, thirteen contractors had signed, and about two hundred of the strikers went back to work. Workers expressed satisfaction with the new working conditions, and one even told a newspaper reporter "that the contractor for whom he worked had expressed regret that the system had not been adopted long ago."[7] Some of the city's wholesale clothing houses even asked their contractors to sign the union agreement, too.

By the second week of the strike, Cilea and her comrades began to see evidence that their bosses had begun to see their own common interests. On July 11 the contractors set up their own organization, the Monumental Tailors' Benevolent Association (MTBA). Baltimore's district master workman of the Knights of Labor, J. G. Schonfarber, spoke to the gathering in favor of submitting the conflict to arbitration. After considerable discussion, the contractors agreed. At the same time, Schonfarber told the contractors that he had warned five Baltimore clothiers that he would pull the clothing cutters, members of the sole remaining Knights assembly (Clothing Cutters' and Trimmers' Assembly 7507), out of the shops of anyone signing the garment workers' agreement. When Schonfarber wrote an article on the controversy for *The Critic* later that week, he laid blame for the trouble on Reichers and commented: "While the Contractors are really the 'sweaters,' they are also men, with families, who . . . are not to blame for the system they work under. . . . Indeed, it is a question whether they are not more sinned against than sinning."[8]

In this setting, arbitration between the contractors and the strikers was anything but easy. The first attempted meeting fell apart when contractors complained about the presence of Secretary Reichers on the garment workers'

6. *Sun,* July 1, 1892, p. 8.
7. *Sun,* July 9, 1892, p. 8.
8. *The Critic,* July 16, 1892, p. 1.

committee. The following week, new committees from the two sides (made up entirely of men) managed to meet together for several hours before they began bickering over the exact meaning of the strikers' demand that all workers be "union hands." Did that exclude members of the Knights, the contractors wanted to know? The MTBA wanted any agreement to use the words "members of organized labor" instead. This issue of nomenclature prevented useful arbitration for the next weeks. Only when other arbitration committees were constituted during the last week of July could negotiations proceed.

Meanwhile, Cilea and her union sisters kept quite busy, even though the arbitration attempts remained an all-male affair. Just as the work teams of coat makers revolved around the male workers' parts of the task, so too were the main public manifestations of the strike run by the men's union. Nonetheless, the women of Local 33 took an active role in soliciting financial support for the strike, an action that was reinforced by sisterly financial aid from the "Women's Branch of the Garment Workers' Union in New York." As secretary of Local 33, Cilea Grott expressed her identity specifically as a female striker when she told a *Sun* reporter: "The woman workers were making a firm stand and were no less determined than the men."[9] At the same time that women like Cilea acknowledged their status as women, in the strike as well as in the shops and the larger Jewish immigrant community, they also saw themselves as part of the larger community of strikers.

Cilea's union announced publicly its decision "not to work as finishers on garments made by non-union workmen" and that many members had agreed "to remain on strike without drawing benefits from the union."[10] When yet another set of arbitration committees met on July 27, the contractors' representatives attempted to divide the strikers along sexual lines, suggesting, as reported by the *Sun*, "that girls who desire to belong to unions can do so, and that those who do not belong be not discriminated against by the union." The members of the union objected, "saying that all girls desiring the work in tailoring shops must belong to the union. They further stated that the girls had stood by them during the strike and the male members of the union would look after them."[11] This immediate reaction from the all-male UGW arbitration committee was ratified by the members of Local 26 the next night, when "the men . . . voted to stand by the girls."[12] On the one hand, this incident reinforced the subordinate position of women in the strike, as male strikers had reached this decision without publicly consulting the women. Yet at the same time it also rewarded the women's continued identifi-

9. *Sun*, July 16, 1892, p. 8.
10. *Sun*, July 20, 1892, p. 8.
11. *Sun*, July 28, 1892, p. 8.
12. *Sun*, July 29, 1892, p. 8.

cation with their fellow strikers. Never again did the contractors attempt to divide the workers in this way.

At the beginning of August, arbitration finally bore fruit, as contractors agreed to virtually all the strikers' demands. Workers would work only ten-hour days, and they would be paid weekly. For their part, the unions agreed to drop their demand for walking delegates, and they moderated their request for bonds from their bosses. Members of the MTBA would only have to pay fifty dollars for each sewing machine operator in their establishments, while nonmembers would pay the full five hundred dollars. The agreement reached on August 2 also included a promise by the contractors to hire only "union hands." All that remained was for both sides to ratify the agreement.

Although approximately one-third of Baltimore's contractors had already signed the original set of union demands, this barely altered version now faltered on the old stumbling block of defining the term "union hands." The president of the MTBA claimed the agreement gave contractors "the right to employ members of any organized labor body; and there is to be no discrimination against Knights of Labor or union men."[13] The MTBA then requested that this reading of the agreement be acknowledged by changing the words "union hands" to "organized labor." The unions denied that this was the proper reading of the arbitration results, and once again the agreement between the two sides fell apart over the issue. The unions then announced that they would no longer deal with the contractors' association but would talk only with individual contractors.

With this breakdown in formal negotiations, the contractors took a surprising step, transforming the MTBA into a local assembly of the Knights: the "Monumental Coat Contractors' Assembly." At this point the strike became "a clean cut [fight] between the Federation and the Knights."[14] A number of contractors who had already signed the union agreement—and paid the required bond—now renounced the agreement as they joined the Knights. Although no inside information that sheds light on the organizational shift of the contractors remains, their alliance with the Knights altered the dynamics of the strike. By the middle of September, one delegate to the Baltimore Federation of Labor complained: "[The] trouble was not between the garment workers and their employers [any more], but between Secretary Reichers, of the international union, and Master Workman Schonfarber, of the Knights of Labor."[15]

Cilea Grott and her comrades, both female and male, must have begun to feel disempowered at this point, and the same was apparently true for members of the Coat Contractors' Assembly. While some contractors closed their shops over the course of September, others opened theirs, operating

13. *Sun*, August 3, 1892, p. 8.
14. *Sun*, August 16, 1892, p. 8.
15. *Sun*, September 15, 1892, p. 8.

under union terms though not necessarily with a signed union agreement. Although negotiations and posturing continued at the leadership levels throughout the fall, hundreds of garment workers returned to work in September. The president of Local 26 reported to the Baltimore Federation of Labor on October 5 that all but about one hundred members were now employed and that all the workers were expected to be back at work after the upcoming Jewish holidays.

Cilea Grott returned to work along with her co-workers. She now worked only ten hours a day, and she could count on receiving regular pay. If her boss did not formally recognize her union, at least he knew its power. She also probably felt more free to speak up at work when conditions bothered her. But the irons were still hot, the windows were still dirty, the men were still in charge.

Many of the clothing industry strikes recounted in this book demonstrate characteristics similar to those seen in Baltimore. Whether affiliated with the United Garment Workers or with the eventual unions of the International Ladies' Garment Workers' Union, strikers joined together in parallel gendered unions to fight for such basic demands as shorter hours and regular wage payment. As in Baltimore, union recognition and formal contracts arose only with more established unions.

Shoes: Chicago, 1892

Workers in the boot and shoe industry had a much longer history of unionism on which to draw than clothing industry workers did. The strike of Chicago shoe workers in the spring of 1892 illustrates some of the differences this history made in the cross-gender struggles of these workers.[16] In February 1892, seventy male lasters in the ladies' shoes bottoming department of the large Chicago factory of Selz, Schwab & Company went on strike for a wage increase and against the use of a new lasting machine. After two weeks, the lasters reached a settlement with the firm, but when they returned to work on Saturday, February 27, they found seven men hired during the strike still at work in the department. The lasters sent a committee to the foreman and to the factory superintendent, who told them that the new workers would not prevent any of the strikers from getting their jobs back and that the new workers would stay. However, this was not good enough for the strikers. According to laster Clarence Moeller, "indignant at the arbitrary treatment we received[,] we left again in a body." By Tuesday afternoon, March 1, the lasters had convinced three hundred male co-workers to attend a meeting at the end of the workday at Bowman's Hall, a saloon and "public hall" down

16. Unless otherwise noted, the story of this strike comes from coverage in the *Chicago Tribune* [hereafter cited as *CTrib*] and the *Chicago Daily News*.

the street at 120 Chicago Avenue. At the meeting, Moeller told the lasters' story, and a man from the stockroom told how lower-paid boys had been substituted for men and how workers were being fined for "trivial mistakes." "After considerable discussion" the assembled workers voted to go to work the next day at the usual hour, but then to "walk out to a man" at 9:00 a.m.[17]

The following morning, alerted by the previous day's newspaper account of the pre-strike meeting, six policemen and a crowd of onlookers gathered in front of the factory at the intersection of Chicago Avenue and Kingsbury Street. At 9:20 some three hundred men walked out of the Selz, Schwab factory, "cheered by the watching crowd." All but the factory's male cutters and female stitchers were now on strike. The top two floors of the factory, as well as the stockroom, were deserted. A meeting of the strikers demanded both wage increases and the settlement of grievances existing in all departments. The same meeting set up three committees to hear grievances from the various departments of the factory, and an executive committee to collect the grievances and negotiate with the firm. The strikers stressed the reasonableness and restraint of the lasters in calling for arbitration of the initial price dispute. In addition, they pointed out that the striking lasters had "behaved like gentlemen, keeping away from the factory, making no threats and molesting nobody in any way, manner, or form, and sustaining their dignity by appeals to their fellow-workmen against the [sic] violence of any kind."[18]

That evening about two hundred of the "women and girls" employed in the factory attended their own after-work meeting at Voltz Hall, two blocks down the street from the men's meeting place at Bowman's. (Voltz Hall apparently did not contain a saloon, which may explain why the women preferred it.)[19] The chairman of the male strikers' committee, James Parker, ran the meeting. He described the situation to the women and encouraged them to join the strike, assuring them that "their grievances would also be presented to the firm for adjustment. No man would go to work unless every woman present, from the youngest to the oldest, had been taken back and given her previous place after the strike."[20] After hearing two other workmen's descriptions of the strike, the assembled women voted unanimously to join the strikers. Six women formed their own "Committee on Grievances." The women followed the men's pattern for their own action, reporting for work the next morning and then walking out as a group at 9:00 a.m. An even larger crowd gathered outside the factory to watch the women leave: "As the women were sighted . . . they were cheered by the spectators, who extended in a line for a block east of the factory. The employes [sic] of the

17. *CTrib*, March 2, 1892, p. 6.
18. *CTrib*, March 3, 1892, p. 9.
19. From *The Lakeside Annual Directory of the City of Chicago, 1892* (Chicago: Chicago Directory Co., 1892).
20. *CTrib*, March 3, 1892, p. 9.

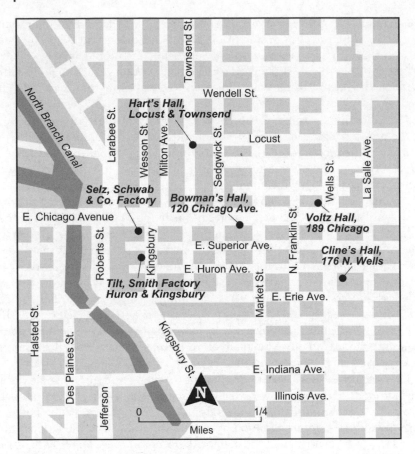

Selz, Schwab & Company shoe strike locations, Chicago, Illinois, c. 1892 (Syracuse University Cartography Laboratory).

Tilt Smith Shoe Company, whose factory is located directly opposite, stopped work and crowded the windows to watch and cheer the strikers."[21] The women proceeded to Voltz Hall to form a "permanent mutual aid association," elect officers, and recite their grievances. In particular, they complained about the company's practice of refusing to admit late workers and of imposing fines greater than the price paid for the work.

Also on Thursday, sixty male cutters at the factory left work, though someone told the *Tribune* that they had left only because their work was of no use if none of the other employees was at work. By the end of the workday, out of 850 Selz, Schwab workers only about thirty remained at work. Claiming that the factory held more than forty thousand pairs of unfinished

21. *CTrib*, March 4, 1892, p. 8.

shoes, strikers announced that competitive pressures would soon lead to their victory over the firm.

The pattern this strike followed was common to strikes of boot and shoe workers. One group of workers, divided from their co-workers by occupation and gender, begins a work action based on their own grievances—in other words, they begin with a relatively narrow sense of solidarity based on occupation. Then, eventually, and fairly quickly in this case, the first group of strikers realizes that it needs its co-workers in order to succeed. These co-workers come to acknowledge their common interests at varying rates of speed, but always through their own occupational allegiances.

This emphasis on specific occupational dividing lines was built into the very nature of the shoe industry at the turn of the century. Even in relatively new shoe factories, such as the Selz, Schwab factory, which was far from the traditional shoe centers of Massachusetts, shoe making was still divided into gendered occupations. Fairly skilled male "cutters" cut out the leather pieces of the shoe; women "stitchers" sewed together the various pieces of the shoe's "upper"; skilled male "lasters" shaped the shoe to its specific size; and finally, male "bottomers" attached the sole of the shoe.[22]

As the Chicago strike illustrates, the architecture of many factories intensified these various occupational divisions. Resolutions by the strikers alternately referred to strikers and their co-workers by occupation or by factory floor and department. The Wednesday strikers passed resolutions in support of "the action of the top floor employés (lasters)" and referred to themselves as "employés of the men's bottoming department and stock room" supporting their "fellow-workmen in the ladies' bottoming department." The three committees appointed to hear grievances were referred to as the "stock cutters," the "men's floor," and the "top floor."[23] The physical layout of the factory reinforced workers' sense of occupational divisions as much as gender did.

In the center of shoe manufacturing in Massachusetts, this division of labor had created similar divisions in workers' organizations. The Lasters' Protective Union (LPU) still represented most Massachusetts lasters in 1892, and many cutters were as likely to belong to separate cutters' unions as to the Boot and Shoe Workers' International Union (BSWIU), which had been formed in 1889 from parts of the Knights of Labor Shoe Workers' District Assembly 216. In all these various shoe worker organizations, workers divided by occupation and by sex attempted to coordinate their activities. While remaining within occupationally defined subunits, various forms of "joint boards" tried

22. See Edith Abbott, *Women in Industry: A Study in American Economic History* (New York: D. Appleton, 1910), pp. 148–85, and Mary H. Blewett, *Men, Women, and Work: Class, Gender, and Protest* (Urbana: University of Illinois Press, 1988), pp. 97–114. Abbott points out that a U.S. Census report found forty-eight individual occupations in the stitching room of a single factory in 1905 (p. 181).

23. *CTrib*, March 3, 1892, p. 9.

to bridge those divisions, particularly in strike situations. In Massachusetts this project enjoyed a long history that can be traced back to the 1860s and earlier.[24]

The Chicago strikers at Selz, Schwab do not appear to have belonged to any of these national organizations before the 1892 strike. Once their strike began, however, they quickly began to organize into the formal labor movement. Within a week of the strike's inception, both male and female strikers at the factory had decided to join the BSWIU, and that organization's general secretary, Henry J. Skeffington, was on his way to Chicago. As in the strike action itself, the male workers, particularly the lasters, led this drive into the AFL-affiliated labor movement.

For the women among the strikers, the trip into the American Federation of Labor was a bit bumpier. As already mentioned, the women formed a mutual aid association, rather than a union per se at their first meeting after the walkout on Thursday. At their next meeting, on Saturday, the leaders of their male co-workers, as well as several local women activists, addressed the striking women. A Mrs. Brown, from the Woman's Alliance[25], spoke about the heroism of the women's strike, telling them:

> You have not gone out for any grievances of your own, but you have gone out to help your brethren. . . . You are not united for your rights only, but also for the rights of the 600 men who work with you: for the rights of many wives and many children who are dependent on them for support. . . . I am glad that such a responsibility rests upon you, and I know you will prove yourself worthy of the confidence reposed in you.[26]

Elizabeth Morgan, a labor activist and wife of Thomas J. Morgan of the Chicago Trade and Labor Assembly, spoke next. She argued that in order to keep themselves from being used to cut wages and replace male workers, women needed to organize, too. Demonstrating an organizational eclecticism that was unusual for the time, Morgan encouraged the women to affiliate with either the American Federation of Labor or the Knights of Labor. She repeatedly warned the women that only organization, and not simply changing jobs, would improve their working conditions, and she repeated her plea again at a meeting on Monday, March 7, once again urging the

24. Gary M. Fink, ed., *Labor Unions* (Westport, Conn.: Greenwood Press, 1977), p. 38; Horace B. Davis, *Shoes: The Workers and the Industry* (New York: International Publishers, 1940), p. 167; Blewett, *Men, Women, and Work*, chaps. 8 and 9, pp. 220–319. See also discussion in chapter 2, below.

25. This is probably Corinne Brown, a former teacher and principal in the Chicago schools, now married to a banker. Brown was, along with Elizabeth Morgan, one of the socialist and pro-union members of the Illinois Woman's Alliance. Meredith Tax, *The Rising of the Women: Feminist Solidarity and Class Conflict, 1880–1917* (New York: Monthly Review Press, 1980), pp. 54, 66.

26. *CTrib*, March 6, 1892, p. 3.

women to join either organization. Even though Morgan had expressed no preference for one or the other organization, the *Tribune* closed its report on the Monday meeting by announcing that both men and women strikers would meet the next day to join the "National Boot and Shoe Workers' Union."[27]

Throughout these early days of the strike, two issues in addition to the organizational issue received the attention of the strikers. The women focused most of their concern on how to deal with strikebreakers. At their Saturday meeting, women strikers showed considerable enthusiasm for printing the names of strikebreakers in the city's newspapers, but strike leaders discouraged the idea. Still, some of the rank and file wanted to publish names. Said one striker, "I think . . . these girls' names ought to be printed. They staid in and worked when we all went out. Some of them hid until we were gone. They say they don't care as long as their names are not published, and I think the only way to shame them is to print their names."[28] After considerable discussion, the women decided to form a committee that would visit the women strikebreakers and "explain to them the error of their ways."[29]

While the women focused on convincing their erstwhile co-workers to join the strike, the men began plotting legal action against Selz, Schwab & Company. On Saturday, March 5, the firm asked workers to come to the factory to receive their final wage payments. On arriving at the plant, strike leader Clarence Moeller received three pairs of damaged shoes and an envelope with payment reflecting his wages minus the cost of the three pairs of shoes. He refused to accept either, informing the cashier that payment of wages in anything other than legal tender was against the law. This prompted a series of court cases against the firm, which apparently had made a practice of fining workers this way. In all, thirty workers, including at least nine women, charged Emanuel Selz with violating the state's new "Anti-Truck Law." Unfortunately for the strikers, the Illinois Supreme Court declared that law unconstitutional on March 26.[30] As a result, none of the cases against the Selz, Schwab company made it through the court system, but the legal challenge took up much of the strikers' time and energy throughout March.

In the meantime, Boot and Shoe Workers' Union leader Henry Skeffington arrived in Chicago on March 10. The strikers held their first joint meeting of both men and women in Cline's Hall at Huron and Wells streets to hear his address. Five hundred people attended the meeting and heard Skeffington

27. *CTrib*, March 8, 1892, p. 7. It is probably this incident that Samuel Gompers referred to in a letter to Skeffington. Gompers asked Skeffington for more details and promised him that if Morgan had "done wrong" he would try to prevent it in the future. AFL Letterpress Copybooks of Samuel Gompers and William Green, 1883–1925, microfilm of originals at Library of Congress [hereafter cited as SG Letterbooks], March 21, 1892, 7:154.

28. *CTrib*, March 6, 1892, p. 3.

29. Ibid.

30. *Shoe and Leather Reporter* [hereafter cited as *S&LR*], March 31, 1892 (53:14), p. 772.

speak about his experiences in strike situations. He urged strikers to continue organizing and to think of themselves as part of a much larger, national movement of shoe workers: "There are differences between the employers and employés in all parts of the United States. Organization is the only means of settling such differences. You have held out as long as you could and at last your wages were cut down so low that you turned against your employers. . . . The main object of organization is to prevent such abuses."[31] Skeffington went on to advise the strikers to maintain order, and he promised support from the national union for their struggle.

As the strike wore on, there were two developments. First, two separate groups of concerned citizens offered themselves as arbitrators of the situation. The first group consisted of religious figures, including Rabbi E. G. Hirsch of Temple Sinai, the Reverend O. P. Gifford of Immanuel Baptist Church, and Walter T. Mills, editor of several religious and prohibition publications. The second group, representing more secular interests, included a member of the Chicago Women's Club, Mrs. Charles Henrotin; Mrs. Henry Wade; and settlement worker Jane Addams.[32]

The company dismissed the latter group quickly, arguing that they had no stake in the situation. The first group accompanied Skeffington and the strike committee to the firm's offices on March 14, where the strikers presented three grievances to the firm: the closing of the gates to late workers, the deduction system for damaged work, and the reducing of wages without consulting or warning workers. Morris Selz and Rabbi Hirsch exchanged quips about the difference between saving "bad souls" and making "good soles" before Selz announced that he was willing to "adjust any differences," but only if the strikers' committee was authorized to reach agreements.[33] The committee reported back to the strikers' meeting in Cline's Hall, and the gathered strikers gave them power to act.

On the following day, the company made the first of several offers reflecting the second development in the strike. Not for the last time, Selz offered to take back all the women workers but only "most" of the men. And also not for the last time, strikers refused that offer. Though at times the strikers continued to meet separately along gender lines, the company's efforts to divide them on the basis of gender failed repeatedly. In fact, at one such point in the strike the women refused such an offer unanimously, while some of the men voted to accept it.

31. *CTrib*, March 11, 1892, p. 2.
32. Identification of individuals made from *The Lakeside Directory of Chicago* (1892), *The Lakeside Chicago, Illinois, General and Business Directory for 1890* (Chicago: Chicago Directory Co., 1891) (www.citydirectories.psmedia.com), and *S&LR*, March 17, 1892 (53:12), p. 644. Mrs. Henrotin also became one of the first members of the Chicago branch of the Women's Trade Union League in 1904. See "National Women's Trade Union League," by Ellen Lindstrom, p. 2, in Rose Schneiderman Papers, Tamiment Library, New York University (microfilm edition of Papers of the Women's Trade Union League and Its Principal Leaders), reel 2, frame 3.
33. *CTrib*, March 15, 1892, p. 3.

The strike wore on for two more months without much comment. Strikers continued to meet, to "brand [the firm] as an enemy to organized labor,"[34] and to hear speakers from the city's labor movement encourage further resistance. The strikers joined the city's May Day parade, although "the conventional red was wanting in the ranks of the shoemakers' unions and Selz, Schwab & Co.'s strikers. They wore blue badges and carried the national colors."[35] Throughout the strike, only two strikers were arrested for assaulting strikebreakers, both toward the end of March. One striker, who had returned to work in late March, made the newspapers in early April when his eldest son died of measles, allegedly made worse by his father's near destitution as a striker. Despite the father's earlier desertion of the strike, strikers passed the hat at their meeting to collect money for the child's burial.

Finally, on May 25, strikers, having dwindled to only about two hundred, struck an agreement with the company. Selz, Schwab agreed to restore the old wages and take back all the women and all but a handful of the men. Even though the *Tribune* termed the strike settlement "a victory for the strikers," many might not have seen it that way.[36] Most workers joined the strike initially, but some returned to work before the strike had officially ended, and others found employment elsewhere. The company, however, did give in to most of the strikers' demands, giving credence to the claim of owner Morris Selz early in the strike that it was "a deep-laid scheme on the part of a few of the leaders who chose the present time when we are exceedingly busy."[37] Whether the lasters, who initiated the strike, had any sort of "deep-laid scheme" is unclear, but they did understand the necessity of choosing optimal strike timing. The strike left at least the kernel of union activity among Chicago's shoe workers as well as, for those who held out to the end, a lesson about solidarity among workers.

Unlike Baltimore's clothing workers, these Chicago shoe workers began and ended their strike with organizations that were defined both occupationally and by gender. That the context for this was both local, in terms of the militance of Chicago's labor movement, and national, with roots in New England shoe union traditions, reinforces the image of the industry's workers as important bearers of union traditions. Not least among these traditions, as we shall see, was that of separate, but allegedly equal, gendered unions.

---

34. *CTrib*, April 2, 1892, p. 3.
35. *CTrib*, May 2, 1892, p. 6.
36. *CTrib*, May 26, 1892, p. 5.
37. *S&LR*, March 10, 1892 (53:10), p. 585.

Tobacco: New York City, 1900

As a very young woman, Bohemian-born Rosie Golden worked for the Philadelphia factory of Harburger, Homan & Company. The superintendent of the factory, Nathan Weiss, prided himself on maintaining a positive environment for his workforce, mostly teenage girls like Rosie. With a piano in the workroom, twice weekly music lessons, and a library for employees on premises, Weiss sought to hire and "create" only "educated, bright, useful women." Perhaps Rosie was even the young girl who sang "That's Why the Cat Came Back" at a reception to celebrate the opening of the company's new factory building in 1898.[38]

Trained in cigar manufacturing in this setting, Rosie must have had a shock when she transferred her life and work to New York City in 1900. Unlike the paradisaical Philadelphia factory, the New York plants of Harburger, Homan & Company provided employee housing that more closely resembled tenement cigar production than welfare capitalism. And that contrast gives us insight into "why the cat came back"—why Rosie Golden traveled to Philadelphia in an attempt to get her former co-workers to strike in support of striking New York City cigar makers in 1900.[39]

The huge 1900 strike of New York City cigar makers began at one of the largest New York manufacturers, Kerbs, Wertheim & Schiffer, which produced a range of products, from the high-end hand-rolled "Spanish" cigars to the cheapest machine-made and tenement-produced stogies. The firm operated its main factory between Fifty-fourth and Fifty-third streets at Second Avenue, but it had branches at Seventieth Street and Avenue A as well as in the Bowery in Lower Manhattan. In addition, it had "country factories" in Lancaster and Harrisburg, Pennsylvania. The firm's Manhattan plants alone employed more than two thousand workers.

At the main Kerbs factory on Fifty-fourth Street, women like Rosie worked at machine bunchers, passing "fillers" on to be bound and wrapped. By mid-March 1900, the workers had been complaining for several weeks about the quality of the raw materials management was giving them. In particular, the quality of the "binders," the second wrapper of a cigar, had been poor, which slowed production. Because all workers were employed on a piece-rate system, under which their wages were tied to output, poor-quality raw materials in effect created lower wages.

A relatively small group of men who worked wrapping the cigars complained of "the present trouble about stock" and gathered to discuss the issue. They formulated a list of demands that, if met, would effectively increase

38. *Tobacco (New York)*, January 14, 1898 (24:11), p. 6. This is probably a reference to the 1893 minstrel hit by Harry S. Miller, "The Cat Came Back." See http://www.melodylane.net/catcameback.html.

39. Unless otherwise noted, the story of this strike comes from coverage in the *New York World* and *New York Tribune*.

their wages. Demands for piece-rate increases for virtually all departments at the factory and for ample good-quality stock were combined with demands for a nine-hour workday and a regular Friday payday for all company shops.[40] The men presented the demands to the firm's owner, Edward Kerbs, at his office on Monday, March 12. When Kerbs refused to consider their demands, the workers threatened to strike. While company officials argued that only a small group of workers actually wanted to strike over these issues, strikers were able to convince first a single floor of the Fifty-fourth Street facility to walk out, then the entire factory, and ultimately workers from all the company's city plants.

Of the more than two thousand workers who struck on March 12, some fifteen hundred were young women like Rosie, for whom the demands for piece-rate increases and regular paydays proved quite appealing.[41] Though few of these young women belonged to the Cigar Makers' International Union (CMIU) at the beginning of the strike, they soon proved to be tenacious strikers and union supporters.

The first mass meeting of strikers was held Monday morning at Hungarian (or Bohemian) National Hall on East Seventy-third Street, which continued to be the main meeting site and the headquarters of the union throughout the long strike that followed. Workers who came together there were reminded simultaneously of several sources of identity: that of Bohemian immigrants, that of Kerbs, Wertheim & Schiffer workers, and ultimately that of strike and union supporters.

Both the cigar makers' union and the city's cigar manufacturers quickly realized that they had in this strike both an opportunity and a problem. For the cigar makers' union, striking against Kerbs, Wertheim & Schiffer, one of the city's largest manufacturers, could increase the strength of the union considerably. But few of the strikers actually belonged to the union.[42] Would strikers be able to hold out without any sort of strike benefits, such as those the relative handful of union members received? The union proposed a unique solution: they quickly promised to pay the nonunion, mostly female, strikers three dollars a week. Though less than the five dollars paid weekly to union members in good standing, this amount provided women with the same percentage (roughly 50 percent) of their weekly wage that union men would receive. This financial outlay by the union worked: it cemented the women's loyalty to the strike cause. For Rosie Golden and her peers, three dollars a

40. New York Board of Mediation and Arbitration, *Fourteenth Annual Report* (Albany: James B. Lyon, State Printer, 1901) [hereafter cited as N.Y. Bd. of M&A, *14th AR*], p. 127; March 9, 1900 (28:18), p. 2. See Patricia A. Cooper, *Once a Cigar Maker: Men, Women, and Work Culture* (Urbana: University of Illinois Press, 1987), pp. 14–18, for a description of cigar making.

41. N.Y. Bd. of M&A, *14th AR*, p. 126.

42. The union estimated that only 400 out of the 2,400 (their number) workers at the Kerbs company belonged to the union at the start of the strike. *Cigar Makers' Official Journal* [hereafter cited as *CMOJ*] 7 (June 1900): 162.

week meant the difference between dinner and starvation. The union strategy, however, would work only if other union members and cigar makers contributed money to the strike cause and coffers.

New York City cigar manufacturers quickly saw the implications of the strike. On the one hand, if the cigar makers' union could gain the support of Kerbs workers, no cigar manufacturer in the city would be safe from the union's "interference." On the other hand, if the Kerbs company could defeat the strike, it would be a fatal blow to the union. Two days after the strike began, members of nine other major cigar firms met with representatives of the Kerbs company at the Hotel Savoy. They all agreed to cut back on production and to put their employees on half-time work, in order to stop monetary contributions from flowing to the Kerbs strikers. Factory doors were locked at noon that day at all nine firms: McCoy & Company, Homan & Harburger, Hirschhorn & Mack, Foster & Company, Levy & Company, Kaufman & Company, Powell & Smith, Schwarz & Company, and the Hilson Cigar Company.

But the manufacturers had not counted on the anger this action would elicit from the workers. With wages cut back to the level of the union strike benefits, many workers chose to join the strike rather than produce what were quickly labeled "scab cigars." As the numbers of strikers increased, the power of sheer numbers began to take over recruitment of more participants. Whether officially on strike or simply idled by the work shutdown, workers moved quickly to join the union. By Sunday, union members meeting at Bohemian Hall represented more than twenty thousand workers. Hundreds watched from the galleries as 105 union delegates (including ten women) promised the striking and locked-out workers collectively payment of $10,000 a week in union benefits.

Although the cigar workers' strike began at a single factory, the actions of both the city's other manufacturers and the cigar makers' union in effect quickly "nationalized" the strike. The actions taken by manufacturers based on their decisions at their Hotel Savoy meeting had unintentional geographical consequences; they shifted the better part of the strike action to the Bohemian immigrant enclave in the upper Sixties and Seventies on the East Side. At the same time, Manhattan residents stretched over fifty city blocks saw evidence of the conflict in the coming months. New York City functioned at this time as the center of the nation's cigar industry, and manufacturers around the world watched the progress of the strike closely. The immediate reaction of the CMIU to this strike of largely unorganized workers shows that the union was well aware of that wider attention. Both sides understood clearly just how much there was to win or lose.

Throughout the strike, the union assigned strikers to picket on the sidewalks in front of the cigar factories, particularly in front of the Kerbs factory on Fifty-fourth Street. Jacob Wertheim described how the picketers functioned:

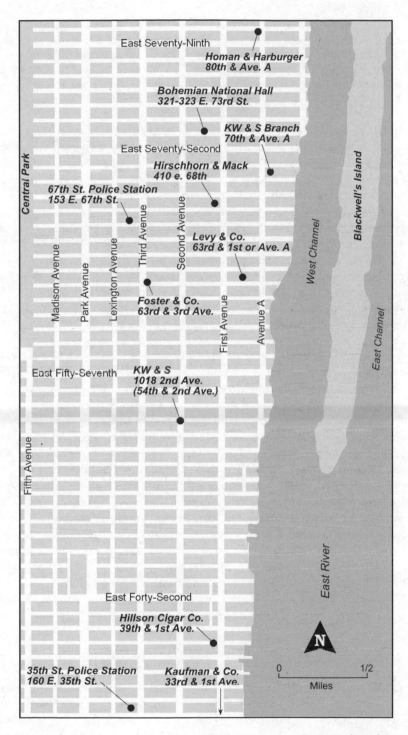

East Seventy-Ninth

Homan & Harburger
80th & Ave. A

Bohemian National Hall
321-323 E. 73rd St.

KW & S Branch
70th & Ave. A

East Seventy-Second

Hirschhorn & Mack
410 e. 68th

67th St. Police Station
153 E. 67th St.

Levy & Co.
63rd & 1st or Ave. A

Foster & Co.
63rd & 3rd Ave.

East Fifty-Seventh

KW & S
1018 2nd Ave.
(54th & 2nd Ave.)

Central Park

Madison Avenue

Park Avenue

Lexington Avenue

Third Avenue

Second Avenue

First Avenue

Avenue A

Fifth Avenue

West Channel

Blackwell's Island

East Channel

East River

East Forty-Second

Hillson Cigar Co.
39th & 1st Ave.

35th St. Police Station
160 E. 35th St.

Kaufman & Co.
33rd & 1st Ave.

N

0   1/2
Miles

1900 New York City cigar strike locations (Syracuse University Cartography Laboratory).

This patrol or picket service . . . consisted of said patrollers loitering and walking slowly and continually up and down in front of the factory, jostling against employees coming in and going out, sneering, hooting and laughing at employees, calling them by vile names and urging them to leave our employment, and persuading would-be employees, by means of argument, threat and fear of bodily harm, not to enter our employment.[43]

In early April, Kerbs, Wertheim & Schiffer petitioned the court for an injunction against such picketers. Although the injunction was granted initially, the superior court eventually overturned it. (The same occurred in the case of another injunction brought against paying out union strike benefits.) In the meantime, the strike hubbub on the streets of New York continued. Rosie Golden might have participated in the picketing, and she certainly would have experienced it because strikers often gathered near the official picketers during opening and closing hours in the factories.

At the same time that the union sought to keep the factories in the city closed down, it also attempted to spread the strike beyond New York City, because many of the struck or locked-out firms continued to supply their customers through production from their Pennsylvania country shops. Thus, the union simultaneously initiated and carried on a strike against the large Kerbs factory in Lancaster.

In the midst of the chaos created in New York by the strike, Rosie Golden quietly slipped out of town. Spending what was allegedly her life savings, possibly as much as eight hundred dollars, on a train ticket to Philadelphia and two thousand half-pound boxes of chocolates, Rosie traveled to Philadelphia to talk with her former colleagues at the Homan & Harburger plant there.[44] In effect bribing the young women to leave the factory, Rosie handed out the boxes of chocolates and gained the attention of about half the plant's one thousand workers. At a nearby hall, she "counsel[ed] peace, and urg[ed] her cohorts to be calm but strenuous," telling them about the trials and tribulations of the New York City strikers. One Philadelphia paper wrote, "She has not been a locked-out worker in New York for nothing. It has developed in her the genius of generalship and she knows that waiting is a good way to win." In the spirit of the struck factory, the speeches were followed by "a versatile young man" who played piano, a program "varied by a short-skirted learner, who sang rag-time ditties with vivacious glee."[45]

"General" of this merry band of strikers or not, Rosie soon returned to New York, reportedly to attend to her ill mother. The girls at the Philadelphia

43. *U.S. Tobacco Journal* [hereafter cited as *USTJ*], April 28, 1900 (44:14), p. 6.
44. A half-pound bar of chocolate cost approximately forty cents in 1900. "Price Lists: Package Goods, Grocery Items and Cocoa Powder," 1901–18, Hershey Foods Corporation Collection Accession no. 85006, box 15, Hershey Community Archives, Hershey, Pennsylvania. Pamela Cassidy Whitenack of the Hershey Archives, William Woys Weaver, and Anne Mendelson all helped track down this information.
45. *Philadelphia Inquirer*, May 15, 1900, p. 1.

Harburger, Homan & Company "cigar girls" on strike in Philadelphia, May 1900 (*Philadelphia Inquirer*, May 15, 1900, p. 1).

Homan & Harburger factory remained on strike for at least six weeks, formulating their own demands for wage increases.[46] On Rosie's return to New York City, the young "Salome" or "Joan of Arc" of the strikers was invited to join the union strike committee there.[47]

The strike in New York wore on through the long, hot summer, with strikers showing no signs of returning to work. Several sources quoted workers making such statements as "We are getting $5 a week not to work and we don't see why we should go into a shop [in] this hot weather. If the unions stop paying us our $5 per we may change our minds. But just now $5 a week for doing nothing is good enough for us."[48] By the end of June, the cigar makers' union began to experience difficulties maintaining the level of strike benefits. Requests to the AFL for assistance were met with a firm refusal from former cigar maker Samuel Gompers, who argued that there

46. *Public Ledger*, May 16, 1900, p. 2. Sources, including coverage in both the *Philadelphia Inquirer* and the *Public Ledger*, as well as reports in the *USTJ*, are unclear on exactly when the Philadelphia strike of Homan & Harburger workers ended. The last reported mention of the strike in any of these sources is a comment in the June 9 *USTJ* (43:20), p. 4, that the strike situation "remains unchanged."

47. The *New York World* quoted one observer likening Rosie to Salome (September 2, 1900, p. 7); the *Philadelphia Inquirer* called her "a Joan of Arc" (May 15, 1900, p. 1).

48. *USTJ*, July 14, 1900 (44:25), p. 5.

were "great industrial disputes going on all over the country" and that prior commitments barred the AFL from assisting the New York City cigar makers. Gompers unofficially added his personal belief that

> the Cigar Makers' International Union is too firmly entrenched to weaken or be seriously injured by the combination of the New York manufacturers; that the latter will have a better recognition of the fighting qualities of our organization than they had immediately previous to the contest; that they will have greater respect for it hereafter, and not provoke any trouble, and that the trade will be more diffused that it was before the present contest, and the cigar makers better organized so as to reap the advantages of higher wages and the permanent establishment of the eight-hour work-day.[49]

In early July, exasperated by the tenacity of the strikers and locked-out workers, some of the companies providing housing to employees began evictions. Homan & Harburger was one of those companies, telling locked-out families living in the company's three tenement houses on Avenue A that they had a simple choice: produce "scab" cigars for Kerbs, Wertheim & Schiffer or face eviction. Out of thirty-nine families listed as living in those buildings in the 1900 federal census, the heads of all were foreign-born, with 85 percent of them coming from Bohemian Austria.[50] These workers refused to leave their homes, claiming that their agreement with Homan & Harburger was that if they lived in the houses they would have steady work with the firm. By refusing to supply such work, they said, the company had broken the agreement, and workers therefore did not have to live up to their end of the bargain. While a committee of three men and three women met with Mr. Homan, the union promised to help the families fight the evictions. Faced with such determination, the firm backed down and the families apparently remained in their homes.

In fact, despite the union's fiscal problems, by the end of August the firms that had locked out workers in sympathy with the Kerbs company fight against the union began to waver. As the support for Kerbs, Wertheim & Schiffer crumbled, other firms agreed to hire none but union workers, granted their workers wage increases, settled various other demands, and reopened their doors to the workers. The union journal explained these deserters as follows: "While these manufacturers made a stubborn fight in one of the greatest battles that has ever been waged in the history of our craft, we congratulate them on the fact that they have sense enough to know when they were whipped."[51] Workers continued their strike against the Kerbs company, although the three city factories belonging to the company "operated at

49. Gompers to G. W. Perkins, SG Letterbooks, June 11, 1900, 35:153.
50. 1900 Federal Manuscript Census for New York County, Borough of Manhattan, E.D. 759, sheets 16B–18B. See also chapter 6 and appendix 2, below.
51. *CMOJ* 25 (September 1900): 9.

Tenement cigar production, East 71st Street, New York City, 1895, perhaps employees of Kerbs, Wertheim & Schiffer (New York Bureau of Labor Statistics, *Twelfth Annual Report*).

nearly full capacity with non-union help" by the end of the year.[52] By the time the February edition of the *American Federationist* went to print, the cigar makers' union could report that it was "free from any serious trade disputes," though the AFL also officially declared the Kerbs company "unfair" in the same issue.[53]

Cigar makers stood at the most unionized end of the spectrum of workers' organization in the tobacco industry. Begun as a largely "pure" craft union, admitting and offering benefits to a small group of the most skilled workers in the trade, by 1900 the cigar makers' union was stretching its definitions of membership. The New York City strike of that year demonstrates how this could bring young immigrants like Rosie Golden to a new appreciation of union membership. As in the case of the Baltimore garment workers, gender and ethnicity reinforced such workers' identifications with the strike and with the union. That very identification propelled Rosie and others to new heights of activism.

Toward the end of the strike, one correspondent for the cigar makers' union paper wrote that, despite partial success, "our soldiers who are carrying on this end of the battle are unable to continue, to carry the burden of this fight against the largest cigar octopus of modern times alone."[54] The leadership of workers like Rosie Golden had inspired many, especially within the ranks of the female and Bohemian cigar makers of New York. Despite the workers' valiant struggle, however, the primary lesson the cigar manufacturers

52. N.Y. Bd. of M&A, *14th AR*, p. 128.
53. *American Federationist* 8 (February 1901): 53, 65.
54. *CMOJ* 25 (September 1900): 6.

learned was that they needed to move business away from New York City. In the years that followed, then, more and more cigar firms began to run "country shops" in Pennsylvania and upstate New York.[55] Rosie's chocolates aside, when this "cat came back" she found her future as a cigar worker tenuous at best. New York City cigar makers found little to sing about in the twentieth century.

Textiles: Lowell, 1903

In the spring of 1902, textile workers in the city of Fall River, Massachusetts, headquarters of the United Textile Workers of America (UTWA), requested and received a 10 percent wage increase.[56] Shortly afterward, the Textile Council in Lowell, Massachusetts, affiliated with the same union, made the same request of their members' employers. Lowell employers, who had operated without strikes for years, refused the Textile Council's request. On Wednesday, March 26, 1902, members of the Lowell Textile Council voted to strike the following Monday, and in response the city's mills prepared to shut down. The acting mayor then appointed a citizens' committee to bring the two sides together to discuss the dispute, ultimately leading the Textile Council to abandon the idea of a strike. Throughout the negotiations, mill spokesmen claimed that because economic conditions for the mills were unfavorable, an increase in wages was impossible.

Almost one year later, on Sunday, February 22, 1903, believing that conditions in the industry had improved, the Lowell Textile Council voted unanimously to request once again a 10 percent wage increase. On February 25 it sent a letter to that effect to the agents of the seven major textile "corporations" in Lowell: the Boott Cotton Mills, the Massachusetts Cotton Mills, the Tremont & Suffolk Mills, the Hamilton Manufacturing Company, the Merrimac Manufacturing Company, the Appleton Company, and the Lawrence Manufacturing Company.[57] Wanting to give mill agents a fair chance to respond unemotionally, and believing that the agents had promised such an increase the year before, the Textile Council put off making its request public.

55. Cooper, *Once a Cigar Maker*, p. 256.

56. Unless otherwise noted, the story of this strike comes from coverage in the *Boston Globe* [hereafter cited as *Globe*], the *Lowell Courier* [hereafter cited as *Courier*], the Massachusetts State Board of Conciliation and Arbitration, *Sixteenth Annual Report for 1902* (Boston: Wright & Potter Printing Co., 1902) and *Seventeenth Annual Report for 1903* (Boston: Wright & Potter Printing Co., 1903), and the *American Wool and Cotton Reporter*.

57. This letter is reported in the *Globe*, March 2, 1903 (a.m.), p. 1, and confirmed by the letter from C. P. Baker to E. M. Townsend & Co., February 26, 1903, Lawrence Manufacturing Company Records, Baker Library, Harvard University Graduate School of Business Administration [hereafter cited as LMCR], MB-13, p. 471.

Unbeknownst to the Textile Council, the mill agents had their own reasons for keeping the wage request quiet. A meeting of the company treasurers on February 27 "agreed that the mills can not afford to grant any increase in wages. The agents were requested to consider the most expedient way of presenting the fact to the Textile Council and also to the general public."[58] The mill agents met on Monday, March 2, when "it was voted to have the Sec'y acknowledge the receipt of the request from the Textile Council and promise a reply letter."

> Mr. Southworth [agent of the Massachusetts mills and secretary of the mill agents' association] had a letter ready refusing their request, but some of us [the mill agents], including him later, thought it would be better to gain time for studying the real temper of the operatives, and to prepare their minds and those of the public for a refusal. . . .
> A too early refusal, without apparent consideration, would . . . precipitate trouble, which time and missionary work may avert.

In fact, the mill agents seem to have believed that a strike in 1903 was less likely than it had been the year before. The Lawrence company agent, Franklin Nourse, commented: "The labor leaders are very quiet, do not talk strike even to the reporters, and are generally acting differently from last year."[59] In other words, what the Textile Council members saw as strategic courtesy the managements of the mills misread as weakness, hesitation, and passivity.

Unlike the other strike stories recounted in this chapter, the Lowell textile strike of 1903 began as a carefully plotted action by the town's organized textile workers, who faced an even more cohesive group of organized textile employers. Though both sides of the controversy began with misperceptions of the actions and strengths of the other side, both sides ultimately had to come to grips with new evaluations of their own strengths and weaknesses. While a core group of union leaders in Lowell had already achieved a high level of union consciousness, many of the town's workers came to recognize their identities as members of various class, gender, and ethnic groups only over the course of the ensuing three-month-long strike.

The material conditions for recognizing such identities can be spelled out in some detail for Lowell. One of the best-documented textile centers in the United States, the city of Lowell is primarily known to history for its earliest cotton mills. In the 1830s, a group of investors known as the Boston Associates developed mills in Lowell, drawing on the young daughters of New England farmers as workers. In Lowell, the Boston Associates formed a number of textile "corporations" with a complex set of interlocking directorships. The various Lowell corporations coordinated their production

58. Letter from C. P. Baker to F. Nourse, February 27, 1903, LMCR, MC-26, p. 182.
59. F. Nourse to C. P. Baker, March 3, 1903, LMCR, MD-79, p. 33.

carefully, with each mill specializing in a different variety of fairly coarse cloth. In this way, the corporations did not so much collude as simply refuse to compete directly with one another.[60] The mills soon became famous both for their cotton goods and for the various educational opportunities they provided female employees. Mill boardinghouses had libraries and pianos, and the young mill workers were encouraged to write for the company-sponsored *Lowell Offering*. Before the Civil War, then, the Lowell mills provided both work and intellectual growth for thousands of young women. By the time of the Civil War, however, the mills had begun hiring the immigrants flooding into the country, and paternalistic offerings ended.[61] By the late nineteenth century, the labor force at the Lowell mills had changed dramatically. Although the mills began with an almost entirely female workforce, by 1900 men easily made up about 40 percent of Lowell textile workers. In that year, the major textile corporations in Lowell employed some sixteen thousand workers, just over one-third (34.4 percent) of the town's employed population.[62]

Laurence Gross, in his book on the Boott mills, argues that "the complex was separated from the community by architecture as well as by ownership."[63] The experiences of workers within the Boott mills were not unique, however, but rather shared by the entire community of textile workers in Lowell. While mill buildings might have cut off pedestrians' views of the Merrimack River and the many canals that powered the mills, most Lowell residents either worked in the mills themselves or had family members or close neighbors who did.

Architecture may have encapsulated the workers in the individual mills and kept them apart from other cotton workers during the workday, but the similarities among mills ensured that Lowell's textile workers understood their commonalities. One mill might offer slightly different employment opportunities than another, but many of the skills learned in one mill could easily be transferred to another. Variations on carding, spinning, weaving, and printing existed in virtually all the mills.

In all the Lowell mills, too, male workers performed the initial step of carding the raw cotton, which was then gathered into loose strands by women ("speeding" and "roving") in preparation for spinning. The original Lowell mills had used ring-spinning machines, which were operated by women, but by 1903 the complex mule-spinning machines common elsewhere began to

60. Laurence F. Gross, *The Course of Industrial Decline: The Boott Cotton Mills of Lowell, Massachusetts, 1835–1955* (Baltimore: Johns Hopkins University Press, 1993), pp. 5–6.

61. Thomas Dublin, *Women at Work: The Transformation of Work and Community in Lowell, Massachusetts, 1826–1860* (New York: Columbia University Press, 1979), chap. 9, pp. 145–64; Gross, *Course of Industrial Decline*, p. 80.

62. U.S. Bureau of the Census, *Occupations at the Twelfth Census* (Washington, D.C.: Government Printing Office, 1904), pp. 598–601.

63. Gross, *Course of Industrial Decline*, p. 41.

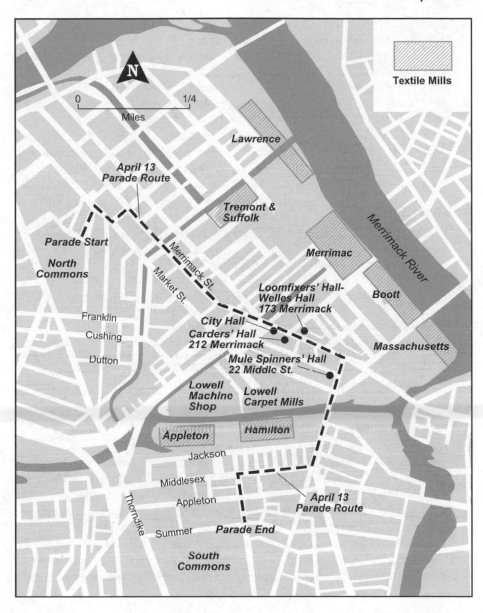

1903 Lowell, Massachusetts, strike locations (Syracuse University Cartography Laboratory).

be used in Lowell as well. Mule-spinning machines were operated exclusively by men, mostly immigrants who had learned their trade in Great Britain. Children of both sexes worked "doffing" filled spindles in the ring-spinning rooms of Lowell mills, while boys served as "piecers," for the mule spinners, both removing completed yarn and serving as general apprentices to the spinners. Female "spoolers," "warpers," and "beamers" prepared the yarn for the looms, and "drawers-in" set up the looms. In the mills' weaving rooms, both women and men worked, though Gross argues that the differential in pay suggests that they worked at weaving different types and qualities of fabric. "Room girls" finished off the pieces and removed the cloth from the looms. The final stages in the production of cloth—sizing, bleaching, printing—were, by 1903, generally performed by men.[64]

These carefully delineated and interdependent work processes suggest a rigid sexual division of labor within the mills. A 1902 report on conditions in the Boott mills, however, reveals how the occupational division of labor by sex might break down spatially within individual mills. This report detailed the haphazard nature of mill growth and its dangers, providing a sense of the work experience of Lowell's textile workers.

The sketch of the Boott mills included in the report conveys the patched-together quality of the mills, illustrating the cobbled-together nature of the complex. Furthermore, the report states:

> Nearly all the Buildings are old, narrow, low-studded, poorly constructed, and so located with regard to each other that daylight is reduced one-half, while in many rooms artificial light is an hourly necessity.
>
> Operatives are not attracted to such rooms, seek employment there only because they cannot get it elsewhere, and are constantly discouraged in an honest effort to do good work. The best of machinery cannot be arranged or operated to the fullest advantage in such mills. . . .
>
> Excessive vibration of floors, and rocking of whole buildings is a common complaint throughout the yard.[65]

The report also pointed out that years of cobbling new structures onto old had created an unsafe and inefficient layout for textile production. In particular, "the most casual observer cannot fail to notice the lack of concentration of machinery belonging to the different processes, for example: There are Cards in 7 different rooms and mills; Roving frames are found in 8 different rooms; Ring Spinning in 7; Mule Spinning in 5; Spooling in 2 places; and the looms are found in 8 different rooms."[66] Going on to propose new mills, the report recommended a more appropriate division of the processes of textile production, with mule spinning on one floor, ring spinning on another,

64. Ibid., pp. 61–66; Melvin Thomas Copeland, *The Cotton Manufacturing Industry of the United States* (New York: A. M. Kelley, 1966), pp. 56–98.

65. Walter E. Parker, "Report on the Condition of the Boott Cotton Mills, Lowell, Mass., 1902," p. 10, Boott/Flather Collection, Center for Lowell History, University of Massachusetts Lowell [hereafter cited as B/FC], box 29B, folder 9B.

66. Ibid., pp. 34–35.

spoolers in one room, rovers in two more rooms, and weavers in a separate building altogether.[67]

The report's proposals, though framed in terms of efficiency and profitability for the mills themselves, unwittingly reveal key aspects of the sexual division of space—or lack thereof—in the Lowell mills. In the haphazard Boott mills, as in many of the others, men and women operated separate machines, but they did so in the same buildings and even within the same rooms. At the very least, they jostled one another as they climbed the stairs and navigated the narrow aisles of the mills. The report also gives an idea of other conditions the workers would share as well. Cramped work spaces, poor light, vibrating floors and walls—both male and female textile workers experienced all these conditions. The secretary of the mixed-gender weavers' union, Annie McMullen, said in 1903, "The life of a mill girl is not an attractive one. . . . It is hard work week in and week out."[68]

The existence of "Lowell mill girls" had changed dramatically over the course of the nineteenth century, increasingly converging with the working conditions of the relatively new "Lowell mill men" alongside whom they worked. In response to their deteriorating conditions, even the workers at the formerly paternalistic Lowell mills sought out the protection of unions. Mill workers' unions in Massachusetts had existed since the 1850s, but they had never been particularly strong in the town of Lowell. The mule spinners of Fall River had established their union in 1858, finally transforming it into the National Cotton Mule Spinners' Association in 1889. Loom fixers similarly established a series of unions from the 1850s on, but only in the 1870s and 1880s did other cotton mill workers begin to form and join unions. Finally, in 1901 the United Textile Workers of America began its attempt to bring together all the various textile worker unions.[69] Although Lowell was not at the center of any of these developments, the member unions of the Lowell Textile Council did affiliate with the UTWA. The purpose of the council was to coordinate activities among the disparate occupationally based unions involved in the city's industry. As such, the council could only make recommendations to member unions, not make decisions on actions. In many ways, the 1903 strike and lockout in Lowell provided the UTWA with its first major test in that city.

The Lowell mill agents finally replied publicly to the Textile Council's request for a wage increase in the middle of March: they would not grant any increase. A Textile Council committee met with the agents on Thursday, March 19, arguing that both improved economic conditions and an increased cost of living justified the wage hike. The mill agents responded with a pre-

67. Lockwood, Greene & Company, "Sketch Plans Showing Proposed Reorganization of Boott Cotton Mills, Lowell, Mass., April 1903," B/TC, box 29B, folder 11.

68. *Globe*, March 30, 1903 (a.m.), p. 2.

69. See Copeland, *Cotton Manufacturing Industry*, pp. 123–24. See also chapters 3 and 7, below.

pared statement repeating their refusal. When the meeting adjourned a little more than two hours after it began, both sides believed that Lowell now faced its first strike since 1875. Though some members of the Textile Council still hoped to avoid such a direct confrontation, they put the question to member unions. Council members believed that the unions of mule spinners, weavers, and loom fixers were fairly cohesive, but they had deep reservations about the potential strike sympathies of most women mill workers, as well as of many of the immigrant workers. Prominent French Americans in Lowell had allegedly come out against the idea of a strike, and the attitudes of the more recent Greek, Portuguese, and Armenian immigrants were unknown to council leaders.

The Textile Council held two meetings on Sunday, March 22. After fully discussing the implications of the conference with the mill agents, the council put the question of a strike to its member unions. Individual unions would meet over the next three nights, following which the council would meet once again to consider the collective decisions.

Though the Textile Council expected a strong vote in favor of the strike from the loom fixers' meeting on Monday night, that group surprised everyone by taking no vote and announcing that they preferred to exhaust all options for compromise before voting. The next night, beamers, carders, and nappers all voted unanimously in favor of a strike in their separate union meetings. Weavers also voted to strike that same night, including Greek weavers who showed up by surprise; the union allowed both the Greeks and other nonunion weavers to vote on the question. Some council members voiced astonishment at the enthusiasm of women workers in the various strike votes. Lowell workers thus began to recognize their membership in discreet occupational groups despite anticipated ethnic and gender divisions. On Wednesday night, a second meeting of the loom fixers voted 248–2 to strike, and the mule spinners joined the pro-strike ranks during their own meeting. The assistants, "back boys" and "piecers," attended but did not vote. Now only a two-thirds vote of the Textile Council stood in the way of a strike declaration.

In the meantime, members of the Massachusetts Board of Conciliation and Arbitration arrived in Lowell and consulted with town officials and representatives of both the unions and the mills. While the board asked the two sides to submit the dispute to them for arbitration, neither side showed much interest in that idea at this point. The mill men felt confident that the strike would either not happen or not be successful, and cited the relatively small percentage of unionized workers. As the Lawrence company wrote to its wholesalers on March 25, "We shall try to run our mill; and as we believe that the knitters will not go out, it is entirely possible that we can keep up a pretty full production."[70] The unions, however, were still leery about outside

---

70. C. P. Baker to E. M. Townsend & Co., March 25, 1903, LMCR, MB-13, p. 491.

interference because of the actions of the citizens' committee the previous year. One union leader noted, "Wise men sometimes are bitten by dogs, but the man who permits the same dog to bite him twice is a fool."[71]

On Wednesday, members of the Textile Council again met with a committee of mill agents to discuss the situation. Both sides went over their views of the situation, unionists explaining their reasoning, and agents clarifying their denial. On Thursday the full Textile Council met to hold a strike vote. Secretary Bernard F. Supple of the Board of Arbitration presented a letter offering mediation and addressed the assembled delegates. According to a newspaper report, "he quoted the old adage: 'Be sure you are right, then go ahead.' He also advised the operatives to exhaust every peaceful means within their power before 'forcing the issue.' " Then, "when he closed he was cheered to the echo and the applause was plainly heard on the street below, although the hall is on the fourth floor."[72] While Supple intended his comments to encourage moderation, workers took the "old adage" as encouragement. They voted unanimously to leave work at noon on Saturday, March 28, and not to return until they had received satisfaction from their employers.

The Textile Council meeting of confirmed union members was followed by a series of meetings of the previously unorganized workers in the mills. Between Thursday night and Monday morning, spoolers, warpers, drawing in hands, slasher tenders, and nappers all met in occupational groups to organize themselves into unions and vote to support the strike. Nonunion spinners and "jack spinners" would attend the next meeting of the mule spinners. A meeting of carders was called for the following Tuesday evening, and Greek textile workers also held their own strike meetings. In other words, organization both by occupation and by ethnicity brought larger and larger groups of workers into the ranks of would-be strikers. Having experienced the dwindling purchasing power of their wages over the previous year, and having watched the deliberations among unionized co-workers and the mill agents over the past month, these workers now stood enthusiastically on the side of striking.

This evidence of increased and unexpected support for the strike movement led mill agents to reconsider their earlier position of disdain. Agents put out feelers among the workers and found that most planned to strike. Accordingly, just before closing on Saturday, the seven mills posted notices stating that the mills would be closed from Monday morning, March 30, until further notice, an action that forced almost twenty thousand out of work. The strike, now transformed into a lockout, was on.

Members of the Textile Council wasted no time. Council President Robert Conroy announced that the workers had won the first round, and assured

71. *Globe*, March 29, 1903, p. 1.
72. *Globe*, March 27, 1903 (p.m.), p. 1.

Lowell mill operatives discuss the contents of their pay envelopes (*Boston Globe*, April 1, 1903, p. 1).

his followers, "This is to be a friendly, manly fight. Our people understand their rights and they will stand up for them."[73] Members of the council organizing committee spent time that weekend talking with Greek, Portuguese, Polish, Syrian, and Armenian workers. They set up headquarters at the carders' union hall on Merrimack Street, where they signed up hundreds of new union members. All would be taken care of during the coming strike, Conroy promised. The Textile Council would meet Monday at 10:30 a.m., and meetings of Greek operatives, mule spinners, ring spinners, warpers, and loom fixers were scheduled for that day as well. Slasher tenders, beamers, nappers, carders, and Polish operatives would hold Tuesday meetings. Council members reminded their constituencies that some workers would report to work on Monday to finish cleaning up their jobs, but that these workers were not deserting the strike. Only at the Lawrence company did a large number of workers report to work, as that company's hosiery knitters

73. *Globe*, March 29, 1903, p. 1.

Lowell mill hands discussing the strike situation (*Boston Globe*, March 30, 1903, p. 2).

were not included in the ranks of the strikers and the company did not plan to close.

The headlines of Monday's newspapers blared the news most Lowell residents already knew: "STRIKE BEGINS," "WHEELS SILENT," "GREAT LABOR CONTEST BEGINS AT LOWELL."[74] Between thirteen thousand and eighteen thousand workers stayed away from their jobs that morning. Police guarded the gates of the Lawrence hosiery mill, whose knitters did not belong to the Textile Council. A small group of Greek workers gathered there to watch the three thousand workers of the hosiery mill walk down Cabot and Suffolk streets to work. Only the yarn department of the mill was shut down by the strike. The only disturbance reported during the first day came when women in the finishing department of the Tremont & Suffolk company peered out their windows to watch the Lawrence workers. Thinking that the finishers were strikebreakers, the crowd of young Greek men began to yell and hiss, but they soon realized their mistake and dispersed.

Several surprises greeted company officials. The Massachusetts mill had not expected its nonunion spinners and Greek, Syrian, and Portuguese workers to strike. A number of Greeks employed in the Lawrence company

74. *Globe*, March 30, 1903 (p.m.), p. 1; *Courier*, March 30, 1903, pp. 1, 10.

dye house also declined to appear for work. Evidence of strike sympathy continued to cascade through the community of textile workers. Back boys and doffers appeared in full at the mule spinners' meetings; Greek operatives surprised all with their group solidarity. And even though the Merrimack company's print works remained open, only six out of twenty-four calico printers, and none of the engravers, appeared for work. One hundred corduroy workers in the Merrimack mills voted to finish the work that was on their frames and then join the strike. A meeting of Polish workers voted to support the strike and chose delegates to the Textile Council. Portuguese workers also held separate meetings. The approximately one hundred slasher tenders in Lowell organized their own union and warned their members, "Whatever you do, act as men. Be manly."[75] Female ring spinners also met and organized a union in the first days of the strike. Twisters and dye-house workers formed unions, too. Through these various occupational and ethnic identities, Lowell textile workers began to evince their recognition of their common interests.

Even the Lawrence hosiery knitters eventually joined the strike. Organized in a union affiliated with the Textile Council the previous year, the knitters in 1903 expressed satisfaction with their wages. According to the Lowell paper, "The efforts to organize these women have not been particularly strenuous, and the reason is not apparent, unless it be that the women are so well satisfied with present conditions that they see no advantage in organizing, and give union people little or no encouragement in this direction."[76] Encouragement or no, the Textile Council called for a meeting of knitters on Tuesday night in Spinners' Hall. The meeting, addressed in both English and French, lasted three hours. While many knitters favored striking, others urged their colleagues to postpone any action.

The following morning, the company fired fifteen knitters who had attended the meeting. Agent Nourse explained to the newspapers:

> We are operating the Lawrence hosiery largely out of deference to the wishes of the men and women employed within the works. Persons who wish to remain out may do so, . . . but it is not our intention to have trouble makers in our employment. An employer, as a rule, dislikes to pay wages to employees who are not working in harmony with his interests. We regard the 15 knitters who were creating dissension as being in that class.[77]

Operatives gathered outside the Lawrence gates on April 1 to discuss the firings, the previous night's meeting, and the planned meeting for that night. The Lowell reporter said:

75. *Globe*, April 1, 1903 (a.m.), p. 7.
76. *Courier*, March 30, 1903, p. 1.
77. *Courier*, April 1, 1903, p. 1.

Meeting of the Lowell ring spinners (*Boston Globe*, April 1, 1903, p. 4).

A visitor . . . would have seen but few signs [of the strike]. . . . To one, however, who had seen these people daily, there were suggestions of restlessness which were partly concealed by the habitual cheerfulness displayed by the operatives when they enter the gates on early mornings. There was a damper upon the ardor of the younger people especially, who gathered in groups and discussed the probable action of their elders. The fact also that there were police upon duty . . . caused a more serious aspect to come over the faces of those who loitered a moment before they entered the mill.[78]

That "more serious aspect" convinced at least some of the knitters to join the strike that night, but only a few dozen stayed off their jobs the following day.

The Lawrence hosiery mills never closed down completely during the strike, although company officials admitted that the spinning department had joined the strike from its beginning. With only three weeks' worth of yarn on hand, the company did not know how long it could keep the knitting departments open. During the first week of the strike, it began to seek out other sources of yarn, telling one possible supplier, "It is a case of necessity, for if we cannot keep our knitters at work, they will go out with the rest of the help at Lowell and join unions."[79] At the same time, however, the company "applied" to

78. Ibid.
79. C. P. Baker to New England Cotton Yarn Co., April 2, 1903, LMCR, MA-34, p. 169.

the collective mills' treasurers for permission to open their spinning departments. Treasurer C. P. Baker reported that his "efforts . . . resulted in a unanimous vote of the treasurers to allow our yarn mill to start and of course we shall avail ourselves of it at the earliest practicable time. We shall start in a very quiet way if we possibly can, and very likely little at present will be said about it in the papers—although I anticipate trouble later on."[80]

By the end of the strike's first week, however, rumors about possible mill reopenings abounded. The agent for Tremont & Suffolk allegedly had men canvassing mill workers, asking whether they would return to work. However, Baker's guess about the plans of the Lawrence mill was realized; no newspaper rumors mentioned any reopening of that mill's spinning departments. Many believed that all the mill gates would reopen within two weeks, perhaps on Easter Monday, because of mill agents' concerns that their most skilled workers would leave town. In fact, once the corporations began paying workers for their pre-lockout employment, some workers did begin to leave Lowell. The French Canadian community in particular became known for returning to the Canadian border in large numbers, with well over one thousand of them leaving Lowell during the course of the strike. Despite this, Council President Conroy said that attempts to reopen the mills would merely show agents just how completely they had misjudged their employees' determination in the strike.

That determination was kept up through the first week or two through almost constant meetings. The Textile Council met daily, often with large audiences. Individual unions of specific occupational and ethnic subgroups also met frequently. Money poured in from union supporters across the state and the nation. The manager of the Lowell baseball league announced that he would organize a benefit baseball game; the Lowell Trades and Labor Council announced a benefit ball; the Textile Council began to plan a mass parade of strikers. Many union meetings ended with music or other entertainment; the cross-gendered weavers' meetings usually concluded with dancing, music provided by one of the older German weavers. The various unions also began to pay out strike benefits, beginning with the mule spinners and carders, who were first paid on Saturday, April 11.

On Monday, April 6, the Massachusetts legislature ordered the Board of Arbitration to investigate the Lowell strike and report back to them on April 22. Although the Textile Council initially bemoaned the narrow parameters of the investigation, arguing that they "would like to see at least one man who knows a spinner from a weaver, or a slasher from a beamer" involved in the inquiry, they pledged total cooperation with the inquiry.[81] The city offered rooms at City Hall for the board to use.

80. C. P. Baker to J. C. Van De Water, April 3, 1903, LMCR, MB-14, p. 1.
81. *Globe*, April 7, 1903 (a.m.), p. 2.

The Board of Arbitration opened its hearings on Thursday, April 9. The executive committee of the Textile Council attended, as did several mill treasurers and agents. Some of the mills agreed on the spot to turn their books over to the board for examination. That first afternoon, the board visited the Lawrence hosiery mill and the Appleton mill, where some looms were operating, and the following week, it would tour several more mills. When the board reconvened on Friday morning, it heard the council's representatives argue that increased prosperity as well as higher wages in both Fall River and New Bedford had led them to make their wage request. Council members also charged that the mill corporations functioned not as individual businesses but as a single, scheming "combination." It was up to the mill agents, unionists argued, to prove their logic faulty.

This the mill agents and treasurers spent the rest of the hearings trying to do. Wage differentials between Lowell mills and the mills in Fall River, they argued, were due to differences in goods produced, consumer demand, and the older age of the Lowell mills and their machinery. The legal representative for the mills, Attorney Frank Dunbar, even argued in his closing statement that the workers themselves in Fall River and New Bedford were better, more efficient operatives and therefore more deserving of wage increases than those in Lowell. The treasurers also repeated emphatically that there was no specious "combination" of the mills.

In the middle of the board's investigation, the Textile Council held its parade and mass meeting. That Monday morning, only the third day of the inquiry, President Conroy was the only member of the Textile Council to show up for the day's testimony. The arbitration board met briefly and then adjourned until later in the afternoon, in deference to the workers' parade.

The parade began at Lowell's North Common, marching to the town's South Common past a reviewing stand of city officials on the steps of City Hall. Just as worker participation in the strike had begun along either occupational or ethnic lines, so the parade adhered to similar lines of distinction. The procession began with a police detail, followed by the executive committee of the Textile Council. A band marched next, followed by the mule spinners' union, the women of the ring spinners' union, the mixed-gender marchers of the weavers' union, and a second, twelve-piece, band. Then came the carders' union, the Polish mill employees, the female "spoolers, warpers, and drawing-in room employes," the male "beamers, slasher-tenders, and dye-house workers," and a third, ten-piece band.[82] Next came the cloth room workers, Portuguese operatives who only joined the procession at Central and Market streets, another twelve-piece band, the Greek operatives, and a final ten-piece band. The loom fixers' union made up the rear.

Marchers wore badges designating their trades and unions and carried American flags and union banners. The Greek contingent also carried Greek

82. *Globe*, April 13, 1903 (p.m.), p. 1.

Lowell women operatives in the April 12 strike parade (*Boston Globe*, April 14, 1903, p. 1).

flags. Many marchers, women in particular, joined the procession en route only after seeing their co-workers in the line. The only carriage in the parade carried two ministers and the elder statesman of Massachusetts labor politics, Frank K. Foster. Altogether, somewhere between five thousand and seven thousand workers marched, with many more lining the streets. The reviewing stand held the mayor, the president of the common council and three aldermen, eight other city officials, and one state legislator.

Once the parade arrived at South Common, high winds reduced audibility to such an extent that three separate speaker stands were erected. Reportedly, fifteen thousand people listened to the speeches there. One speaker stand addressed the Greek contingent, while the others addressed strikers more generally. Virtually all pointed out that if the strikers had organized earlier they might not have had to strike. Several state representatives spoke, one reminding the strikers, "You are not going into this trouble for yourselves, but for your children. If you receive your just dues your children will not wear their lives out at the loom."[83] State Representative Samuel Ross, national secretary of the mule spinners' union, assured the strikers that financial assistance would arrive from the labor movement and encouraged them to continued their struggle at the ballot box as well. Council President Conroy promised that another such event in the near future would celebrate their joy at receiving a 10 percent increase in wages.

83. *Globe*, April 14, 1903 (a.m.), p. 2.

Unfortunately, Conroy's optimism was not borne out by subsequent events. On April 22 the Board of Arbitration submitted its report to the state legislature. Their investigation had shown that Lowell workers had received wage increases since 1898 of 14 to 24 percent. There was no "combination" of the mills, as the Textile Council had claimed. Lowell's competition was not the mills of Fall River and New Bedford but the mills of the southern states, where wages were considerably lower. The arbitration board concluded that, out of the seven mills, only the Lawrence company could afford to give its workers an increase. Conroy immediately returned to his pre-inquiry suspicion of the board, announcing that he had expected this conclusion and calling the hearings a "farce."[84]

Meanwhile, officials of the Lawrence company expressed their outrage at the ruling of the Board of Arbitration. On the first day of the hearings, Lawrence Treasurer Baker had written to the company's wholesalers about the inquiry, expressing his confidence that the board would support the mills.[85] After the report came out, Baker wrote to virtually everyone about errors the board had made and alleging that the board had used "figures [that were] incorrect in every particular."[86] As late as May 6, Baker wrote to a confidant who had promised to speak to the governor on behalf of the mill. In a ten-page letter, Baker outlined his side of the mill's interactions with the board, explaining various "misunderstandings" about the time period the board's inquiry covered. He concluded: "I am not surprised that a mistake should be made in the case of some one of the companies. The whole investigation was a hurried affair from beginning to end; and, as we are all subject to errors, it is easy to understand how one could have crept in." The problem he identified was that the board would not recognize its "errors" and that "they disliked to acknowledge publicly the errors discovered afterwards."[87]

Though binding arbitration had never been requested or intended, Baker's virulent response to the board's findings suggests that those involved in the inquiry had expected the board to wield at least considerable moral force in the settlement of the dispute. This was true for Lowell businessmen, for the corporations, for the members of the Textile Council, and for the strikers in general. The board's findings now suggested that there was no easy way out of the situation. Strikers found that they would need considerable assistance in order to continue the strike. During the next month, controversies over

84. *Globe*, April 23, 1903 (a.m.), p. 4.
85. C. P. Baker to E. M. Townsend & Co., April 9, 1903, LMCR, MB-14, p. 6.
86. C. P. Baker to E. M. Townsend & Co., April 25, 1903, LMCR, MB-14, p. 24. See also C. P. Baker to State Board of Conciliation and Arbitration, April 24, 1903, LMCR, MA-34, p. 197; C. P. Baker to G. A. Copeland, Night Editor, *Boston Daily Advertiser*, April 27, 1903, LMCR, MA-34, p. 201. See also E. M. Townsend & Co. to C. P. Baker, April 25, 1903, LMCR, ML-3, p. 245; W. A. Reed to C. P. Baker, April 24, 1903, LMCR, MAD-48.
87. C. P. Baker to Arthur H. Lowe, May 8, 1903, LMCR, MA-34, pp. 210–19, quotations from pp. 218 and 219.

the level of support union members would receive and attempts to obtain financial assistance for nonunion strikers gained center stage in the Lowell strike. The council began to admit that it was having a difficult time providing benefits for all the new union members since the strike began. Some even suggested that the strike might have to scale back, with only the original member unions of the Textile Council participating. Council representatives now placed priority on seeking financial donations from both regional and national sources. By May 1, city officials announced that applications for relief had increased in Lowell. At the same time, many strikers had reportedly gained employment elsewhere and left town. Polish and Armenians had allegedly left for Lawrence, Massachusetts, and about one thousand Greeks and at least as many French Canadians had left town since the strike began. Many corporation-owned tenements stood empty, and the city lost population every day.

The first weekend in May, AFL President Samuel Gompers traveled to Boston. He met with Conroy for some time, but he spoke to the city's Central Labor Union mostly about a controversy among boot and shoe workers. He did not appear in Lowell during this trip, leading some there to believe that his endorsement of the strike was only lukewarm. Many began to fear that assistance from the AFL would be negligible. However, Gompers returned to Massachusetts on Sunday, May 24, and spoke to a crowd of five thousand on the Lowell South Common. In his speech, he commented on his earlier failure to visit Lowell:

> It has been said that I did not want to be attached to a losing cause and for that reason did not come here. I do not think this contest in Lowell is a losing one. Allowing, for the sake of argument, that it might be a losing struggle, I say it is well it was made. It is possible that if the contest was not made . . . a reduction [in wages] might have been ordered. . . . I have been associated with many union men and women in defeats they sustained and have been as proud of the struggle they made as I have of other contests where victory was won.[88]

Gompers promised financial assistance to the strikers, and in fact, the next day, the executive committee of the AFL sent an appeal for donations to its member unions.[89] Most of those gathered on the South Common, however, must have felt the strike's ignominious end in the pits of their empty stomachs as they listened to Gompers.

---

88. *Globe*, May 25, 1903 (a.m.), p. 5.
89. Samuel Gompers to "Officers and Members of Organized Labor," May 25, 1903, and Albert Hibbert to Gompers, May 16, 1903, both in *The American Federation of Labor Records: The Samuel Gompers Era* (Madison: State Historical Society of Wisconsin, 1981), microfilm edition (Microfilming Corporation of America), reel 43. Gompers had expressed reservations about the Lowell strike to Lowell Trade and Labor Council President Dennis Healey several weeks earlier. See Gompers to Healey, April 17, 1903, SG Letterbooks, 70:15.

Immediately after the AFL president's visit to Lowell, the corporations began to plan the reopening of the city's mills. Other than the Lawrence hosiery mill, the corporations had consistently argued that they would not even consider opening their doors until their "skilled help"—particularly the male mule spinners and loom fixers—agreed to return to work. Though no official message to that effect had been received, a meeting of the mill agents on Monday, May 25, discussed the possibility of reopening the mills. The corporation treasurers met the next day and voted to reopen the following Monday, June 1.

Throughout the last week of May, then, the various unions of the Textile Council met once again in their occupational and ethnic configurations. The Greeks voted to return to work, but the female ring spinners voted to remain on strike and to post the names of any who returned to work. Some estimated that as many as four thousand workers had left Lowell, and President Conroy optimistically argued that the remaining seven thousand skilled workers would not give up the fight. Some skilled operatives, however, told reporters that they had lost the struggle and needed to admit defeat now. Even Conroy admitted that the corporations could easily replace their unskilled workers. Lawrence Corporation agent Nourse believed that "none of the unions will stay out solidly, and that some of all, including the mule spinners, will go back to work. . . . If this happens, the others will follow very soon."[90]

On Monday, June 1, the mills opened "with a little less than half of their usual help."[91] Over the next two weeks, workers drifted back into the mills, until by June 15 the *Boston Globe* estimated that 70 percent of the mill hands had returned to work. On Sunday, June 21, by unanimous vote of its fourteen-member unions, the Textile Council declared the strike over. The corporations immediately announced that they would fire no strikebreakers in order to return jobs to strikers. On June 26, the Lawrence company treasurer wrote to a customer: "The strike in Lowell is settled, but the mills are not yet in full operation."[92] They soon would be, though, with little change in conditions. Strikers had not received any wage increase; instead, they had lost more than eight weeks' worth of wages. The Lawrence and Massachusetts mills replaced some of their mules with ring-spinning machinery, but even they continued to use skilled male mule spinners alongside their female ring spinners. Although competition with new textile mills in the South had barely been mentioned during the course of the strike, the Lowell corporations' insistence on continuing much as they had since before the Civil War meant that they would never be able to compete successfully with southern textile mills, even without any meaningful union presence in the town.

90. F. A. Wilcox to C. P. Baker, May 28, 1903, LMCR, MA-34, p. 248.
91. F. A. Wilcox to C. P. Baker, June 2, 1903, LMCR, MA-34, p. 253.
92. C. P. Baker to Messrs. J. H. Lane & Co., June 26, 1903, LMCR, MA-34, p. 274.

Unlike the other strikes recounted here, the Lowell strike began as an of-fensive action, when workers demanded a pay raise. The strength of the strike among skilled male workers such as mule spinners and loom fixers, and the skepticism of those groups about the allegiance of co-workers defined by gender or ethnicity as "other," appears as well in many other strikes and industries. In the Lowell strike of 1903, unionists in the textile industry at-tempted to overcome some of their skepticism and prejudices. Their shaky attempts to do so in this case reflect the problems and opportunities faced elsewhere as well.

The above account of the strikes in Baltimore, Chicago, New York City, and Lowell highlights the ways in which strikers' actions reflected both their circumstances and their resources. In all four of the industries examined, workers faced particular yet similar situations. As event compounded event in each strike, workers recognized and acted on their membership in different groups. Both the events and how the workers experienced them were bound by the material circumstances of their daily lives. The sexual division of labor, the geography of their home and work lives, the financial and cultural re-sources they had to work with—all these things created the arena within which workers, both female and male, had to work out their relationships with co-workers and employers.

None of these four strikes resulted in clear-cut victory for the strikers, though none was an unmitigated disaster. As Samuel Gompers had pointed out to the Lowell strikers, no strike was a total failure for workers, for every strike increased workers' consciousness of their economic power.[93] From the moment workers put down their tools or stepped away from their machines, they experienced an empowerment that was very different from their daily subservience to their employer and his overseers. Although, especially in protracted strikes, other lessons about gender or ethnicity might be learned, the initial recognition of class identity could be built on later to strengthen union organization. In this way, Gompers was right: no strike was ever a total defeat for the workers.

Not only strikers learned from the strike experience. Workers' organizations and their leaders also learned valuable lessons from strikes. Out of all these experiences they would attempt to mold more effective unions. The dialectical exchange between workers and their unions, which grew out of myriad strikes like those in this book, shaped the labor movement of the future. In the case of cross-gender strikes in particular, the movement and the workers who participated in it also shaped and reshaped their assumptions about both women and men. We now turn to just how this ongoing construction of gender occurred.

93. *The Samuel Gompers Papers*, vol. 3: *Unrest and Depression, 1891–94*, ed. Stuart B. Kaufman and Peter J. Albert (Urbana: University of Illinois Press, 1989), p. 569.

2 The Knights of Labor

What the labor organizations *might* have been . . .
—*Shoe and Leather Reporter*, March 24, 1887

Known for its paternalism, the Harmony Mills Company cotton factory in Cohoes, New York, included six separate mills and employed more than three thousand people.[1] As one observer noted, although skilled workers were generally well paid in the Cohoes/Troy area, cotton mill workers were an exception to the rule: "These may be classed with the hardest worked and poorest paid operatives in the United States."[2] This situation led weavers in two of the mills to approach Superintendent David J. Johnston with a request for a 10 to 27 percent increase in wages in March 1887. The weavers claimed that this increase would merely make their wages equal to those in the "eastern mills" of Massachusetts, while the company argued that their wages already matched or exceeded those in the surrounding areas. The two sides continued to meet over the wage issue throughout the spring. Master Workman Murray of the District Assembly of the Knights of Labor attempted to keep the situation as calm as possible.

The spark igniting the strike in Cohoes occurred at the beginning of July, when weavers in one of the mills refused to "scrub out" under their looms any longer and walked out on strike. On Saturday, July 2, a meeting of Harmony Company weavers vowed to remain out until what they termed an "obnoxious rule" was abolished. On Monday, July 4, strikers stopped production in all but one of the company mills.[3] The following day, some two thousand operatives gathered outside the one operating mill and convinced all but one hundred of that mill's employees to join the strike.

The reigning organization of workers in the mid-1880s was the Noble and Holy Order of the Knights of Labor. Established with a broad definition of "producers" eligible for membership, the Knights welcomed into its ranks the skilled and the unskilled, blacks and whites, immigrants and native-born, and males and females. In fact, all but social parasites (most notably, gamblers, bankers, saloon keepers, and lawyers) were admitted into local assemblies

---

1. Unless otherwise noted, the story of this strike comes from coverage in the *Troy Daily Times* [hereafter cited as *TDT*] and from New York Bureau of Labor Statistics, *Fifth Annual Report* (Albany: Troy Press Co., 1888) [hereafter cited as N.Y. BLS, *5th AR*].

2. *Journal of United Labor* [hereafter cited as *JUL*], June 25, 1887 (7:41), p. 2439.

3. *TDT*, July 5, 1887, p. 3.

of the Knights. These Local Assemblies (LAs) reported to District Assemblies (DAs), which began with geographic boundaries but by the 1880s included craft boundaries as well, in the form of National Trade Assemblies (NTAs). Annually, representatives of the assemblies met in a "general assembly"; in between those annual meetings, an elected general executive board made decisions and oversaw the Order. As part of a late nineteenth-century world rife with fraternal orders and their rituals, the Knights took on much of that world's forms and symbols, including a level of secrecy and a complex initiation rite. In addition, the entire organization was administered by its Grand Master Workman. While many of the Order's early historians belittled the emphasis on such ritualistic mutualism,[4] more recent historians have celebrated the successes the Knights had in the realms of labor activism and electoral politics, suggesting implicitly (and sometimes explicitly) that the former contributed to the latter.[5]

In 1884 the Federation of Organized Trades and Labor Unions (FOTLU), an organization formed largely in opposition to the Knights of Labor, called for a nationwide strike in favor of an eight-hour workday, to be carried out on May 1, 1886. While the national leaders of the Knights of Labor, most notably Grand Master Workman Terence Powderly, did not support the strike call, many members of the Knights in cities and towns around the nation joined both unorganized workers and members of trade unions in striking in the days surrounding May 1. The months around May 1 saw a huge increase in membership in the Knights of Labor, a membership that soon dwindled in the acrimonious aftermath of the eight-hour-day strikes. Labor historians still differ about the causes behind this decline in Knights' membership, but they all agree that disagreements over the eight-hour-day strikes within the organization played an important role. The "Great Upheaval," as it came to be called, certainly played a role in both the rise and the fall of the Knights of Labor.[6]

While historians have discussed the impact of the events of 1886 ad nauseam, few studies of women in the Knights of Labor have ventured beyond 1886 to examine the strengths and weaknesses of the Knights vis-á-vis women

4. Gerald Grob, *Workers and Utopia: A Study of Ideological Conflict in the American Labor Movement, 1865–1900* (New York: Quadrangle, 1969), and Norman J. Ware, *The Labor Movement in the United States, 1860–1895* (New York: Vintage, 1964).

5. Richard Oestreicher, *Solidarity and Fragmentation: Working People and Class Consciousness in Detroit, 1875–1900* (Urbana: University of Illinois Press, 1986); Leon Fink, *Workingmen's Democracy: The Knights of Labor and American Politics* (Urbana: University of Illinois Press, 1983); Robert E. Weir, *Beyond Labor's Veil: The Culture of the Knights of Labor* (University Park: Pennsylvania State University Press, 1996).

6. See Oestreicher, *Solidarity and Fragmentation*; Grob, *Workers and Utopia*; Kim Voss, *The Making of American Exceptionalism: The Knights of Labor and Class Formation in the Nineteenth Century* (Ithaca: Cornell University Press, 1993); Robert E. Weir, "Powderly and the Home Club: The Knights of Labor Joust among Themselves," *Labor History* 34 (Winter 1993): 84–113; and idem, *Knights Unhorsed: Internal Conflict in a Gilded Age Social Movement* (Detroit: Wayne State University Press, 2000).

after that momentous year.[7] In fact, as the strikes presented in this chapter demonstrate, gendered interactions within the Knights of Labor in their later years provide insight into the decline of the Knights and their ultimately being overwhelmed by the American Federation of Labor.

Classic examples of "women's strikes" in the Knights of Labor are the 1887 strikes of cotton mill workers in Cohoes, New York, and of glove makers in San Francisco, both of which demonstrate many of the characteristics Susan Levine describes in her study of women in the Knights. In particular, these strikes show how the Knights allowed women to participate in working-class militance within an ideology that viewed women's wage work as temporary and that revered their domestic roles. As Levine put it, in this way "the Knights offered an unprecedented integration of women's roles in the home, the community, and the workplace."[8]

At the same time, both these strikes included men as well as women. Attention to the gendered dynamics of these strikes nuances the usual picture of the Knights as a potential haven for women workers. The narrative of the Worcester County, Massachusetts, boot workers' strike similarly adds to skepticism about this image of the Knights. In the Worcester County strike, women were effectively blotted out of the picture, while the male posturing of bickering Knights' leaders took center stage. In the cases of the 1892 Baltimore strike, discussed in chapter 1, and a nearly identical Boston strike the same year, the divisions within the Knights were overwhelmed by a rivalry with one of the newest unions of the AFL, the United Garment Workers of America (UGW). In all the strikes discussed in this chapter, the men of the Knights of Labor maintained careful control over the strike activities of female co-workers.

The story of the Cohoes strike illustrates the control Knights leaders wielded over strikers, both male and female. During the second week of that strike, F. F. Donovan of the New York State Board of Arbitration visited Cohoes to make a preliminary investigation. He met with Master Workman Murray and other labor representatives and then announced that the full board would come to Cohoes the following week to attempt to settle the strike. When the board met in the Harmony Hotel on July 19, one of the first witnesses was Murray, speaking on behalf of the strikers. He announced

---

7. Susan Levine, in *Labor's True Woman: Carpet Weavers, Industrialization, and Labor Reform in the Gilded Age* (Philadelphia: Temple University Press, 1984), and Carole Turbin, in *Working Women of Collar City: Gender, Class, and Community in Troy, 1864–1886* (Urbana: University of Illinois Press, 1992), end their examinations in 1885 and 1886, respectively. Mary H. Blewett, in *Men, Women, and Work: Class, Gender, and Protest* (Urbana: University of Illinois Press, 1988), continues her story of Lynn shoe workers past 1886 but does not comment on the interaction between what happened in Lynn and what was going on in the Knights nationally. Ardis Cameron's discussion of the 1882 strike of textile workers in Lawrence, Massachusetts, in chapter 1 of *Radicals of the Worst Sort: Laboring Women in Lawrence, Massachusetts, 1860–1912* (Urbana: University of Illinois Press, 1993), barely touches on the organizational role of the Knights.

8. Levine, *Labor's True Woman*, p. 10.

that the strikers were willing to submit the dispute to arbitration. William E. Thorn, Harmony Company treasurer, countered by stating that the company "had nothing to submit for arbitration."[9] The investigation continued that afternoon in the Cohoes common council chambers, when seven operatives, including one woman, testified about their continued efforts to increase wages and complained about unfair discharges and the scrubbing-out issue.

On the second day of the board's investigation, strikers brought in as witnesses several children who testified that they had been hired when they were under the age required by state law. Board member Robertson pointed out that this issue had nothing to do with the strike, and he suggested that it be brought before a grand jury instead. The Harmony Company submitted a copy of a printed notice stating New York State child labor laws, which hung in every room of the mills, and announced that the company's books and payroll would be open to the board at any time. The board's investigation of the Cohoes strike then ended without reaching any definite conclusions.

In the meantime, the strikers, with the aid of the Knights, attempted another strategy. A few days after the strike began, a rumor appeared in the *Troy Times* that the national office of the Knights would soon send a letter to every Knights local assembly in the nation, asking for assistance in finding other work for the Harmony strikers—"the idea being to depopulate Cohoes and get even with the employers."[10] This effort received a fair amount of publicity (relative to the strike in general), but it is unclear exactly how many Harmony employees actually ever left Cohoes, or even how much of the exodus could be attributed to the Knights' plan. Observers reported later that some hands had "gone away to Montreal and elsewhere," but those were probably French Canadian workers who could return home easily; their exodus was not necessarily engineered by the Knights.[11] Ironically, a group of more than fifty Irish families (about four hundred operatives in all) did travel from Cohoes to Manville, Rhode Island, on the advice of Cohoes Master Workman Murray, to replace striking French Canadians in a mill in Manville.

Around the same time, mild violence between strikers and nonstrikers broke out several times. The day before the Board of Arbitration began its brief investigation, Cohoes police arrested several boys gathered outside the Ogden mill, and the day after the investigation ended, one young woman was arrested for slapping another. Other than the arrests of two men for disorderly conduct at a July 30 benefit picnic, however, these were the only recorded outbreaks of temper during the strike.

By the end of July, the position of the Harmony management was hardening. The company had always been proud of its relations with employ-

---

9. *TDT*, July 19, 1887, p. 3.
10. *TDT*, July 8, 1887, p. 3; quotation from N.Y. BLS, *5th AR*, p. 311.
11. N.Y. BLS, *5th AR*, p. 312. See chapter 4.

ees, and the strike was threatening its entire way of doing business. Superintendent Johnston said:

> The interference of labor committees with the internal workings of our business has at last reached a point where we are compelled to make a final resistance. We have at all times tried to exercise the utmost fairness toward our employés, and in the future we have determined that in no way shall we listen to committeemen, and if we know it they will not be allowed within our works.

Johnston announced that, depending on market conditions, the mills would reopen after the annual repairs were made in August. He stressed that "those employés who have entered into this misguided movement must learn by experience that the Harmony mills company asks nothing unreasonable, pays them better and looks after their interests more carefully than uninformed and irresponsible labor agitators."[12]

In response to Johnston's public statements, District Master Workman Murray pointed out that Harmony operatives were still leaving town. By his count, only 23 of 113 mule spinners remained in Cohoes, and there were now few ring spinners as well. Murray claimed that some one thousand workers had left the town, and he assured his audience that the strikers could still last for weeks.[13]

The final break in the strike occurred after the annual August drawing of the water from the Cohoes canals. For ten days between August 10 and 21, all the mills and most other factories in Cohoes shut down. Before the canals were drained, the Harmony Company attempted to reopen one mill, and in the last week before the canal repairs, that mill ran with about forty looms in operation. After the canals reopened, the company resumed full operations in the Ogden mill. On the same day, several overseers went to see Superintendent Johnston, saying that "the help" had come to them and asked them to seek the reopening of the mills. Reportedly in response to these pleas, the company reopened another mill and announced that a third would reopen in the next few days.

By the first week of September, all but one of the Harmony mills were open. The final mill to reopen began production at noon on Monday, September 12. The next Thursday, a committee of strikers met with Superintendent Johnston to ask for reinstatement. Johnston replied that "individual applications would be received and acted upon." On the following Sunday, September 18, strikers held a meeting at which they called off the strike.[14] By Monday, September 19, virtually all the striking operatives of the Harmony Company had returned to work. Once again, "during the day the tenements [of Harmony Hill were] deserted; the occupants [were] within the

12. *TDT*, July 29, 1887, p. 3.
13. Ibid.
14. *TDT*, September 17, 1887, p. 3.

four walls of Harmony No. 1, or 2, or 3, as the case may be, wearing out their brief span of years for the beggarly pittance that is doled out to them."[15]

Several characteristics of the Cohoes strike make it a classic Knights of Labor strike. The workers, and their Knightly representatives, attempted to arbitrate their differences with the company both before and after the strike began. The Knights also appealed to the public's sense of morality, with their charges of illegal child labor. The attempt to find employment elsewhere was also a common tactic of the Knights, even when, as in this case, this might involve strikers from one location functioning as strikebreakers at another location. In this strike, as in others, there was little sense of any solidarity along trade lines beyond the immediate strike locality. While the emphasis the Knights put on local ties among workers of different trades might create a "subculture of opposition" in particular localities and circumstances, it rarely encouraged workers to view themselves as members of a wider industry community.[16] Instead, the Cohoes weavers came to see themselves as beleaguered and underpaid Harmony Mills employees, without extending their sense of solidarity beyond their own locality.

Furthermore, unlike the more documented examples of the Lynn shoe workers and Philadelphia carpet weavers described by historians Mary Blewett and Susan Levine, in the cross-gender strikes examined in this chapter women workers rarely speak in their own voices. Instead, male "Master Workmen," usually not even from the same industry, spoke for the strikers—both female and male. Does this mean women demonstrated less militance than men did? Some two-thirds of Harmony's workers were female, and while 22 percent of the male workers joined the strike, more than 27 percent of the women did.[17] Clearly, women's militance in Cohoes was at least equal to that of men.

Finally, the Cohoes strike, like many others under the direction of the Knights of Labor, ended in defeat for the strikers. Despite the well-known victory of the Knights in the 1886 Gould strike, most strikes carried out by local assemblies went down in defeat.[18] One Troy spinner explained that he had opposed the strike from its beginning. With a wife and five children, the two oldest of which also worked in the Harmony mills, he had returned to

15. N.Y. BLS, *5th AR*, p. 313.
16. Oestreicher, *Solidarity and Fragmentation*, p. 60.
17. U.S. Bureau of Labor, *Tenth Annual Report: Strikes and Lockouts* (Washington, D.C.: Government Printing Office, 1896) [hereafter cited as U.S. BLS, *10th AR*], pp. 638–41.
18. This was not true of Knights strikes only; most strikes in the 1880s failed to achieve workers' objectives. Voss found that 63 percent of New Jersey strikes ended in defeat for workers in 1887 (Voss, *Making of American Exceptionalism*, p. 132). The two studies of strikes and lockouts by the U.S. BLS in 1886 and 1894 report that only 44.5 percent of all strikes between 1881 and the middle of 1894 could be termed successful; a similar proportion (45.0 percent) of strikes in this study's four industries could be termed the same. See U.S. Bureau of Labor, *Third Annual Report: Strikes and Lockouts* (Washington, D.C.: Government Printing Office, 1888), pp. 838–39; and U.S. BLS, *10th AR*, pp. 1564–65.

work because the Knights offered no financial assistance. He wanted higher wages but believed that the mills provided his best employment opportunity. Precisely because the Knights included semiskilled workers in their ranks, many felt these types of pressures.

Some of the same characteristics also appear in the markedly more cosmopolitan setting of San Francisco. San Francisco glove makers began their march toward a work stoppage when they presented a new "schedule of prices" to their employers in early fall 1887. Unlike many strikers who joined the Knights only after walking off their jobs, the young glove makers by the Bay had already organized themselves into Local Assembly 7546, the glove makers' assembly. Their employers acted like many others confronted by the Knights and other labor organizations: they formed an employers' association—the Glove Manufacturers' Association—and developed their own schedule of prices, announcing that the new prices would go into effect on Wednesday, October 12.[19]

It took another week and a half, and at least one full paycheck, before glove makers decided to strike. On Monday, October 24, employees of "nearly all" the city's principal glove manufacturers struck, claiming that the new schedule reduced the wages of most glove workers, and the wages of all the women workers, by 15 to 50 percent.[20] By the next day, the strikers had organized what they called the Glovers' Protective Union (GPU), and by the middle of the week almost 350 of 400 glove workers were on strike. Women made up almost two-thirds of the strikers, while nonstrikers included about fifty male cutters.[21]

The *San Francisco Chronicle* reported: "The reduction chiefly affects the girls, who have seldom made over $10 per week and as low as $4, 'and now they propose to cut them down lower still, as if that was not near enough to starvation,' indignantly exclaimed the Secretary [of the GPU], 'and we don't propose to stand it.'"[22] In a statement issued by the Glovers' Protective Union on October 26, the new union said that the strike was being waged mainly for the benefit of the women and girls in the glove factories, "a class of society that already have difficulties enough to contend with in the shape of cheap competing labor and the efforts on every side to reduce their wage to a mere pittance."[23] An 1881 trades assembly report had listed gloves as one of the trades employing Chinese workers, the bane of existence for San

19. Unless otherwise noted, the story of this strike comes from coverage in the *San Francisco Chronicle* [hereafter cited as *SFChron*].
20. *SFChron*, October 26, 1887, p. 3; California Bureau of Labor Statistics, *Third Biennial Report, 1887–1888* (Sacramento: State Printer, 1888) [hereafter cited as Ca. BLS, *3rd BR*], p. 158.
21. U.S. BLS, *10th AR*, pp. 46–49. See also *SFChron*, October 26, 1887, p. 3, and October 31, 1887, p. 8.
22. *SFChron*, October 26, 1887, p. 3.
23. Ca. BLS, *3rd BR*, p. 159.

Francisco's less-skilled workers.[24] The glove makers, like other women workers in the city, faced sharp—and "cheap"—competition for their jobs.

During the first week of the strike, some manufacturers announced that they were taking on "apprentices" to replace the strikers. A week into the strike, a Mr. Blumenthal stated that his apprentices were doing well and that he would "have everything running in good order in a few weeks."[25] The Leak Manufacturing Company announced that it was operating with about half its workforce, including its regular number of male cutters, who had not gone out with the others. Some work was being done by hand and some by machines run by newly hired apprentices. A member of the firm said the company would be glad to take strikers back but that it could also do without them. It would not make any concessions to the strikers.

On Wednesday, November 2, the cutters at Leak's factory joined the strike, complaining that they had been asked to do scab work from Blumenthal's factory. The men said that, although they were satisfied with their own wages and conditions, the request that they "help out another firm in a fight against their fellow-workmen" [*sic*] had propelled them to action. Strikers announced that they would make "a strong effort" to get cutters in a third factory to join them as well.[26]

Meanwhile, some of the original strikers began to find jobs in other industries in the city. As November wore on, the glove makers began to plan for an "entertainment" to benefit the strikers on December 14. When members of the GPU then approached members of other unions in the city and asked them to buy tickets to the entertainment, most of the unions also passed resolutions of sympathy for the strikers. By November 25, the glove makers had sold more than 1,300 tickets for the ball to be held at Odd Fellows' Hall. A committee of "young ladies" continued to sell tickets and promote the idea of the benefit.

While the union's benefit ball took place in December, by the end of November the city's glove factories were all open, staffed by returned workers and a few replacements. In its report on the strike, the California Bureau of Labor simply said: "The strike was a failure, and all the glove-makers, who could do so, returned to work at the old rates."[27]

Like the Cohoes strike, that of the young San Francisco glove makers ended in failure. Though this group of workers started out with greater organization, they ended in similar defeat, largely because the semiskilled nature of their jobs made them all too easy to replace. The glove makers also ended as muted as their Cohoes counterparts had been, subject to the assumptions of both

24. Alexander Saxton, *The Indispensable Enemy: Labor and the Anti-Chinese Movement in California* (Berkeley and Los Angeles: University of California Press, 1971), p. 169.

25. *SFChron*, October 26, 1887, p. 3.

26. *SFChron*, November 3, 1887, p. 6.

27. Ca. BLS, *3rd BR*, p. 159.

the press and the Knights' leadership that young women could not speak for themselves despite the audacity their striking displayed.

The Knights have generally been touted by historians as being much more welcoming to women than other labor organizations of the time. Because the Order prided itself on welcoming all "producers" to membership, they officially allowed women to join as either wage workers or unwaged household producers (housewives). Most female Knights were industrial workers, but the rhetoric of the Order often addressed women's domestic roles more than their industrial roles. Mary Blewett suggested in her book on shoe workers:

> The ideology of the Knights of Labor represented two conflicting positions on women's involvement in their organization: a general commitment to equal rights and a moral critique of capitalism based on values shaped by family life and domesticity. Although the Knights welcomed all women into their ranks, the natural sphere for women remained the home, not the workplace.[28]

One of the most vivid examples of this type of rhetoric appears in A. W. Wright's speech to the 1890 General Assembly in Cincinnati. Often interrupted by applause, Wright told his listeners: "If you break up a home you take away the only place where the principles of liberty can be taught the rising generation. . . . Nations no more than individuals can afford to sin against the homes of the land." Those who would teach "the principles of liberty" to children should be their mothers; those "breaking up" homes were first of all the employers who replaced male workers with inadequately paid women operating new machines. But equally important to Wright was that "when we buy the cheap clothing, when we buy the cheap boots and shoes and hats and shirts, . . . then we are the ones who are employing these girls and cutting down their wages."[29] As Grand Master Workman Terence Powderly had put it two years earlier, "The Order was founded to make the workman's home prosperous and happy. It was the intention to prevent misery from stalking through the workman's door at the bidding of an employer."[30]

This type of rhetoric served a complex dual purpose for the Knights. On the one hand, it appealed to women both as workers and as wives and mothers by condemning the low wages women received and simultaneously elevating the roles of women as wives and mothers. On the other hand, such rhetoric also appealed to male workers with its defense of their jobs and wages. Virtually all the Knights' discussions included similar rhetoric with similarly complex layers of understanding.

28. Blewett, *Men, Women, and Work*, p. 248.
29. *Journal of the Knights of Labor* [hereafter cited as *JKL*], May 10, 1890 (10:41).
30. *JUL*, March 3, 1888 (8:35), p. 2586.

At the same time, the Knights demonstrated complexity in much more than rhetoric. An examination of strikes under the leadership and general umbrella of the Order, such as those in Cohoes and San Francisco, reveals the actual actions workers took as members of the Knights. The two major historians of women in the Knights of Labor, Mary Blewett and Susan Levine, both address a similar project, Blewett through examining the shoe workers of Lynn, Massachusetts, and Levine by looking at carpet weavers in both New York and Philadelphia.[31] However, Levine does not carry her study beyond the peak of the Knights' membership in 1886, and Blewett does not address more generalizable issues in the later years. The present study begins at precisely that point. One thing we see is that the later gendered image of the Knights is much less complimentary than the earlier one. As the Knights fractured into competing factions and faced competition from the new AFL unions, the dynamics of organizational disputes left little room for independent women's voices.

Nowhere is this more obvious than in the 1887 strike of boot workers in Worcester County, Massachusetts, an action that provides a counterexample to Blewett's bold "lady stitchers" of Lynn. On January 26, 1887, the boot and shoe shops of Worcester County, Massachusetts, posted the following "iron-clad" notice:

> Recognizing the fact that justice can only be obtained by according to both the employer and the employee the right of individual contract for his or her labor, this factory will hereafter be open only to such operatives as will agree to deal individually with the firm or its accredited representative.[32]

This move on the part of Massachusetts manufacturers began one of the last great battles waged by shoe workers in District Assembly 30 of the Knights and the Lasters' Protective Union. The *Shoe and Leather Reporter* intoned in one of its last reports on the strike, "So far as the shoemakers are concerned, the Knights of Labor is a dead Order in Worcester County. Hardly a man could be found among them willing to join in giving it a decent burial."[33] Though the strike actually did not spell the end of the Knights, many saw it as marking the end of the hold that District Assembly 30 had over Worcester County boot workers. As such, the strike tells us much about the decline of the Knights of Labor, as well as the role that gendered workers played in that decline.

---

31. See Blewett, *Men, Women, and Work*, and Levine, *Labor's True Woman*.

32. Quoted in *Shoe and Leather Reporter* [hereafter cited as *S&LR*], March 24, 1887 (43:12), p. 349. (Also quoted in *JKL*, April 2, 1887 [7:29], p. 2338, cited from *New York Herald*.) Unless otherwise noted, the story of this strike comes from coverage in the *S&LR* and the *Boston Globe* [hereafter cited as *Globe*].

33. *S&LR*, June 23, 1887 (43:25), p. 1208.

Worcester County was a center of boot manufacturing in particular. As the industry journal put it, "the Worcester County boots are generally recognized as of a quality not readily paralleled."[34] In North Brookfield, a small town of about four thousand in 1890 just north and west of the city of Worcester, E. & A. H. Batcheller & Company was reputed to be the largest boot factory in the world, employing more than two thousand workers. When Batcheller's closed down in 1902, locals warned that the town would come to "be known as the deserted village."[35]

In mid-December 1886, boot workers in Spencer, Massachusetts, represented by the Knights and the Lasters' Protective Union, asked their employers for higher wages for workers who were paid by the piece. As one worker explained, piece workers had to work more than twelve hours a day during the busy season. Workdays that began at five o'clock in the morning would end as late as eight or even ten o'clock at night. "If our employers don't know of this, the night watchman does, and also do our wives and children."[36] The ensuing strike was therefore waged on behalf of a little less than two-thirds of the workforce. Though only 8 percent of the workers supported by the strike were women, more than twice as many of the strikers (17 percent) were women.[37] Just over three-quarters of Spencer's female boot workers joined the strike.

The boot manufacturers of Worcester County held a meeting in Boston on Saturday, January 22, at which they agreed on the wording and posting of the "iron-clad" notice cited above. The manufacturers explicitly viewed this as forcing the issue of "whether the men who work for wages shall govern their employers or be governed by them."[38] One leading manufacturer said:

> Our workmen have declared themselves exempt from any obligation to do as we want them to. We are expected to pay *their* schedule prices, to adopt the hours for a day's work *they* prescribe. . . . The work-folks have driven us to take steps to maintain our independence of their dictation. When they come to us and tell us what "we have got to do," we think it high time we set about putting a stop to that sort of business.[39]

Behind manufacturers' frustrations were two organized groups of workers: the Lasters' Protective Union and the Knights of Labor. Both responded to the employers' "iron-clad" notice by calling their members out on strike.

---

34. *S&LR*, March 17, 1887 (43:11), p. 499.
35. *Pawtucket Evening Times*, April 18, 1902, p. 11.
36. *Globe*, January 27, 1887 (a.m.), p. 5.
37. Based on figures given in U.S. BLS, *10th AR*, pp. 366–69, line 1. Women made up approximately 20 percent of the boot workers in Spencer factories (U.S. BLS, *10th AR*, pp. 362–65).
38. *S&LR*, February 3, 1887 (43:5), p. 209.
39. Ibid., p. 210.

Well over four thousand workers in the villages of Brookfield, West Brookfield, and Spencer, as well as in the town of Worcester itself, went on strike.[40]

The unions involved in the Worcester County walkout brought with them into the strike fairly long histories of both cooperation and disagreement. Shoe workers had always played a large role in the Knights of Labor. After the Civil War, male shoe workers had formed the Knights of St. Crispin, soon joining with female co-workers in the corresponding Daughters of St. Crispin. Hammered by the devastating depression of the 1870s, the Crispins threw their lot in with the new secret labor organization, the Noble and Holy Order of the Knights of Labor. Shoe workers quickly formed one of the largest occupational groups within the Knights. Among female Knights, the proportion of shoe workers was even greater.

The other main union involved in the Worcester strike was the Lasters' Protective Union, which had organized in Lynn, Massachusetts, in 1879. Though often cooperating with other unions in the shoe industries, the Lasters also displayed a certain aloofness, often taking markedly independent stances. Lasters, almost all male in the late nineteenth century, viewed themselves as more skilled and more indispensable to production than any other group within the industry. In 1887 they ended years of loose affiliation with the Knights and officially join the American Federation of Labor, amalgamating with the AFL's Boot and Shoe Workers' Union in 1895 before striking out as an independent organization again in 1898.[41]

Faced with the apparent determination of united employers to function without union representation, both the Knights and the Lasters of Worcester County ordered their members to walk out. Workers did this slowly, many remaining at work until they had completed current tasks. Two weeks after the employers' "iron-clad" notice was posted, the strike reached its full force. Newspapers reported that daily meetings of strikers were well attended, crowded "to the door."[42]

By mid-February, Worcester County manufacturers began to reopen their establishments with strikebreakers. Unlike in the case of the San Francisco glove makers, these strikebreakers appear to have had previous experience in boot or shoe making. Most of the replacement workers came from other parts of New England, with Maine often mentioned as the most common point of origin. Along with the introduction of strikebreakers came violence and threats of violence against these "scabs."

40. U.S. BLS, *10th AR*, pp. 365, 369, reports 4,343 strikers; S&LR counted more than 15,000 (February 3, 1887 [43:5], p. 210); the *Globe* reported more than 8,000 (January 30, 1887, p. 2). Much of this wide variation may be due to either overcounting or undercounting the number of hand workers who worked in their own homes in the surrounding countryside.

41. Blewett, *Men, Women, and Work*; Horace B. Davis, *Shoes: The Workers and the Industry* (New York: International Publishers, 1940), pp. 165–66, 177.

42. *Globe*, February 4, 1887 (p.m.), p. 1.

As firms filled up with replacement workers, owner Batcheller commented that his treeing department, "long named the 'County Kerry shop,'" now housed an "entire new class of bright, capable workmen."[43] In fact, employers and their spokespeople commented repeatedly about the tenacity of these "foreigners" among the strikers. In the city of Worcester alone, foreign-born individuals made up 37 percent of male boot and shoe workers; of those, 46 percent were Irish and another 30 percent were French Canadian. Only 17 percent of women were foreign-born, but fully 65 percent were the daughters of "foreigners."[44] Employers' diatribes against the foreign-born workers probably included these young hyphenated Americans. The city of Worcester also saw the most explicit display of ethnic solidarity in the strike. Early in February, Worcester ethnic and fraternal organizations, including the Highlands and the Ancient Order of Hibernian Guards, sponsored a benefit dance that netted about one thousand dollars for the strikers.[45]

French Canadians also played a role in the ethnic dimensions of the strike. The town of Spencer was said to be almost half French Canadian. The manufacturers complained that the French workers "cannot read, some of them cannot talk English" and that "in the main they hear but one side of the story—what their leaders choose to tell them." While the *Shoe and Leather Reporter* proudly recounted the story of how a "jolly old Frenchman" had returned to work in Spencer, they continued to bemoan the loyalty these workers had to their labor order: "Altogether, it is a phase of human experience which it is difficult to comprehend."[46] In Spencer at least, French Canadian ethnic ties and union membership, in either the Knights or the Lasters, reinforced each other.

By mid-March, employers began to replace the striking "foreigners" with more than replacement workers. On March 17, Batchellers' North Brookfield plant reported that twenty-four of its twenty-six new lasting machines were now in operation. Though some of the county's boot makers expressed doubt about the possibility of replacing hand-lasted boots with machine-lasted ones, by the end of the strike virtually all the manufacturers had installed the new lasting machines. Worcester County's boot makers had begun their strike as relatively skilled workers, but the manufacturers were clearly eager to replace them with less-skilled machine tenders.

National leaders of—and national debates within—the Knights also began to enter the strike picture in March. On March 26, Thomas Barry, a member of the general executive board and an opponent of Grand Master Workman Terence Powderly, arrived in Massachusetts from Michigan to help with the

---

43. *S&LR*, March 3, 1887 (43:9), p. 402.
44. U.S. Department of the Interior, Census Office, *Report on Population of the United States at the Eleventh Census: 1890* (Washington, D.C.: Government Printing Office, 1895), pp. 742–43.
45. *S&LR*, February 17, 1887 (43:7), p. 306.
46. *S&LR*, May 5, 1887 (43:18), p. 857.

strike. Along with other speakers from the geographically based District Assembly 30, Barry addressed strikers in Spencer on Saturday and in Worcester on Tuesday, then left to report to the board in Philadelphia at midnight. On Thursday, industry scuttlebutt reported that Powderly, not trusting the report from his nemesis, Barry, had written to a "fair and impartial" manufacturer who allegedly "command[ed] the respect both of the workmen and the manufacturers," to get the story of the strike.[47]

The Worcester strike played into one of the greatest controversies within the Knights at the time: Should "national trade assemblies" be formed? Because the Knights had always attempted to encourage mutuality among workers of different trades, Powderly and many other leaders of the Knights encouraged the formation of "mixed" local assemblies—that is, local organizations that included members from a number of different occupations and industries. However, from the organization's very beginning, many of the local assemblies were in fact "trade" assemblies, in which most or all members belonged to a single occupation or industry. In 1881 the Knights' General Assembly voted to allow establishment of national trade assemblies, a move that was reaffirmed and strengthened again in 1886.[48] As much as such organizations helped prevent the exodus of Knights to the growing trade unions of the time, whether these national trade assemblies should be established continued to be a point of contention. Faced with continuing competition from the unions of the American Federation of Labor and its predecessor, the Federation of Organized Trades and Labor Unions, the national leaders of the Knights attempted in the late 1880s to use the national trade assemblies as a way to stem the tide. By the time of the General Assembly of 1887, some twenty-two trade assemblies were represented. It is thus fitting that the general executive board voted to allow establishment of a shoe workers' national assembly in the midst of the Worcester strike. The founding convention of that assembly was held in early June less than one hundred miles away in Brockton, Massachusetts, and included votes of support for the Worcester strikers.[49]

The founding convention of the shoe workers' NTA 216 foreshadowed several problems the General Assembly would ultimately have with the national Knights' leadership. Assembly leader Henry Skeffington spoke to this in his opening remarks: "That we seek a change of form in our organization

47. *S&LR*, March 31, 1887 (43:13), p. 591. (Probably Isaac Prouty? See "Among the Factories. Spencer," S&LR, March 24, 1887 [43:12], p. 573.)

48. Weir, *Knights Unhorsed*, p. 36; Grob, *Workers and Utopia*, p. 102. Grob notes that such a vote was first passed in 1879 and then overturned less than nine months later.

49. *Globe*, April 1, 1887 (p.m.), p. 5; Knights of Labor, National Trade Assembly No. 216 (Boot and Shoe Workers), *Report of the First Annual Session of the Boot and Shoe Workers' of the U.S. and Canada [1887]* (Boston: L. E. Cowles, 1887), p. 17, microfiche edition, *Pamphlets in American History: Labor*, L3364 (Sanford, N.C.: Microfilming Corporation of America, 1979). [Report hereafter cited as "KoL, NTA 216, *Report* (1887)."]

must not be interpreted to mean that we are tired of the Knights of Labor."[50] On the second day of the convention, delegates voted to request a charter from the Knights' executive board, threatening to "form some other organization" if the board failed to grant the charter.[51] It is also telling that Terence Powderly soon decreed that preexisting local assemblies already affiliated with a district assembly would have to get permission from that district assembly in order to switch allegiance to any national trade assembly. In other words, Worcester County boot makers, who already belonged to Massachusetts DA 30, would remain in that assembly rather than automatically be transferred to the new NTA 216.[52]

During the middle week of June, the Massachusetts Board of Arbitration traveled to Worcester to investigate the strike, announcing that the "exhaustion" of the strikers made it clear that the strike was over. The board then received a communication from the chairman of the joint local executive board of the Knights asking that the state arbitration board intercede. The arbitration board responded that they did not believe they could do any good at this point. DA 30 then sent a message to the strikers from Boston encouraging them to return to work if possible. This letter, as well as the letter from the arbitration board, were read to a meeting of workers on Monday, June 20. At that point, all workers present except the bottomers and lasters voted to return to work, and before the week was over, these last two groups of skilled male workers began to apply for work in the boot factories as well.

The Worcester strike story demonstrates the byzantine contortions Knights leaders took as the organization began its decline into both petty squabbling and serious dissension in the years after 1886. By the early 1890s, the Knights, while still formally existing, would be all but destroyed.

How did women function, and how did the Knights treat them during this decline? The basic outline of the Worcester strike tells us little about the role of women in the county's boot industry. During the strike, there were few comments about female strikers, though the *Shoe and Leather Reporter* told its readers that the Batcheller company lacked only "a few of the French and Irish girls" from the upper fitting room; the company reported that the heeling department adhered to the strike more forcefully, as "the girls were well organized, and all went out."[53] In late March, the *Boston Globe* focused briefly on women workers, commenting that in the George H. Burt & Company plant of Brookfield virtually all the "ladies" employed in stitching uppers and in heeling ("a small army of them") quit work when the ironclad notice was posted. When three of the young women talked with a *Globe* reporter, they were

50. KoL, NTA 216, *Report* (1887), p. 9.
51. Ibid., p. 15.
52. This issue ultimately led NTA 216 to break with the Knights. See Davis, *Shoes*, p. 166.
53. *S&LR*, March 24, 1887 (43:12), p. 573.

not particular when they return to work, as they live at home, and there is no immediate need of their doing any work. Others, who are not so fortunately situated, are quite as firm not to return to work, and in this resolve they are aided and abetted by their companions, and furnished with sufficient money for their support by the labor organizations. The girls as a class, are well educated and fine appearing, and with that obstinacy peculiar to their sex, stand out strongly for their rights. If anything, they are more obstinate than the men, and it would be interesting to see how quickly they would relinquish the acquaintance of anyone who abandoned the organization.[54]

Despite this hint at the militance of the women, however, neither the rhetoric of the Knights nor that of the newspapers fully acknowledged the participation of women workers in the strike. When the Spencer town select-men appointed forty special police officers on February 25, strikers asked to be allowed to appoint seventeen of their own, "to protect their wives and children from the convicts and State Prison birds whom the manufacturers are bringing to town."[55] This imagery also paralleled that of the manufactur-ers, who, even while acknowledging that the "young people" who held out the longest as strikers included girls as well as boys, argued that as "younger people . . . left the village to find work elsewhere," young women stood at greatest risk: "Young girls are away from home for the first time in their lives, subject to influences with which they might never have been brought in contact if they had staid at home. Among those who remain the demoral-izing tendencies of idleness are perceptible."[56]

Unlike the militant "lady stitchers" found in Lynn by Mary Blewett, the young women of Worcester's boot industry kept a low profile during the strike. To the extent that they participated in strike activities, they did so as members of the Irish and French Canadian communities of the boot towns. Female shoe workers from other communities offered both financial and moral support as fellow women workers, but the female strikers in Worcester apparently acted as members of local and ethnic communities rather than as specifically *women* strikers.

Like the Cohoes and San Francisco strikers, women in Worcester County were effectively silenced by the more vocal male leadership of the Order. While manufacturers in the county seem to have recognized women's milit-ancy in the strike, male Knights demonstrated no recognition of that charac-teristic. The focus for both the Knights and the lasters' union remained on the skilled male workers rather than on the less-skilled women. At the same time, while the Knights often held contradictory views of women, the Order

54. *Globe*, March 26, 1887 (a.m.), p. 5.
55. *S&LR*, March 3, 1887 (43:9), p. 402, and June 16, 1887 (43:24), p. 1182, on "boys and girls" in the strike.
56. *S&LR*, March 24, 1887 (43:12), p. 573.

still had a vision of organizing not only women but also less-skilled workers more generally. Perhaps the Knights' main problem only arose when "less skilled" and "female" coincided.

In her study of New Jersey Knights, political scientist Kim Voss argues that by the 1880s the experiences of male skilled and less-skilled workers converged in significant ways and that because many factory operatives were now men, skilled workers no longer had to overcome gender prejudices in order to combine with operatives. As Voss puts it: "An alliance between male factory artisans and male operatives required that artisans overcome only one prejudice—that against the less skilled, but an alliance between male factory artisans and female operatives necessitated a rethinking of two—against working women and against the less skilled."[57]

Voss also found that ethnicity was less significant than gender in keeping skilled and less-skilled workers apart. In fact, her statistical work on New Jersey found that "separate ethnic communities might encourage unity as well as fragmentation." But, she says, "workers were rarely able to bridge the distance between male and female workers."[58] In addition, Voss found that it was easier for the Knights to organize the less skilled (and often female) workers within their own community rather than within their own industry.[59]

In other words, Voss would argue that we should not expect the Knights to be "inclusive" when it comes to cross-gender strikes like that of boot workers in Worcester County. As the Knights continued to crumble, this became more and more true.

By the early 1890s, the disintegration of the Knights' relationship with women workers had deepened. Both the Baltimore garment workers' strike of 1892 and a similar strike of Boston's garment workers that same year demonstrate this. On Wednesday, October 5, 1892, the United Garment Workers went on strike in two shops in Boston.[60] They demanded that work hours be reduced to fifty-eight hours a week and that union members receive the same pay for working on summer clothes as they received for working on winter clothes. Two days later, seven more shops struck as well.[61]

On the following Saturday, members of the Boston Clothing Contractors' Association (CCA) initiated a lockout in thirty of their shops, which immediately put more than one thousand men and women out of work. Almost two weeks later, with new members joining the union, and union officers unable to "take their initiation fees fast enough,"[62] General Secretary Charles

---

57. Voss, *Making of American Exceptionalism*, pp. 58–59.
58. Ibid., p. 179.
59. Ibid., p. 182.
60. Unless otherwise noted, the story of this strike comes from coverage in the *Boston Globe*.
61. Massachusetts State Board of Arbitration, *Seventh Annual Report for the Year 1892* (Boston: Wright & Potter Printing Co., 1893)[hereafter cited as Ma. Bd. of Arb., *7th AR*], p. 147. They called this demand "equal pay for equal work."
62. *Globe*, October 17, 1892 (a.m.), p. 3.

F. Reichers of the UGW showed up in Boston. He called the battle a "test case" for the new union and said that it might be for the better if some of "the sweaters" were forced out of business.[63]

In the middle of the third week of the strike, a committee of the Clothing Contractors' Association approached members of the state Board of Arbitration. On Saturday evening, two contractors representing the CCA, Isaac L. King and Maurice Greenbaum, met with three workmen representing the Independent United Garment Workers' Association of Boston. The clerk of the state arbitration board witnessed their agreement, which defined fifty-eight hours as a week's work, promised the same wages in winter as in summer, and raised no objection to members of other organizations working along with them.[64] Reichers immediately erupted, proclaiming, "The organization with whom a 'satisfactory settlement was reached' has since exploded like a toy balloon."[65] "The Independent," he explained, was affiliated with the Knights of Labor. In the meantime, fourteen contractors had already signed union agreements with the UGW. By Friday, October 28, only three shops had yet to sign. On the following day, the rest of the shops signed the union's agreement, and both the strike and the lockout officially ended.[66]

The Baltimore strike, similar in some ways to this Boston strike in that it involved workers in both the UGW and the Knights, was described in detail in the last chapter. Here I simply point out the significance of the details having to do with the Knights for understanding gender and the decline of the Order. Over the course of the Baltimore strike, the AFL's United Garment Workers of America came into direct and messy conflict with the Knights of Labor. The clothing cutters in the struck contractors' shops were organized into Clothing Cutters' and Trimmers' Assembly 7507 of the Knights of Labor, and this organization, backed by its district assembly, threatened to withdraw from the shops if they signed the UGW contract calling for employment of none but "union hands"—code words for the UGW. The *Baltimore Sun* noted that this turned the strike into "a clean cut [fight] between the Federation and the Knights."[67] On July 14, UGW leader Reichers told the *Sun* that it was "only a question of a little time when the Knights of Labor will consist of middlemen and the Federation of Labor of the workers."[68] As if to prove Reichers's words true, in the middle of August the Contractors' Association organized itself into a local assembly of the Knights: the Monumental Coat Contractors' Assembly.[69] By September, instead of keeping the

63. *Globe*, October 17, 1892 (p.m.), p. 5.

64. Ma. Bd. of Arb., *7th AR*, pp. 148–49; *Globe*, October 22, 1892 (p.m.), p. 4.

65. *Globe*, October 24, 1992 (a.m.), p. 5.

66. U.S. BLS, *10th AR*, p. 435, line 37.

67. *Baltimore Sun*, August 16, 1892, p. 8. Unless otherwise noted, the story of this strike comes from coverage in the *Baltimore Sun* [hereafter cited as *Sun*].

68. *Sun*, July 14, 1892, p. 8.

69. *Sun*, August 16, 1892, p. 8.

focus on workers' disagreements with their employers, the Baltimore strike had disintegrated into an interorganizational dispute.

The trouble between the Knights and the UGW in Baltimore that summer, and in Boston the following fall, took on a form that was becoming all too familiar in the 1890s as the unions of the AFL and the Knights of Labor competed for the same groups of workers in an increasingly sleazy manner. The ways in which this conflict was played out in the Baltimore garment strike, however, suggest some interesting—and perhaps unexpected—ways in which the two organizations would differ.

Throughout the strike, both the workers (male and female) and the national office of the UGW shared a main concern: they wanted to bring an end to the competitive chaos of the city's clothing sweatshops. Though the Baltimore strike was virtually a strike against sweatshops, the UGW did not waste much time railing against sweatshops in general. The workers already understood the problems with the coat contractors' shops, and the union helped them formulate those problems into demands. Therefore, all the union had to do was run the strike. In mid-July, the UGW helped establish cooperative shops that would operate along the lines demanded by the strikers. Reichers insisted on calling the first of these a "factory" and proudly described how its production would be organized. The establishment of such shops, Reichers continued, meant that "much more has been accomplished for the garment-workers than was originally expected."[70]

Co-ops such as those set up by the UGW during the Baltimore strike have usually been associated more with the Knights of Labor than with AFL unions. In fact, the Knights had established a cooperative shirt factory in Baltimore just four years earlier, in 1888. Rather than setting up their co-op on the "modern" basis preferred by the AFL, however, the Baltimore Knights had quickly "decided . . . to abolish the factory system and permit the girls to do the work at their homes."[71] The Knights' sense of morality, in other words, found home work, often seen as an indicator of sweatshop systems of labor, more acceptable for young women than factory work. But the UGW sought to place all workers in factories rather than in the homes of workers or in the homes and sweatshops of their employers. This distinction between the two organizations sums up not only many of the differences between them but also many of the differences in their attitudes toward and treatment of women workers.

The Baltimore Knights' DA 41 had previously included a local assembly made up of female "sewing machine operatives," but this district assembly had withdrawn from the Knights in November 1891, after writing several letters to Master Workman John W. Hayes in which they asked the general

70. *Sun*, July 22, 1892, p. 8.
71. *JUL*, November 22, 1888 (9:21), p. 2740. The Knights' co-op closed less than a year after its opening (*JUL*, July 11, 1889 [10:2], n.p.).

executive board to appoint someone to the Woman's Department of the Knights. District Master Schonfarber later said that the workers left the Knights because the Knights were "too conservative" for their taste.[72] He held that the conservatism of the Knights was one of its benefits, a characterization with which the city's wholesalers probably agreed, once their subcontractors joined the Knights as a way to battle the strikers of 1892. Women workers, however, could very well view the Knights as conservative because of their attempts to return and confine women to the domestic sphere. (Hayes's reputation as a womanizer merely reinforces this view.)[73] Once in the UGW, women workers would belong to their own Local 33 of the union, the Women's Branch.

The AFL's UGW, in other words, treated the presence of women workers in the industry and in the union seriously. The Knights of Labor, however, nominally sought to gain the support of non-wage-earning women but did little to address the concerns of women workers in the Baltimore coat industry in 1892. In mid-August, DA 41 announced that it was in the process of forming "neighborhood clubs" to enforce boycotts of non–Knights of Labor goods. About a week later, the mayor received a letter purporting to be from strikers' wives. Signed by two hundred women, the letter stated: "We have small children . . . and we are all starving." The letter implied that the women's husbands wanted to return to work but were prevented from doing so by members of the UGW. Reichers himself wrote to the mayor the following day, denying responsibility for the problem and suggesting that the letter from the "Wives of Strikers" was in fact written by someone who was against the strikers.[74] Certainly this appeal to public' sympathy sounds more like the Knights' sense of morality than anything connected to the militant community of strikers.

Contrary to popular historical belief, the UGW appears to have given women a much fuller role in their organization than the Knights did in Baltimore. By the time of this strike, the main strength of the Knights lay in the Clothing Cutters' Assembly. In organizing this highly skilled, all-male occupation, the Knights actually hewed to craft union lines more closely than the UGW did. When Terence Powderly spoke at the Knights' Labor Day celebration in Baltimore in 1892, he specifically discussed the role of women in the Order in part of his speech: "The Knights of Labor say to all men who cross the threshold of their order that all men are brothers and all women are sisters. . . . While the man is fighting for his eight hours a day woman's work often begins at 5:30 o'clock, when she gets her husband's breakfast,

72. Jonathan Garlock, *Guide to the Local Assemblies of the Knights of Labor* (Westport, Conn.: Greenwood Press, 1982), p. 180; Letter from Mamie N——ay to John W. Hayes, January 20, 1891, John William Hayes Papers, microfilm edition (Sanford, N.C.: Microfilming Corporation of America, 1975), reel 7; Sun, August 17, 1892, p. 8.

73. Weir, *Knights Unhorsed*, p. 156.

74. *Sun*, August 24, 1892, p. 8, and August 25, 1892, p. 8.

and does not end until late at night, when she must sit down to mend his clothes while he is asleep."[75] This view of "woman's work" as the work of a wife may suggest a real openness to women in their family roles, but it completely disregards the situation of most employed women. How welcome would the young and single feel in an organization that so explicitly celebrated women's unpaid domestic roles? The UGW did offer these young women an alternative activist role.

The Baltimore strike thus suggests some of the ways in which the rhetoric about women of the Knights and the AFL might have led to quite different reactions toward the two organizations by women workers. The Knights of Labor, with their vague anticapitalist sentiments, believed that the moral and economic problems of women workers began when their productive work was removed from the home. Four years earlier a supporter of the Baltimore shirt cooperative put it this way: "Brothers, do you wonder at our sisters being tempted and led from the paths of virtue, when their battle for bread is surrounded by so many hardships, and their very environment such as are calculated to lead them from the monotony of a factory life into the gilded dens of vice?"[76] The problem was as much the factory as it was low wages or exploitative bosses. For the Knights, women—and their work—belonged at home.

These later cross-gender strikes under the auspices of the Knights of Labor highlight several developments and issues. Just as in the 1887 strikes that began this chapter, the strikes of the garment workers five years later demonstrate the ways in which both women workers and rank-and-file workers in general continued to be silenced by the efforts of "Master Workmen" to speak on behalf of the strikers. The efforts of the Baltimore and Boston Master Workmen to negotiate deals with employers while disregarding strikers' demands reinforces the idea that such spokesmen for the Knights often shared virtually nothing with strikers because they themselves usually came from very different trades. The mixed results of the Boston and Baltimore strikes also remind us of the problems the Knights faced in their dealings with poorly paid, semiskilled operatives in the earlier strikes. That women made up the majority of this group of workers reinforces Kim Voss's warning against expecting male workers to span the gaps of both skill and gender simultaneously. Many of the male workers in this chapter's strikes had valuable skills within their industries, but even they faced increased mechanization of their tasks, as in the case of the Worcester boot makers.

Do these stories therefore outweigh the more optimistic view of the attitudes of the Knights toward women, as seen in Levine and Blewett? Even a historian of the Knights' demise, Robert Weir, argues that "the KOL did more to organize women . . . than any other male-dominated labor organiz-

75. *Sun*, September 6, 1892, p. 8.
76. *JUL*, September 20, 1888 (9:12), p. 2704.

ation of its time."[77] How much of the discounting of women's roles in the strikes under consideration here arises from the fact that the strikes all took place after the Knights had begun to decline as an organization? While it is difficult to give a single, blanket answer to this question, the case studies presented here suggest that the Knights' descent from labor supremacy made some of the organization's most troubling qualities worse. Internal factionalism and external threats reinforced the tendency of the confusing structure of the Knights to limit free speech and democratic decision-making by its members. Furthermore, the growing desperation of the Knights becomes apparent as they sought to maintain membership levels by, in Samuel Gompers's words, "admitt[ing] to membership . . . others than wage-workers."[78] When the Knights brought strikebreakers together in the Independent United Garment Workers' Association of Boston, or formed the Monumental Coat Contractors' Assembly among the struck employers in Baltimore, they effectively moved their organization further away from its original vision of a "Cooperative Commonwealth" of producers. Neither female nor male workers would be served by such actions.

In addition to these actions provoked by the organization's sense of crisis, the Knights relied increasingly on their domestic ideology of "woman's place." Easily viewed in the earlier years as Levine's "unprecedented integration of women's roles in the home, the community, and the workplace,"[79] this ideology was by the early 1890s a much clearer though even more impossible attempt by the embattled leadership of the Knights to restore economic equity by returning women to the homes in which they belonged. Such a stance might appeal to male Knights and their wives, but it left little room for organizing and action by women workers.

If the Knights believed that women belonged at home, then where did women belong in the eyes of its organizational nemesis, the American Federation of Labor? Charles Reichers of the Garment Workers would have argued that they belonged in a new, "modern" factory run under union conditions. For many others in the craft unions of the AFL, as we shall see, the question would result in more ambiguous answers.

77. Weir, *Knights Unhorsed*, p. 158.
78. "A Circular Issued by the Executive Council of the AFL," in *The Samuel Gompers Papers*, vol. 2: *The Early Years of the American Federation of Labor, 1887–1890*, ed. Stuart B. Kaufman (Urbana: University of Illinois Press, 1987), p. 117.
79. Levine, *Labor's True Woman*, p. 10.

3 *The American Federation of Labor*

Strong hands to aid the weak
—*The Tailor*, July 1890

On Saturday, December 6, 1890, Herbert Walmsley, superintendent of the Clark Thread Company mills in Kearney and Newark, New Jersey, fired Frank Hatfield, "an elderly English [mule] spinner," when his spinning mule broke down. Forty of Hatfield's fellow spinners in the company's Mill No. 2 left their work at noon on Monday to protest the discharge.[1] This was only one of a long series of disputes the mule spinners had been having with Superintendent Walmsley. From issues of wages and work speed-ups, to complaints about the abusive "tyranny" of Walmsley and his overseers, mule spinners had kept up a litany of complaints since the previous March. In mid-November, following what they felt were the unjustified firings of two other spinners, the mule spinners had written to the executive council of the National Cotton Mule Spinners' Association (NCMSA) in Fall River, setting forth their concerns and requesting assistance in case they had to strike. The firing of Hatfield apparently served as the final straw for the spinners. When they met with Walmsley to discuss this latest discharge, he "told the men that if they did not like his management they could put on their coats and leave."[2] Spinners in the company's other two mills then met and voted to join the work stoppage. At 1:00 p.m. all 120 mule spinners at Clark's refused to return to their work. With that action a large number of ancillary workers, including women, were unable to continue working.

On the following Tuesday, approximately eight hundred of the more than two thousand employees stayed away from work, which meant that the spinning departments of all three Clark mills closed down. At the end of the workday, the company posted notices at the mills that all departments would close for an indefinite length of time. When the striking mule spinners announced on Wednesday that they would receive financial assistance from their union, their acknowledgment of their fellow workers combined a mix of solidarity, condescension, and indifference. "Of course," commented one spinner to the *New York Times*, "we fell with the 2,700 operatives who are

---

1. Unless otherwise noted, the story of this strike comes from coverage in the *Newark Daily Advertiser* [hereafter cited as *NDA*] and the *New York Times* [hereafter cited as *NYTimes*].
2. *NYTimes*, December 9, 1890, p. 2.

not organized, and who will not receive any pecuniary assistance. We'll do what we can to help the boys and girls who have widowed mothers or others who cannot help themselves depending upon them by organizing entertainments. But the shut-down will not drive us from our purposes."[3]

In several ways, the actions of the Kearney mule spinners and their union illustrate the principles of craft unionism. The doughty mule spinners attempted to settle their disputes with their employers, requested permission from their union to strike, and restricted the ensuing receipt of strike benefits to members of their union only, defined narrowly as only members of their craft, that of mule spinning.

The unions of the American Federation of Labor claimed fundamental differences from the Knights of Labor. Rather than admitting all "producers" into loose-knit local assemblies, the craft unions of the AFL followed skill and occupational lines in forming their unions. Selig Perlman and Philip Taft argued in 1935 that the solidarity of the AFL "was thus a solidarity with a quickly diminishing potency as one passed from the craft group—which looks upon the jobs in the craft as its common property for which it is ready to fight long and bitterly—to the widening concentric circles of the related crafts, the industry, the American Federation of Labor, and the world labor movement."[4]

The cross-gender strikes examined here give Perlman and Taft's comment about the "diminishing potency" of solidarity new meaning. Mechanization threatened the "common property" of skill at the turn of the century, but that property was also threatened by other things. All too often, it was women who worked at the new machines. Manhood too functioned as a type of "common property" that might be defended through the use of solidarity.

The various ways that unions conflated—or refused to conflate—skill and manhood appear throughout the strikes discussed in this chapter. Beginning with the strike of Clark's workers in 1890, this chapter examines the implications of craft unionism in all four industries. The organizational exclusiveness of the mule spinners shifted over the years and with geographical location, as seen in a 1902 Rhode Island strike of thread mill workers. The role of gender and skill is similarly traced in the cases of shoe workers in Chicago in 1892 and in Maine in 1893. In both the textile and shoe industries, mechanization played a complicating role in the stories. Strikes of custom tailors in Nebraska and Ohio illustrate the gendered issues confronting that group of skilled workers as they attempted to knit their organization together. Finally, strikes of cigar makers demonstrate some of the ways their union attempted to cope with rapid changes in both the mechanization and the

3. *NYTimes*, December 11, 1890, p. 2.

4. Selig Perlman and Philip Taft, *History of Labor in the United States*, vol. 4: *Labor Movements, 1896–1932* (1935; reprint, New York: A. M. Kelley, 1966), p. 9.

feminization of their work, at times accompanied also by new waves of immigrant workers.

The mule spinners' strike at the Clark thread company highlights issues of inclusion and exclusion in craft unions' organizing of workers that the union recognized as highly skilled. While the mule spinners' union followed craft and occupational lines in organizing, the work lives of its members illustrate the interdependence of different groups of workers. Accordingly, the strike demonstrates the potential not only for the economic strength of craft unionism but also for its possible divisiveness, as well as the dangers lurking in continuing technological change.

The mills of the Clark company in New Jersey reportedly employed 2,400 individuals before the strike of the winter of 1890/91. Of these, less than one-third were men and boys, while two-thirds were young women—"girls."[5] These workers faced a sexual division of labor that made them highly interdependent. Female carders and framers prepared raw materials for spinning. Mule spinners and their assistants, all male, then worked the cotton into yarn. Another group of female workers then applied themselves to the more-mechanized ring-spinning process, turning the men's yarn into fine thread. Though the sexes worked in completely separate workrooms—and even buildings—within the factory complex, the labor of both sexes was required to complete the work. If one group stopped production, the other usually had to follow suit in short order.

Within this sexual division of labor, workers at the Clark thread mills in New Jersey found themselves divided along ethnic lines as well. The male workers in the mills tended to be Protestants from England and Scotland, while the young female workers were overwhelmingly Irish Catholics.[6] Furthermore, the history of the mule spinners' union itself was firmly connected to the migration of Lancashire immigrants to the United States.[7] Both occupationally and organizationally, then, gender operated in tandem with ethnicity in the New Jersey mills. This conflation of gender and ethnicity almost guaranteed that the proud mule spinners would make the condescending statements about and dismissive actions toward their female co-workers that occurred in the course of the strike.[8]

5. U.S. Bureau of Labor, *Tenth Annual Report: Strikes and Lockouts* (Washington, D.C.: Government Printing Office, 1896) [hereafter cited as U.S. BLS, *10th AR*], p. 592.

6. U.S. Department of the Interior, Census Office, *Report on Population of the United States at the Eleventh Census: 1890*, part 2 (Washington, D.C.: Government Printing Office, 1897), pp. 698–99; U.S. Bureau of Labor, *Fourth Annual Report of the Commissioner of Labor, 1888: Working Women in Large Cities* (Washington, D.C.: Government Printing Office, 1889), pp. 236, 274–75. Also see *New York Daily Graphic*, January 25, 1888, p. 617.

7. See Mary H. Blewett, "Deference and Defiance: Labor Politics and the Meaning of Masculinity in the Mid-Nineteenth-Century New England Textile Industry," *Gender and History* 5 (Autumn 1993): 398–415, and Mary H. Blewett, *Constant Turmoil: The Politics of Industrial Life in Nineteenth-Century New England* (Amherst: University of Massachusetts Press, 2000), pp. 264–65, 312, 320–21.

8. See chapter 4.

In the four-month-long strike at Clark Thread, the mule spinners' view of their less-skilled co-workers (female and male) never wavered, though the actions of the other workers varied considerably. The mule spinners' union would assist the spinners' male "helpers," paying them strike benefits, though not at the same level as those of the spinners themselves. As for the female workers in the mill, one spinner explained that two years earlier they had attempted to help the women organize. A local newspaper reported: "He said that now they would make no effort at organizing the other employees, but would depend entirely on themselves."[9] While the mule spinners remained true to this sentiment, they were not above using the unorganized women workers in their appeals to public sympathy. This was particularly true when the AFL's executive committee declared a nationwide boycott of the mill's products. The boycott call, in February 1891, claimed: "The men struck work and have now been out gallantly, heroically fighting for their own and labor's rights, to organize, to maintain their manhood, to protest against injustice and wrong."[10] Though the AFL's boycott was officially only on behalf of the organized male mule spinners, the strikers repeatedly used Walmsley's abusive treatment of the women workers as the most prominent example of the "system of tyranny and persecution" at the thread mills.[11]

For their part, women workers began to organize almost immediately when the strike began. At their meetings, these women drew up lists of demands, formed committees, helped organize benefits, and solicited donations. As Christmas approached, efforts to raise additional financial contributions for the strikers and their supporters increased. Women workers canvassed door-to-door, and one local saloon keeper offered to contribute all his Christmas earnings to the relief fund. Women also approached New York City and national unions for their support. These various fund-raising efforts were soon embroiled in controversy, however, as out-of-work women claimed that they did not receive any of the funds from the various benefits. Newark newspaper accounts in late December repeatedly discussed the "considerable feeling among the thread mill girls" about the "efforts for relief made in their behalf by the public" and from which they received little benefit.[12]

At the end of December, the Clark company began importing yarn from its Scottish mills, claiming it was responding to the public outcry over the condition of the women workers who were out of work because of the mule spinners' strike. As one newspaper reporter put it, "The girls wanted to stand

9. *NDA*, December 12, 1890, p. 1.
10. Samuel Gompers to AFL Executive Council (EC), February 4, 1891, AFL Letterpress Copybooks of Samuel Gompers and William Green, 1883–1925, microfilm of originals at Library of Congress [hereafter cited as SG Letterbooks], 5:408; Gompers to Henry A. Woods, Kearney, N.J., February 5, 1891 (5:413). Boycott circular from AFL EC, in *The Tailor* 2 (April 1891): 6.
11. See *The Tailor* 2 (April 1891): 6; *Seattle Post-Intelligencer*, March 16, 1891, p. 8.
12. *NDA*, December 27, 1890, p. 1, and December 26, 1890, p. 1.

by the spinners, but the wolf was growling outside the door, so they had to bury their wishes and return to work."[13] The women worked for three days with the imported yarn but were told on New Year's Eve that the mills would close until the first Monday of the new year. Monday, January 5, described by a Newark reporter as "a cold bitter morning," witnessed a "touching scene" at the mill gates as several hundred women workers gathered to plead for their jobs back. Many told observers that the "scanty assistance" received from the relief funds forced them to return to work, even if, as rumored, they would be working with imported strikebreakers.[14]

As the company intermittently opened various mill departments, female employees faced difficult decisions. Should they accept employment alongside strikebreakers in order to gain much-needed wages? Or should they support the striking mule spinners and refuse to work on "scab products"? Even though the mule spinners had shown little support for the women thus far, over the remaining months of the strike women workers in the mills decided to walk off their jobs a surprising number of times. Though it is difficult to understand where the women's sense of solidarity came from, given the deep divide between them and the male strikers, at least some of it was rooted in the main focus of the male spinners' cause: the women's nemesis, Superintendent Herbert Walmsley. In 1888 the company's female employees had struck on their own, complaining of the treatment they received from Walmsley.[15] When it became clear in March 1890 that Walmsley would remain as the mills' superintendent, more than one hundred women decided to quit work, arguing that "their earnings had been so miserably small since the strike as not to tempt them to handle material prepared for them by 'scab' hands. . . . There was to be no escape from Walmsley, and they could not reconcile themselves to the idea of permanent servitude to such a boss."[16] The women's interests in the strike were therefore simultaneously financial, solidaristic, and selfish. Over the course of the strike, women workers would alternately join the male spinners' strike and then resume work.[17]

The strike at the Clark mills ended officially in April, when Massachusetts state senator and longtime NCMSA leader Robert Howard negotiated terms for the mule spinners' return to work. The *New York Times* reported: "Even Superintendent Walmsley has agreed to make things as comfortable as he can for [the men who are taken back]."[18] Just as the mule spinners' union had ignored the financial needs of the unorganized female workers throughout the strike, the strike's settlement ignored them as well. The women

13. *NYTimes*, January 4, 1891, p. 16.
14. *NDA*, January 5, 1891, p. 1.
15. *New York Daily Graphic*, January 25, 1888, p. 614.
16. *NYTimes*, March 12, 1891, p. 1.
17. U.S. BLS, *10th AR*, pp. 592–93, reports all female workers as strikers.
18. *NYTimes*, April 19, 1991, p. 8.

of the Clark mills would remain aware of their own role in the strike if only because their male co-workers largely refused to acknowledge their existence.

The strike, however, reinforced the tendency of the mule spinners to cling to their union and to their proud and lonely stance as the only economically important group of workers in the mills. The National Cotton Mule Spinners' Association embodied the independence of the mule spinners. The mule spinners believed that they could act without the cooperation of their co-workers, and their union similarly believed that it could act independently of any given larger union movement. The mule spinners' union thus became an organizational free agent moving from independent status into the Knights of Labor, then into the AFL, back into the Knights, to independence, and ultimately into the AFL again.

In this way, the mule spinners' union was organizationally similar to the Lasters' Protective Union. Both the Lasters and the Mule Spinners believed not only that they did not need the cooperation of co-workers in strikes but also that they did not need the support of other unions of skilled workers. Using the mule spinners to begin this chapter on the AFL is therefore somewhat ironic. While the union demonstrates many of the key qualities of the AFL's distinctly gendered form of craft unionism, the mule spinners' fundamental sense of independence made it a less-than-ideal member of the Federation.

By 1901, however, the National Mule Spinners' Union, as it now called itself, had negotiated a merger of sorts with the newly formed United Textile Workers of America (UTWA). It would retain its independent charter with the AFL while affiliating loosely with the new union.[19] The implications of this can be seen in the 1902 strike of workers at the J & P Coats Company thread mills in Pawtucket, Rhode Island.[20]

Early in April 1902 the mule spinners' union of Rhode Island demanded a 10 percent wage hike for Coats thread mill spinners in order to bring wages in line with those of mule spinners in the region's cloth mills. The management of the Coats Company quickly became the first Rhode Island employer to grant the demand. Virtually simultaneous with this, a fifty-eight-hour-workweek act for the labor of women and children went into effect in the state. Because of the interdependence of workers in the industry, this meant that all workers' hours would decrease from sixty to fifty-eight. Coats announced the new hours and noted that these shorter hours would be accompanied by a 3.5 percent wage decrease for all their workers. When Coats employees received their first diminished paychecks, the spinners' checks still reflected a 6.5 percent increase over previous pay, while the rest of the company's workers received smaller checks.

19. The complex story of textile unionism and the mule spinners role in it is told more fully in chapter 7.
20. Unless otherwise noted, the story of this strike comes from coverage in the *Pawtucket Evening Times* [hereafter cited as *PET*].

Workers at Coats did not, however, strike immediately. It was more than a month later, at 2:00 p.m. on May 20, that female twister tenders in Mills 4 and 5 refused to work any longer. The women claimed that since the company had deducted the two hours' pay from their wages, it had also sped up the machines, causing the workers to work harder and to produce at least as much as they had produced under the old sixty-hour workweek. The following day, more twister tenders joined the strike. Workers dependent on the work of the twisters, described by the newspaper as being "mostly boys," were also thrown out of work by the strike.[21] Many in Pawtucket believed that the well-known "liberal" treatment of workers by the company, combined with the strikers' unorganized and leaderless state, would prevent the strike from lasting very long.[22] Despite this belief, the strike continued to spread as the week progressed, so that by Friday more than one thousand workers were on strike. Many more, including the company's 150 mule spinners, were idled by the strike as well.

Strikers now demanded that the company match the mule spinners' 10 percent wage increase for all the mills' workers, in addition to restoring the lost 3.5 percent. They held the strike's first mass meeting on Friday evening, deciding to stay out and begin the work of forming a branch of the United Textile Workers' union (UTWA). Now under the leadership of Rhode Island mule spinners' union secretary James Cliffe, a committee of strikers met on Saturday with Coats' Mr. Arnold and proposed that if the company would restore the original two hours' pay, workers would return to work and give the company four weeks to consider the demand for a 10 percent wage increase for all employees. Arnold responded by suggesting that workers return to work Monday morning, promising they "would be treated fairly." A meeting later that afternoon heard the committee's report and voted "to stay out and to proceed with the work of forming a branch of the United Textile Union."[23]

What is interesting here is the role of the mule spinners, largely in the person of James Cliffe. Though Cliffe lost four children to diphtheria over the course of April and May, he also attended the mule spinners' union national convention in Boston, helped form Pawtucket's AFL-affiliated Central Labor Union, helped his co-workers join with the UTWA, and received his commission as a "deputy organizer" for the AFL. Throughout all this activity, Cliffe's goal seems to have been to assist other workers, including women workers, in re-creating their own versions of the mule spinners' careful craft unionism. Cliffe's own union had no argument with the Coats management; its members had, after all, already received their own pay increases. Perhaps Cliffe understood, though, the increasingly tenuous position of his own craft.

21. *PET*, May 21, 1902, p. 9.
22. *PET*, May 22, 1902, pp. 5, 8.
23. *PET*, May 26, 1902, p. 10.

New technologies, any one of which might undercut the economic strength of this "most skilled" group of workers in the mills, were being developed every year. At the same time, textile workers in general were becoming more active in the labor movement, and the formation of the UTWA in 1901 was but the organizational form of that activity.

At the Rhode Island mule spinners' union meeting of May 1, gathered members had read and discussed a letter from the UTWA requesting their assistance in organizing other textile workers. The meeting had tabled the issue for future discussion.[24] Before that discussion could take place, though, the actions of the twister tenders intervened. In this case, faced with their co-workers' strike, Cliffe and the other mule spinners took up the cause of the strikers and helped organize them into the "appropriate" AFL union. Why did these spinners react so differently toward female co-workers, compared with their New Jersey brothers a decade earlier?[25]

The answer is found in two developments over the decade: the mule spinners' union had gradually accepted adherence to the AFL as a federation of craft unions and the existence of the UTWA as a craft union of "textile operatives." While the mule spinners' union retained a state of semi-independence within the textile workers' union, its affiliation with the union allowed members to support co-workers' participation in the union without feeling that such membership threatened their own identities as unionists.[26]

The mule spinners' hope for the textile workers' union was that it would act as its Pawtucket members did: just like mule spinners. The Pawtucket strike continued for only one more week after the first meeting with Arnold. In the middle of the strike's second week, a four-person committee, including Cliffe, two women, and one man, once again met with the company's management, though this time in the person of Alfred M. Coats. The committee told Coats that it had decided not to ask for the 10 percent wage increase but that it did want the two-hours' pay restored. Coats's reply, as reported, sounded slightly whiney: "He said the employees had not shown the consideration to the concern that might reasonably have been expected. The concern had always treated its employees fairly and generously and the grievances should have been stated before they quitted work."[27]

The committee responded by assuring Coats that this inconsideration on their part was due solely to inexperience and that from now on they would

24. *PET*, May 2, 1902, p. 14. See chapter 7.
25. The role played by ethnicity remains murkier for Pawtucket than it was for Kearney and Newark. I had hoped to compile a data set from the 1900 Federal Manuscript Census in order to explore this question, but census enumerators in Pawtucket had made no distinction between different types of textile production, let alone between different occupations. See appendix 2 for a description of other data sets compiled.
26. The mule spinners would ultimately withdraw from the UTWA on the eve of World War I; see Gary M. Fink, ed., *Labor Unions* (Westport, Conn.: Greenwood Press, 1977), p. 353. See also Blewett, *Constant Turmoil*, pp. 313, 386–87.
27. *PET*, May 29, 1902, p. 9.

present grievances "properly." By the end of the meeting, Coats suggested that if all strikers returned to work the following Monday he would show no discrimination and treat them fairly. If the same committee returned to him at that time, he promised to "give the matter consideration."[28] A meeting of strikers later the same day voted unanimously to return to work under those conditions.

On Monday, June 2, 1902, all the strikers returned to work at the Coats mills.[29] At 5:00 p.m. one week later, the Coats Company posted notices that wage rates would be returned to the sixty-hour-a-week level and would be in force retroactively to April 7, when the fifty-eight-hour workweek law had gone into effect. (No mention was made of the alleged speed-up of the work; presumably, workers continued to produce sixty hours' worth of work in fifty-eight hours.) As reported, workers were pleased with the decision: "Employees of the concern readily admitted that they have been treated fairly by the corporation in this matter and that the amicable relations which existed up to the strike have been restored and are likely to be continued for years."[30]

The following day, June 11, James Cliffe presented UTWA Local 348 with the charter he had received a week earlier from national headquarters. The union then set about the business of craft unionism: electing officers, setting meeting dates, voting their thanks to the mule spinners' union. If Cliffe's goal here was to make sure that his co-workers became firm subscribers to AFL-style unionism, it is telling that he did not separate them out into occupationally divided subunits of the United Textile Workers. Cliffe's own mule spinners' union remained such a semi-independent unit of the larger union, but in his and other mule spinners' eyes their co-workers did not possess that most valuable of properties: skill.

Mule spinners joined with Samuel Gompers and others in the AFL in arguing that one of the critical factors allowing the young federation to survive the depression had been its careful adherence to the defining principle of craft unionism: organizing workers along lines of occupational skill, or "craft."[31] Workers who possessed crucial skills in any given industry retained a level of economic power against their employers, because they could not easily be replaced during strikes. However, as the cross-gender strikes under consideration here demonstrate, definitions of "skill" often became entangled in workers' definitions of "manliness." Such strikes required workers to spell out—for themselves as much as for the public—their understanding of the

28. Ibid.

29. Rhode Island Bureau of Industrial Statistics, *Sixteenth Annual Report* (Providence: E. L. Freeman & Sons, 1903), p. 151.

30. *PET*, June 10, 1902, p. 3.

31. See, for example, an interview in the *Indianapolis Sentinel* with Gompers, January 5, 1896, quoted in *The Samuel Gompers Papers*, vol. 4: *A National Labor Movement Takes Shape, 1895–98*, ed. Stuart B. Kaufman et al. (Urbana: University of Illinois Press, 1991), pp. 112–13; AFL, *Report of the Proceedings of the Thirteenth Annual Convention*, 1893, p. 12.

bounds of solidarity. Just who would be included and who would be excluded? Virtually all cross-gender strikes in the early years of the AFL craft unions sooner or later required workers to figure out just who belonged to their specific craft or skill group and who did not.

Strikes monitored by the national unions of the AFL also demonstrate the sometimes tenuous nature of what it meant to workers to belong to national organizations. In their attempts to respond to and control members' often-precipitous actions, the national craft unions promulgated their own definitions of what constituted both skill and manly behavior. The union as a whole would be strengthened when the definitions of national union leaders coincided with local union members' definitions. Similarly, the national unions might gain strength if members simply believed that they shared a gendered craft identity with their union brothers around the nation.

For the mule spinners of New Jersey in 1891 and Pawtucket in 1902, such an overlapping definition of skill and manhood created no great problem, no worrying dissonances. Shoe workers confronted issues of skill and gender in similar ways. The AFL's Boot and Shoe Workers' International Union (BSWIU), developed out of the long traditions of the Knights of St. Crispin, the Knights of Labor, and the Lasters' Protective Union. Mary Blewett shows how Massachusetts shoe and boot workers fashioned a complex strategy in which they organized workers largely along separate occupational lines but then coordinated the activities of the various unions.[32] Ideally, this meant that all occupations and all skill levels, as well as both women and men, would address their own particular issues while still uniting to fight employer resistance. Skilled male lasters, cutters, and bottomers could and did acknowledge the skills of female stitchers, and all these gendered groups of skilled workers operated in their unions in coordination both with one another and with less-skilled co-workers, both male and female.

Initially, coordination of the actions of male and female shoe workers derived from a mutual acknowledgment of workers' skills, but by the 1880s, mechanization had made major inroads into those skills.[33] While the shoe workers of eastern Massachusetts might still call on traditions of cross-gender craft cooperation to hold together their union strategy, shoe workers elsewhere worked in shops without those older traditions, both within and outside the workshop. In this context, cross-gender unionism in other areas of the nation faced a rockier road.

The Chicago strike of 1892, described in chapter 1, demonstrates this. Beginning with male lasters, the strike first spread to other men in the factory.[34] It took several days before the male strikers began to pay attention

32. Mary H. Blewett, *Men, Women, and Work: Class, Gender, and Protest* (Urbana: University of Illinois Press, 1988).

33. Ibid., pp. 226–29.

34. Unless otherwise noted, the story of this strike comes from coverage in the *Chicago Tribune*.

to their female co-workers. Once women were encouraged to join the strike, however, they became firm strike supporters. Thus far the story appears to follow the example of New England shoe workers; though workers struck and presented grievances along the lines of occupations and sex, they seemed to be united in their efforts. This unity held throughout the two months of the strike, although cracks soon began to appear. Early meetings of the women strikers often featured speeches by local union activist Elizabeth Morgan, who urged the women to organize in order to prevent wage cuts and to avoid being used as strikebreakers. Male strike leaders certainly supported this sentiment. However, Morgan also encouraged the women to affiliate with either the AFL or the Knights of Labor. Male unionists, including Henry Skeffington of the AFL union, were unhappy with Morgan's ecumenical view of the women's organization, even though eventually the women did affiliate with the AFL union.[35]

The strikers' employer soon sought to take advantage of splits between male and female strikers, offering to take back all the women but only the men who had not been replaced already by strikebreakers. This offer was repeated several times during the strike, and each time it would be refused by the women. These women workers clearly agreed with the woman who told them she saw their actions as "heroic": "You have not gone out for any grievances of your own, but you have gone out to help your brethren."[36] At several points in the strike, speakers reminded workers of a strike the previous year in nearby Elgin, Illinois, which had been lost because the women were not united. This memory clearly influenced the male strikers in Chicago in their efforts to include women in their activities, and those efforts paid off: the strikers won their battle in late May. The lasters who began the strike were thus rewarded for the confidence they placed in their female co-workers. These Chicago shoe workers found that unity across gender lines worked much better than did the strict adherence to occupational craft unionism, such as that practiced by Kearney's male mule spinners.

The example of the 1892 Chicago strike therefore supports Blewett's view of cross-gender craft cooperation in the shoe industry. This single strike suggests that the shoe industry was the exception that proved the rule of the limiting effects of gendered unionism. At the same time, the Chicago strike sounds a warning to the historian: after all, the strike's positive conclusion appears to be based at least in part on the workers' absorption of a recent—and geographically close—counterexample. Furthermore, though the Boot and Shoe Workers' Union could successfully navigate the shoals of gender divisions in this particular strike, it based its very organizational

35. Letter from S. Gompers to E. Morgan, March 11, 1892, in *The Samuel Gompers Papers*, vol. 3: *Unrest and Depression, 1891–94*, ed. Stuart B. Kaufman and Peter J. Albert (Urbana: University of Illinois Press, 1989), pp. 154–55; Samuel Gompers to H. J. Skeffington, SG Letterbooks, March 21, 1892, 7:154.
36. *Chicago Tribune*, March 6, 1892, p. 3.

structure on the sexual division of labor as presented at the workplace. Would unity also prevail in strikes initiated by women workers? Would male workers themselves prove worthy of women's confidence?

In early August 1893, female stitchers in a shoe shop in Auburn, Maine, refused to sign the new, lower, price list—the price rates offered for various jobs—presented by their employers.[37] Throughout the next week, workers held meetings along occupational (and therefore, gender) lines. All expressed sympathy with the skilled female stitchers, and most of them, belonging to the Boot and Shoe Workers' International Union, voted that week to strike in support of the women. The male lasters, members of the Lasters' Protective Union, and male shoe cutters, members of their own Boot and Shoe Cutters' Union, took longer to decide finally to strike on behalf of the women.

The lasters, whose union most closely resembled that of the mule spinners, walked out of their jobs only after the combined Auburn shoe manufacturers had escalated the strike considerably. When the lasters finally did strike, employers fought back in two ways: by importing immigrant Armenian lasters to work as strikebreakers and by installing new lasting machines in several of the shops. Though mule spinners too faced both technological and ethnic replacements, the reluctant lasters of Auburn and elsewhere faced these trends even more over the following years.[38] The impact of this did not become clear in the Auburn strike, however. The strike occurred just as the depression of the 1890s began. Even if the strikers had cooperated fully with one another, the quickly worsening economic conditions would have doomed the strike to failure. The unresolved gender issues of the Auburn strike lingered for years, until a combination of new technologies and a resulting new sexual division of labor within the shoe industry erased the efficacy of the nineteenth-century gender-based unions.

If the mule spinners and lasters faced similar problems of skill, gender, and mechanization and came to similar conclusions, the issues for other AFL unions were less clear. Two of the earliest and most central AFL unions, that of tailors and that of cigar makers, demonstrate the possible problems. Both these groups experienced much more blurring of the lines of craft and skill, a blurring that could often coincide with definitions of manliness in disturbing ways.[39]

The Journeymen Tailors' Union of America (JTUA), established in 1883, voted in 1887 to join the recently formed AFL. The tailors' union serves as

37. Unless otherwise noted, the story of this strike comes from coverage in the *Lewiston Evening Journal*.

38. John T. Cumbler, *Working-Class Community in Industrial America: Work, Leisure, and Struggle in Two Industrial Cities, 1880–1930* (Westport, Conn.: Greenwood Press, 1979), p. 82; Blewett, *Men, Women, and Work*, p. 268.

39. What follows on the tailors' union is taken from Ileen A. DeVault, "'To Sit Among Men': Skill, Gender, and Craft Unionism," in *Labor Histories: Class, Politics, and the Working-Class Experience*, ed. Eric Arnesen, Julia Greene, and Bruce Laurie (Urbana: University of Illinois Press, 1998), pp. 259–83.

a model of early AFL craft unionism in several ways. Made up of workers in the custom-tailoring trade, the union sought to control both entrance into the trade and wage levels. A complex set of membership dues established a financial basis for payment of strike benefits, although the union's executive board had to approve local strikes before benefits would be paid.[40] During the early years of its AFL membership, the tailor's union remained a loyal member of the Federation, with the two organizations sharing the services of John B. Lennon, the Denver tailor who served as tailors' union general secretary from 1887 to 1910 and as AFL treasurer from 1888 to 1917.[41] Through this connection, that union enjoyed a close working relationship with activists in other AFL unions.[42] The tailors' union thus provides a particularly appropriate example of the construction of the AFL as a gendered union movement in the late nineteenth century.

The national officers of the tailors' union repeatedly and officially urged members to accept women as full and equal union members.[43] At the union's 1891 convention, Lennon discussed the role of women in the union. Chastising the locals that failed to provide women with the same benefits and protection as men, Lennon argued that "women are in the trade and they are in to stay." The proper response to this situation, he continued, was to strive to attain equal pay for women and men. If every union member worked to improve the condition of women, Lennon promised them they would have "the respect of all mankind, and greater power to elevate the condition of all custom tailors."[44]

Such rhetoric aside, in strike after strike of tailors' union members, both the question of equal wages for women and the question of whether women were in fact qualified for membership in the union remained unsettled. Lennon and others did not call for equal status for *all* women; instead, they attempted to define membership in the union—and in "the trade"—so narrowly that many, if not most, women performing tailoring tasks would be effectively excluded.

Custom tailors saw themselves as participants in a trade as highly skilled as any. However, they acknowledged a crucial difference between their trade and many others. One tailor put it this way: "Tailoring is entirely different

---

40. See Charles Jacob Stowell, *Studies in Trade Unionism in the Custom Tailoring Trade* (Bloomington, Ill.: Journeymen Tailors' Union of America, 1913), pp. 71–72, 88; Charles Jacob Stowell, *The Journeymen Tailors' Union of America: A Study in Trade Union Policy* (1918; reprint, New York: Johnson Reprint Corp., 1970), pp. 54–55.

41. Stowell, *Studies in Trade Unionism*, pp. 60, 100, 93–94; *The Samuel Gompers Papers*, vol. 2: *The Early Years of the American Federation of Labor, 1887–90*, ed. Stuart B. Kaufman (Urbana: University of Illinois Press, 1987), p. 451.

42. See, for example, the "Secretary's Report" at the 1889 JTUA Convention, at which Lennon thanked Samuel Gompers, Adolph Strasser, and P. J. McGuire by name ("Proceedings of the Convention," in *The Tailor* 2 [September 1889]: 1).

43. See, for example, "Women in the Tailoring Trade," *The Tailor* 1 (November 1888): 7 ("Frauen im Schneidergeschaft," p. 3); and *The Tailor* 1 (April 1889): 4.

44. *The Tailor* 3 (August 1891): 2.

to many other skilled trades, in this respect, that the work is easily port-
able. . . . Tailors . . . can take their work under their arms and sit down almost
anywhere and make it."[45] This portability of the tailor's work stood at the
heart of one of the union's primary goals: to abolish home work and replace
it with "free back shops" provided by the employer.[46] While gaining such
shops became a central goal of the tailors' union, members insisted that
working in these shops was not in and of itself a defining characteristic of
their skills. A series of painful struggles resulted, which involved not only
the place of work but also the tailor's role within his family and women's
role within the union.

The Omaha strike of 1889 illustrates some of the difficulties raised by the
home work issue for the tailors' union.[47] In mid-February, five of the firms
belonging to Omaha's Merchant Tailors' Exchange announced a wage reduction of 10 percent. The subsequent strike of ninety tailors, including three
women, thus began with a demand for restoration of the earlier price list.[48]
In addition, leaders of the Omaha union insisted that all work be done in
shops rather than in the homes of the tailors.[49] In this the Omaha leaders
followed the spirit of a resolution passed at the tailors' union 1887 convention, which called for "the gradual substitution [for 'having the work done
in our homes'] of the system of workshops provided by the employers of
trades."[50]

While all the Omaha tailors supported the restoration of wages, some
found the attack on home work unacceptable. The union members who
worked in their own homes with the assistance of members of their family
and others left the tailors' union local when it raised this issue, and formed
a rival union.[51] Members of the new union proceeded to return to work for
the members of the Merchant Tailors' Exchange. In the ensuing rhetorical
battle, JTUA members called the rival union's workers "scabs" and explicitly
evoked their own manhood in contrast. At the beginning of the strike's fifth

45. Alex. S. Drummond, "The Eight-Hour Question as Applied to Tailoring," *The Tailor* 3
(September 1891): 1.

46. The debate over this issue in the 1880s and 1890s is a variation of what Joan Scott found
among Parisian tailors in the 1840s. Scott argues that, for French tailors in these years, "skill"
became synonymous with "the shop." See Joan W. Scott, "Work Identities for Men and Women,"
in *Gender and the Politics of History* (New York: Columbia University Press, 1988), p. 100.

47. Unless otherwise noted, the story of this strike comes from coverage in the *Omaha Daily
Bee* [hereafter cited as *DB*].

48. U.S. BLS, *10th AR*, pp. 558–61. The striking tailors argued that the cut was actually
closer to 20 percent. See *The Tailor* 1 (April 1889): 4; *DB*, February 19, 1889 (a.m.), p. 2.

49. Letter from Beerman, in *The Tailor* 3 (June 1893): 5.

50. Constitution and By-laws of the Journeymen Tailors' National Union, adopted August
1887, in "American Labor Unions Constitutions and Proceedings," microform edition (Ann
Arbor: University Microfilms, 1980s–) [hereafter cited as "Constitutions and Proceedings"],
pp. 19–20.

51. Nebraska Bureau of Labor and Industrial Statistics, *Second Biennial Report for 1889
and 1890* (Lincoln, 1890), p. 337.

week, the Omaha newspaper published a letter from "The Striking Tailors" that reiterated the strikers' demands: that the shops of the Exchange stop utilizing scab labor and that employers establish workshops in which they could "sit among men and make [their] work." The Merchant Tailors' Exchange responded scathingly:

> Now, men of the union, will you be truthful enough to state to the much-abused public how you find it degrading to sit among the so-called scabs! As a matter of fact, they are composed of good ex-union men—some of them that were such as late as two weeks ago; and, as a matter of truth, have you not . . . had your walking committee call on all so-called scabs and beseech them to join your union, which would, at once, transform them into men and first-class tailors, regardless of merit! So much for your pride.[52]

The scorn of the Exchange helped neither the Exchange nor the now-divided union. Though the Omaha tailors eventually won their strike, for the next two and a half years the "men and brothers" of the original union would have to deal with the "cutthroats and pirates" of a "scab union."[53]

When they affiliated with the JTUA, Omaha tailors joined an organization that understood the complexities of the home work issue for tailors but also took a firm stance in favor of free back shops. The columns of the union's journal, *The Tailor*, were filled with admonitions against home work[54] and calls for the establishment of back shops. Back shops, ran the usual argument, would enable union members to control working conditions; they would be able to tell exactly how much was being produced, who was producing it, and how much they were being paid. This would help minimize the effects of seasonal unemployment, allow tailors to enforce an eight-hour day, and in general further the cause of unionization.[55]

In addition to the pragmatic organizational implications of home work, however, the issue had an emotional side. As one union member put it, "The sacred and endearing associations that cluster around the word home, are prostituted to the basest purposes when the workman is forced to convert his home into a workshop."[56] Back shops would make tailors' homes more pleasant and raise the moral standards of their families.[57] Home work,

---

52. *DB*, March 18, 1889 (p.m.), p. 8.

53. *The Tailor* 2 (March 1890): 4.

54. "Fillers" in the union's journal, *The Tailor*, often commented on the evils of home work. For example, "Tailors, is it not about time for you to place yourselves on a level with other mechanics and stop working in your homes?" (*The Tailor* 1 [November 1887]: 4; see also 1 [October 1887]: 3; 1 [March 1888]: 8; 1 [April 1888]. 6).

55. See, for example, "Back Shops," *The Tailor* 1 (June 1888): 4, and "Can the Workers of Our Trade Be Benefitted by the Eight-Hour Movement?" *The Tailor* 3 (October 1891): 4.

56. *Proceedings of Convention of the JTUA*, 1891, in "Constitutions and Proceedings," Resolution on Back Shops.

57. *The Tailor* 1 (December 1887): 4, "Back Shops vs. Home Work" ("Back-Shops gegen Hausarbeit," p. 2); *The Tailor* 1 (May 1888): 6.

however, "begins the destruction of what makes life worth living, a happy home. . . . Every consideration is subordinated to this work; the meals of the family, cleanliness, care of the babies, schooling of the children, loving inter-course between husband and wife, recreation, home comfort and all that sweetens existence."[58]

Despite such reverberating emotional appeals, tailors continued to work at home. Sometimes, as in Omaha, they resisted attempts by their unions to change the system. It was not that union members really wanted "to make a factory of their houses,"[59] but rather, as one union author pointed out,

> they have their wives and daughters working with them. They can take all the hours God gives them, and make the whole family do the chores for them by running to and from the stores. So you can plainly see what you have to contend with in doing away with the home work. It is almost traditional with some of our members, and they know right well that it will never be changed while asking the employers for what our members themselves don't want.[60]

Though rarely addressed directly, this partially acknowledged production by wives and daughters lay at the root of the general reluctance of rank-and-file tailors to put a stop to home work. As the Omaha union had learned, threatening this source of additional income could provoke strong responses.

While the home work issue raised questions about the role of members of tailors' families, the union always framed the issue in terms of the location of work rather than of the participants in that work. Officially, the union had already resolved the issue of the role of wives in the union, if not exactly their place in the tailoring trade. In November 1890 the Springfield, Missouri, local posed a question to the general executive board of the national union. The local had passed a resolution stating that all tailors' helpers should join the union, but now they were puzzled over whether the resolution covered tailors' wives as well. The board ruled "that unless the wife devotes her entire time to working as a helper she should not be compelled to join; that is, in case the wife does her own housework and helps her husband in her spare time, she should not be compelled to join the union."[61] For wives whose tailor husbands worked at home, then, the line between helpmate and helper would have been blurry and difficult to cross.[62]

58. "An Open Letter to the Chicago Drapers' and Tailors' Exchange and to the Public," printed in *The Tailor* 3 (September 1892): 2.

59. "Back Shops," *The Tailor* 1 (June 1888): 4.

60. "On Back Shops," *The Tailor* 3 (November 1891): 1.

61. *The Tailor* 2 (December 1890): 4.

62. This was the unspoken rationale behind the "Wife's Funeral Benefit" and its unequal application. The heirs of a male JTUA member received $100 on the member's death, and the member himself received $75 if his wife died. The heirs of female members of the union received only $75 on the member's death, and there was no benefit for a husband's funeral. See *The Tailor* 2 (March 1891): 6, *The Tailor* 3 (June 1893): 3.

The issue of the role of "helpers" in the tailoring trade (and in the tailors' union) involved questions of both the use of wives as helpers for home workers and the use of unrelated women as helpers in other settings. In spring 1887 the tailors' union local in Knoxville, Tennessee, found itself dealing with the complexities of the intersection between the two. At the time, union members reported that roughly one-quarter of them worked at home, while the rest worked in employers' back shops. The local union secretary reported: "Some of the men employed women help, the men working home had help from their wives, one in particular had a jour[neyman] help with his wife. Some of the bosses employed female help in their back shops . . . but with the exception of one shop (F. I. Callan) not to an extent to hurt the interest of the jours."[63]

At this point, Callan began to expand his business and hire additional women. The union, arguing that employing lower-paid women was equivalent to "having work made under the bill," demanded that Callan fire all but one of his women workers. Callan refused, pointing out that "he had as much right to work a woman for profit as the jour, and if the union expected him to discharge his women he would consider the necessity of doing so when they, his jours, first set him the example." The union held a special meeting at which it decided that members would "give up their female help" and stop working at home, demanding that all bosses provide back shops. A union committee gave Callan one week to comply with the union's demands. As they had in Omaha, responses of Knoxville union members varied. Some home workers refused to begin working in back shops and were expelled from the local. Other men working for Callan "discharged their women at the specified time only to see them transfer their services to Mr. Callan in accordance, it was then seen, with a pre-arranged plan." An apparently successful strike ensued, and a year later Callan was "running his trade without woman help."[64]

The Knoxville story highlights several important aspects of the "helper" issue. Home workers used wives and daughters as helpers without paying them in any formal sense. These family members helped the home-working tailor complete more work and therefore earn more money. Alternatively, some individual journeymen employed unrelated helpers. The journeyman then paid these helpers out of the money he received from his employer.[65] In effect, the individual journeyman acted as a subcontractor.

If the difference between casual assistance by tailors' wives and the more regular employment of female helpers by tailors was difficult to discern, the line between female helpers and "tailoresses" was equally so. The role of

---

63. Letter from A. Todlenhausen, Knoxville, *The Tailor* 1 (March 1888): 7.
64. Ibid. The union was not, however, successful in bringing the men expelled from the union back into the JTUA.
65. Helpers appear to have been about 8 percent of the workers in the custom tailoring trade by the turn of the twentieth century. Stowell, *Studies in Trade Unionism*, pp. 24–25.

women in the trade and in the union became an increasingly controversial topic in the late 1880s and early 1890s as the clothing trade underwent continual changes. The problem, explained a Denver tailor in 1887, was not women per se. Women working under what he called the "piece master system" often did not realize that they were taking work away from men. Skilled women, however, should be admitted to the union:

> If a woman can make a coat, pants or vest to the satisfaction of the employer and the customer, for what reason is she not entitled to the same amount of pay for the same amount of work? . . . I would never fear the woman who gets as much as I do for the same amount of work as myself, but it is the woman who is unable to get the same pay who is an injury to the tailors.[66]

The complexities of the issue of equal pay arose in an 1890 strike in Columbus, Ohio.[67] In mid-April of that year, members of tailors' union Local 27, acting with the approval of the national union, struck against thirteen shops belonging to the Columbus Merchant Tailors' Exchange. The union had presented a new wage bill to the Exchange shops, requesting a wage increase for union members who worked on pants and vests—a segment of the trade made up of women. The strikers reportedly included eighty men and thirty-four women, or almost all of the 130 union members in Columbus.[68]

The union's public appeals for support continually portrayed the women as helpless and at the mercy of men. The members of the Exchange were the "bad" men, unfairly forcing honest and hardworking women into prostitution; the male members of Local 27 were the self-styled "good" men who provided vigorous material support for the women—in fact, "waging a bitter war" on their behalf. The picture of feminine vulnerability painted by the union officials is belied somewhat even by their description of the strike. The men, "having worked and associated with these women in the shops for many years," did not initiate the movement for improving the women's wages. Rather, the women themselves "agitate[d] the movement of joining the Union, and finding that there was no opposition to the movement by our organization, . . . they requested the Union to admit them as members." The union's appeal presents Local 27 as the agent of the "forcible" strike action, but it also provides information that allows us to suspect that the women were themselves capable of taking forcible action.[69] Though we do not directly

66. *The Tailor* 1 (January 1888): 7.

67. I am grateful to Grace Palladino for the initial research she did on this strike while annotating it for *Samuel Gompers Papers*, 2:343. Unless otherwise noted, the story of this strike comes from coverage in the *Daily Ohio State Journal*, the *Columbus Evening Post*, *Der Ohio Sonntagsgast*, and *The Tailor*.

68. U.S. BLS, *10th AR*, pp. 972–73; Ohio Bureau of Labor Statistics, *Fourteenth Annual Report for the Year 1890* (Columbus, 1891), p. 35.

69. All quotations are from *The Tailor* 2 (June 1890): 4.

hear their voices, these do not seem to be passive, dependent, women. After all, the women had sought out union membership in order to support their demands for better wages.

Despite the unity of male and female workers, the Columbus strike ultimately failed. While tailors' union secretary Lennon praised the strike to the national union as "one of the most just and honorable ever engaged in by any union in America,"[70] the JTUA's varied experiences with the Columbus "tailoresses" did not leave the union with an untroubled position on the question of women's union membership and their wages. Even while the national union officially supported tailoresses' claims for wages equal to those of tailors, the failure of the Columbus strike exposed the difficulty in realizing such a goal. Soon after the Columbus defeat, the Nashville local petitioned the national union's executive board for support in its demand that women receive "the bill in full." The executive board advised the local "to act with caution, and send the Board fuller information as to the number of members that might become involved."[71] Theoretically enthusiastic about equal pay for women and men, the leadership of the tailors' union was also pragmatic. They would not encourage their locals to embark on a series of long, expensive—and probably unsuccessful—strikes.

In these various local conflicts the tailors' union worked out three possible roles for women, both in the tailoring trade itself and within the national union. As "tailoresses," co-workers with skills equivalent to those of many journeymen tailors, the union welcomed women as (almost) equal members. This welcome stemmed from an uneasy mix of an acknowledgment of their status as wage earners and a fear of their competition as low-wage workers.

As "helpers," women were also to be allowed into the union on a par with male apprentices. This admittance of women arose from concerns of male tailors that conditions smacking of "sweating" cheapened the trade as a whole, risking their skills and livelihoods. Finally, as wives and daughters of journeymen tailors, women were expected to benefit passively from the union status of the male members of their family, even while contributing actively to the male-earned family income. While the tailors' union attempted on a national level to regulate each group in various ways, the exact moment at which a wife became a helper, or when a helper became a full-fledged tailoress, would be worked out by the local unions.

All three of the women's roles in custom tailoring revolved around the tailor himself. The union believed that it was the male tailor who possessed the skills necessary for satisfactorily creating men's clothing. Lennon could thus argue that limiting the number of female helpers allowed a union tailor "deprives him of work that should be *made by him*, but is now made by

70. *The Tailor* 2 (May 1890): 4.
71. *The Tailor* 2 (November 1890): 6.

persons who have really no skill as tailors."[72] The union tailor had such a high level of skill, in other words, that his very *supervision* of the work process would itself ensure that that skill was embodied in the clothing produced. It was that ability to be the very personification of skill that supplied much of the force behind the "manly virtue" represented by the tailors' union as a craft union. Even when they acknowledged women as tailoresses, male co-workers viewed women's skills as limited, leaving them "at the mercy of their greedy employers" and in need of male union protection.[73]

The tailors' union recognized that it needed "to bring the extreme localities of this vast Continent together so that when a union is assailed in California, the members of our craft in the remotest part of the Continent will feel its effects."[74] One crucial way of doing this was to call on a common sense of "manhood." At the same time, precise definitions of manhood grew out of different local experiences. The national union called on the commonalities among those experiences to build a sense of solidarity—a sense of literal brotherhood. Union membership would instill a sense of "sitting among men," of sharing certain skills and attitudes, across the entire nation.

The tailors' union was confronted with trade-specific issues in its efforts to define manhood in ways that would knit the union together rather than tear it apart. Yet its attempts to do this were echoed in other trades in which AFL-affiliated craft unions operated. The most direct parallels to the tailors' union appear in the cross-gender strikes under the direction of the Cigar Makers' International Union (CMIU). The leaders of these two national unions were close colleagues and friends, and they and their industries defined similar roles for women workers.

In the 1880s and 1890s, cigar makers, like tailors, faced an industry that used women simultaneously in the segments of the industry dominated by home work (called "tenement-house work" by the CMIU) and in the sectors of the industry that were becoming increasingly reliant on new machines and an increased subdivision of the labor process. As in the tailors' union, in their attempts to negotiate these issues the cigar makers were confronted with combined issues of skill and gender.

Eileen Boris demonstrates how the cigar makers' union ultimately rejected a legislative strategy for dealing with the problem of tenement-house work in the late 1870s and early 1880s. Under the leadership of Adolph Strasser and Samuel Gompers, the cigar makers' union turned to an economic strategy premised on basic trade union principles. Similar to the tailors' strategy on home work, the CMIU ruled that "locals with any tenement house workers . . . were forbidden to maintain such workers in good standing as long

72. *Proceedings of the 1889 Convention of the Journeymen Tailors' Union of America, Columbus, Ohio,* "Constitutions and Proceedings" (emphasis added).

73. *The Tailor* 2 (June 1890): 4.

74. *Proceedings of the 1891 Convention of the JTUA, St. Louis, Mo.,* "Constitutions and Proceedings."

as they labored at home." Boris contends that "such a stand committed the CMIU against organizing the less skilled."[75] Cross-gender strikes in the cigar industry paint a much more complicated picture.

While similar to the tailors' union, the cigar makers differed in a key way. Though tailors' employers certainly colluded with their workers in allowing home work that they knew probably incorporated the labor of family members, home work in the men's custom clothing industry formally acknowledged only the male tailor as a wage earner. The tailor himself often made the decision to participate in home work. In tenement-house cigar making, the employer determined both the site of production and the identities of the producers. Cigar manufacturers would buy or lease a tenement and rent its apartments to chosen families, who then would make cigars in order to pay their rent. Employers expected all but the very youngest members of the family to participate in cigar production. While manufacturers assumed that husbands would head the cigar-making "teams," they retained the right to inspect work performed in the tenements.[76] By so doing, they ensured that women working under this system would see themselves as employees. As a result, women and men working under the tenement-house system continued to strike throughout the later 1880s and 1890s.[77] A series of strikes in New York City during the first months of 1888 illustrates some of the ways in which the cigar makers would grapple with issues of skill, gender, and home production.

In early January 1888, several New York cigar manufacturers threatened either to reduce wages by 25 percent or to return to tenement-house production. Union members accordingly applied to the union for permission to strike.[78] At noon on Friday, January 6, twenty-seven men pushed the first boulder down the hill, walking off their jobs at David Hirsch's Defiance Cigar factory. Six months earlier Hirsch had agreed to try paying the union's requested wage rates for a trial period, but when the trial period expired he announced to the workers that he was going back to the previous wages. Hirsch was well known among cigar manufacturers as the first of them to fight against the tenement-house production system in New York City. At a city Board of Trade dinner, Hirsch had told the city's mayor: "I am opposed to [tenement cigar making] . . . but there are 6,000 cigar makers idle in this city, and I think it better to resume the system than to let these men starve."[79]

---

75. Eileen Boris, "'A Man's Dwelling House Is His Castle': Tenement House Cigarmaking and the Judicial Imperative," in *Work Engendered: Toward a New History of American Labor*, ed. Ava Baron (Ithaca: Cornell University Press, 1991), p. 139.

76. Ibid., pp. 119–20.

77. Ibid., p. 139.

78. Unless otherwise noted, the story of this strike comes from coverage in the *New York Sun* [hereafter cited as *Sun*].

79. *Sun*, January 7, 1888, p. 1.

In fact, Hirsch neither resumed tenement-house production nor let "his" men starve. Instead, he gave in to his workers' demands and restored their wages. Two days after their strike had begun, it ended. The Defiance strike was only the first of the new year, though. On the night of Wednesday, January 11, five hundred to six hundred cigar makers gathered in Cooper Union heard speakers discuss their plight. Resolutions "calling the attention of the public to the evils of the tenement house system, as inimical to the interest of workingmen, detrimental to the health of the city, dangerous to public morals, and disgraceful to republican institutions" combined with those calling for the use of the cigar makers' union "blue label." The strike committee announced that they had received permission from the national union for four more factories to go on strike.[80]

Now the strikes began in earnest. On January 17, workers at S. Ottenberg & Company, members of both the CMIU and the Knights of Labor, struck against a fifty-cent-per-thousand pay decrease. Similarly, the same day, five hundred workers at Sutro & Newmark struck against a decrease. Less than a week later, four hundred more at the Kerbs & Spies factory struck, as did two hundred employees of Jacoby & Bookman. Some twelve hundred cigar makers were now on strike at factories ranging along fifty blocks of Second Avenue. Most fought against wage decreases, but the strikers at Jacoby & Bookman also charged that the firm insisted that workers return to tenement production.

These various strikes intertwined with one another so thoroughly that it is often difficult to unravel exactly what happened in each. They also brought together both tenement-house and factory production, as well as the role of gender, in the two systems and in the cigar makers' union. One of the larger companies involved, Kerbs & Spies, began to replace strikers with new bunch-making and wrapping machines. They would hire to work at these machines not the men who might join the union but boys and young women. The most notorious of the tenement producers, Jacoby & Bookman, commented: "It is competition with this machine which has driven the manufacturers in this city to go back to the tenement house work and to reduce wages, but if the machines once get in general use even tenement house work cannot compete with them."[81]

While the system of tenement-house production presented the cigar makers' union with the most problems, it also created the best publicity for the strikers. When Jacoby & Bookman instituted eviction procedures against striking families in early February, New York newspapers had a field day. By the time formal evictions actually took place in the middle of the month, strikers were ready with pageantry and pathos. A "tremendous crowd" made up of idle cigar makers, the soon-to-be-evicted families, and hundreds of the

80. *Sun*, January 12, 1888, p. 1.
81. *Sun*, January 28, 1888, p. 5.

residents of the neighboring houses gathered outside the three tenement houses owned by the firm. A "platoon" of police officers "with night sticks" policed the crowd, "vent[ing] their surplus energy on hustling small boys along." Accompanied by "a strolling band of Germans . . . engaged . . . to enliven the scene," the crowd ate lunch and drank free beer served by "the Cesky Hastinec or Hungarian tavern of Josef Masin." When the sheriff and his assistants arrived, the band broke into "The Marseillaise" and "The Dead March," "and when the first goods were brought out they played 'The harp that once thro' Tara's halls.' It was the only Irish air they knew." Shouts like "This is not Ireland. Strangle the landlords!" broke into the music. As twenty-one families had their furniture removed, reporters commented: "The most noticeable pieces of furniture on the street were cradles. Every family had at least one cradle and from two to five children." The firm itself had no comment, simply referring inquiries to the sign on their door: "WE HAVE NOTHING TO SAY."[82]

The strikes of 1888 evoked the horrifying images of filthy, unhealthy tenement-house production that had provoked the CMIU's great campaigns against the system in the 1870s. Members of the union remembered well the dangers of competition from tenement-produced cigars for those made under union conditions and prices. Some three-quarters of the strikers that early winter of 1888 were women, and the cigar makers' union aided male and female strikers without prejudice. Women picketed shops, sometimes with babies in their arms, and in return received two dollars a day from the union. At times they chased strikebreakers "with rotten eggs an' bits of ice and snowballs"; at other times they were arrested by police for verbally abusing the scabs.[83] When the Jacoby & Bookman evictions took place, the union acquired new rooms for evicted families, rooms for which employers would no longer garnish their wages.

The union stood staunchly by the New York City strikers, even though most had never belonged to the union. Between January 17 and February 29 alone, the union collected more than $2,300 in aid for the strikers, most of it coming from assessments levied on members of local unions across the nation. Though the money flowed in, many union members worried about its efficacy. Several correspondents argued in the pages of the union journal that the money would be better spent on pushing the union label. "Look how the label boomed two years ago, when we put three men on the road," argued one. "The bosses came begging to us for the use of the label on our own terms, and it looked as though we were going to drive the cheap rubbish

---

82. All from *Sun*, February 15, 1888, p. 3, except the mention of "The Marseillaise" and the shout about Ireland, both from *Tobacco (New York)*, February 17, 1888 (4:15), p. 3.
83. *Sun*, February 5, 1888, p. 11.

Evicted family, similar to those involved in the 1888 New York City strike, as portrayed by C. Broughton, c. 1892 (courtesy of UNITE Archives, Kheel Center for Labor-Management Documentation and Archives, Cornell University Library).

out of the trade."[84] Was the "cheap rubbish" here the inexpensive "working-men's" five-cent cigar? Or was it the nonunion workers, mostly immigrant women, who made that cigar?

The cigar makers' union confronted this issue in 1891, when they voted explicitly to deny union membership to tenement-house workers. Two local unions in New York City raised the issue when the union's national executive board told them that workers employed in tenement production could not reap any of the benefits of union membership. In other words, for all intents and purposes they would lose union membership.[85] The two locals fought back under the appeal process of the international union, arguing that the union constitution did not support such expulsions. Instead, they argued, the relevant clause of the constitution read simply that "all persons engaged in the industry shall be eligible to membership." Local 141 went on to point out, "There is no clause in this article which provides where applicants for membership must live or where he [sic] must work. . . . If there is no room

---

84. *Cigar Makers' Official Journal* [hereafter cited as *CMOJ*], 13 (March 1888): 6, letter from Sam Ball, New York, March 1, 1888. Others supported this basic argument; see, for example, the letter from "Members of Union 179" (Bangor, Maine), in the same issue, p. 5.

85. *CMOJ* 16 (February 1891): 1.

in the International Union for people that work where they live, then it must be plainly stated in the Constitution."[86]

The New York City unions argued that they had done just what the union had suggested. After fighting tenement production in the legislature and the courts, they "tried another way":

> We have organized them. We have raised their wages to the level of shop workers, . . . and if we protect the organization we will be able to raise the wages still higher, and in that way force the bosses to give it up themselves, for it will not pay them. If we should suspend them it will have a demoralizing effect upon them, and what will be the direct result? Reduction after reduction of wages will follow and who will suffer by it utmost? The cigar makers in the city and country as well, for it will enable manufactures [sic] to flood the market with cheap labor as they done [sic] before, and the country members will not be able to hold their own. By having them organized and keep on raising their wages, we will compel the bosses to give it up themselves . . . and if given up that way it will never be revived again. We never expected that we will be condemned for the action we took in the matter. We expected praise and got condemnation for it.[87]

The elected officials of the international union replied:

> While any and every cigarmaker could become a union member, it does not follow, that after joining the Union he can continued to work as a tenement-house slave, by turning his so-called home into a tenement-house cigar factory, in which he works from twelve to eighteen hours per day, and occasionly [sic] on Sundays. If he intends to retain his membership in the Union, he must work under the system which is not prohibited by the Constitution.[88]

Ultimately, the leadership's arguments swayed the union membership as a whole. The final vote saw almost six thousand members vote to change the relevant constitutional clause to read "All persons engaged in the industry shall be eligible for membership, except Chinese coolies and tenement-house workers."[89] With this constitutional change, it appears that the union viewed the tenement-house workers themselves as at least part of the "cheap rubbish."

Even as the cigar makers' union denied membership to tenement-house cigar makers, it had already made the opposite decision about members affected by increased subdivision of the labor process and mechanization in

---

86. *CMOJ* 16 (June 1891): 10.
87. Ibid.
88. Ibid., p. 11.
89. *CMOJ* 17 (January 1892): 7; 16 (October 1891): 5. The reference to Chinese coolies was proposed by San Francisco's Local 228 months before the tenement-house issue appeared in the pages of the union journal. See *CMOJ* 16 (February 1891): 1.

factory production. The activities enshrined as "skilled" by the union produced the entire cigar from prepared tobacco leaf.[90] As some factories began
to use molds to form the tobacco into the basic cigar shape, the cigar makers'
union insisted that such cigars were inferior to handmade ones. At the same
time, union leaders phrased this denial in terms of the machines themselves
rather than the person—or gender—of the machine operators. The national
union left the decision on machine operators' union status up to the local
unions. The fact that women made up many of the mold operators means
that women's union status depended on decisions made by local unionists.

The operation of this policy could already be seen in 1886 in Davenport,
Iowa, where, under special conditions, the union granted use of the CMIU
label to a cigar factory utilizing molds. The local allowed the factory to pay
one dollar less per one thousand cigars than was paid by other local union-
label factories, "considering his system of manufacturing (bunch-making
and rolling separated)."[91] However, the union only slowly tried to enroll all
the workers in the factory. In 1888 the union embarked on an unsuccessful
strike to force the factory's packers to join the union, but the factory workers,
both male and female, had a relatively tenuous relationship with the union.
The fragility of the bonds among the factory's workers and among those
workers and other members of the union in Davenport contributed to the
ultimate failure of the strike. By pursuing a strategy of selectively granting
use of the union label for factories using molds, and therefore making exceptions to their usual rules governing both labels and membership, the union
in effect created a second-class category of members. The union allowed
some women working in specific factories and performing mechanized tasks
into its ranks, but it did so by making local exceptions rather than by changing its general rules.

The Iowa strike also brings into focus one of the favorite organizing tools
of the cigar makers' union: the union label, or, as they preferred to call it,
the "blue label." Unionists argued that the label campaign made unionization
a benefit for manufacturers rather than a detriment. Consistently throughout
the time period covered by this book, the cigar makers touted their union
label. What this campaign might mean for women workers can be seen in
the major strike of Detroit cigar makers in 1895.[92] During May 1895, Detroit
cigar makers took up the spirit of the CMIU's "blue label" campaign and
began to agitate against the city's nonunion shops. According to the Detroit
unionists, the city's cigar manufacturers were rushing pell-mell to replace
(skilled) male hand cigar rollers with "women and children" operating machines. The Detroit union labeled the shops in which this took place "angel"

90. Patricia Cooper, *Once a Cigar Maker: Men, Women, and Work Culture* (Urbana: University of Illinois Press, 1987), pp. 50–54.
91. *Davenport Evening-Democrat Gazette*, February 16, 1888, p. 1.
92. Unless otherwise noted, the story of this strike comes from coverage in the *Detroit Free
Press* [hereafter cited as *DFP*], June 5, 1895, p. 5.

or "annex" shops. As obedient members of their national union, the Detroit cigar makers requested permission from the executive board of the CMIU to strike, receiving such in early June. Local President William Strauss "at once ordered all union men out of the open shops." At noon, Wednesday, June 5, "over 350 men and girls walked out."[93]

In many ways, the Detroit strike provides a classic example of the cigar makers' union struggle for the union label. Strikers demanded that employers pay the union scale of wages; in return, the company would be allowed to affix the union's blue label to its products. In the course of their campaign, Detroit's unionized cigar makers approached liquor dealers and other retailers, local parks, and various local unions to ask that only blue-label cigars be smoked or sold. The twist in this case came with the "angel" shops. The AFL's John McBride gave the following description:

> When a cigar manufacturer runs a "Union shop" and employs union men and women he is allowed the use of the Cigar Makers' International Union blue-label, which guarantees to the public that the cigars having this label upon the box have been made by well paid, clean and skilled labor, but when a manufacturer having the use of the Union Label runs an Annex or Angel shop, on the quiet, and takes the cigars made therein, by underpaid women and children, and mixes them with the cigars made by union labor in his regular shop, he not only takes advantage of the helpless women and children, but aims to reduce wages and impare [sic] the standard of workmanship of union labor, and through false pretenses defrauds the smokers of Union labeled cigars by leading them to believe that they are patronizing the product of clean, well-paid cigarmakers.[94]

In fact, the "girls" of the strike once again proved to be much more active than the epithet "helpless women" would suggest. In the first phase of the strike, women canvassed confectionery and drug stores touting the blue label. Though no women appear to have held official positions on the strike's advisory board, women took on most of the planning for various benefits throughout the summer, leading Samuel Gompers, when he visited Detroit, to "pa[y] a high compliment to the ladies who are engaged in the present difficulty."[95] A demonstration and mass meeting featured a parade that began with four carriages for the women strikers, followed by their fellow strikers and other Detroit trade unionists. The evening's theme was "Against Child Labor," and slogans carried in the parade included not only "Blue Label, forever," but also "Shall the father support the child, or the child support the father?" The machinists' union carried their own sign: "We make machines, but don't smoke machine-made cigars."[96]

93. Ibid.
94. John McBride to N. Jackson, C.I.U. Advisory Board, Detroit, September 4, 1895, SG Letterbooks, 11/12:386.
95. *DFP*, June 30, 1895, p. 11.
96. *DFP*, July 7, 1895, p. 8.

In mid-July, some two hundred additional strikers, including women, marched to the struck factories en masse and removed their tools. When several factory managers subsequently invited strikers to return to work, none did. Toward the end of August, the Brown Brothers' Company recruited more than fifty "Spaniards, Cubans and Mexicans" to work in their plant. Met at the train station by a committee from the union, several of the Cubans were reported to have said that "they had been deceived and that they would not work together with girls." J. H. Brown denied that these men would replace any of the women at the plant, claiming that he had brought them to Detroit only in order to add production of the high-end "clear havana cigar" to his plant's production. "Many of the strikers regard the arrival of these Cubans as the death-blow to their strike, fearing that the girls at Brown Bros. will have to make way for them and thus make matters worse for the strikers."[97]

As the strike wore on into September, tempers became increasingly ragged. Manufacturers began to use more strikebreakers, which led to increased clashes outside the factories. Despite the increased violence, few of the initial strikers abandoned the strike, though many found employment elsewhere. On September 21, the Cabinet Cigar Company agreed to the strikers' demands, announcing that they would run a union shop from September 25 on. Cigar makers continued their battle, gathering information on child labor in the factories and passing it on to the state's factory inspectors. A year after they began their strike, Detroit cigar makers voted 242–87 to "continue the bitter struggle to the end."

> [In the] presence of Mr. G. W. Perkins, President Cigar Makers' International Union, Mr. Sam Gompers, President American Federation of Labor, Mr. L. E. Tossy, President Michigan Federation of Labor, and Mr. John C. Dernell, our agent, the cigar makers discussed the advisability of calling our strike off. This was defeated by a vote of 242 to 87, which shows conclusively that our members are determined to continued this fight until at least our union will be recognized.[98]

Like the Columbus tailors, Detroit cigar makers were willing to fight to the bitter end for their union and for their female co-workers. The Detroit men would have recognized the sentiment expressed in a poem written in honor of the Columbus strikers:

> O, brave and noble men! to seek
>   For honest rights that were not thine;
> For thy strong hands to aid the weak   `
>   Is surely glorious and divine.

97. *DFP*, August 28, 1895, p. 5.
98. *CMOJ* 21 (June 1896): 7.

. . . .

Thank God, that you did rise
    To take the toiling women's part;
I know that in their loving eyes
    The grateful tears will kindly start.

Fear not to due [sic] thy duties well
    While earthly days and years go by;
For angels will thy story tell,
    And noble deeds shall never die.[99]

For many other union men, however, the promise of reward in heaven would not be enough to carry them toward support for female co-workers. The Kearney mule spinners, for example, would have laughed at such sentiment, scoffing at the idea that any type of rewards came to anyone other than those who helped themselves. Such, they would have said, was the very essence of membership in the American Federation of Labor.

The craft unions of the AFL were based on a decidedly masculinist definition of "skill." The craft union notion of some workers' proprietorship of the socially constructed category of "skill" ensured continuing debate over the nature and content of that skill. In her study of nineteenth-century American fraternalism, Mary Ann Clawson argues that "fraternalism publicly affirmed the values of a patriarchal society in which social adulthood, proprietorship, and masculinity were inextricably linked."[100] Late nineteenth-century AFL unions shared this fraternal linkage and fraternalism's qualities of exclusion. Though union members would have argued that the individuals they excluded were merely unskilled, and not any particular group (such as women, blacks, or immigrants), unions' social construction of skill as an inherently gendered quality ensured the de facto exclusion of women from the nation's major craft unions.

Craft unions based on workers' possession of the bundle of physical abilities known as skills had a number of implications for union strength and power. Whether they were custom tailors faced by the new "sweated" trades producing ready-made clothing, cigar makers undermined by simple machines and tenement-house production, shoe lasters confronting new technology and new immigrants, or mule spinners simply being mechanized out of existence, clinging to gendered definitions of skill ultimately undercut the economic power of all their unions. A nongendered definition of skill still would have left these workers open to the threat of mechanization, but the intrinsic gendering of skill raised the specter of replacement by "mere women" as well. The concurrent racialization of skill turned immigrants and other racial

99. *The Tailor* 2 (July 1890): 5.
100. Mary Ann Clawson, *Constructing Brotherhood: Class, Gender, and Fraternalism* (Princeton: Princeton University Press, 1989), p. 46.

groups into additional threats to these workers and their unions.[101] The problem faced by these unions therefore became much larger than Perlman and Taft's concern with "a solidarity with a quickly diminishing potency as one passed from the craft group."[102] The craft—and its cousin, the skill—became simultaneously the source of the AFL unions' economic power and the source of their greatest weakness. Appeals to male workers' sense of gendered skill could strengthen ties among union brothers, but it also implicitly excluded women workers and their concerns from many AFL unions. Nowhere is this clearer than in the stories of the cross-gender strikes told here.

Working out the balance between male property in skill and the presumed female lack thereof became even more complicated when ethnicity entered the picture. Whether strikebreakers were Armenian or Cuban, whether strikers were Bohemian, or Jewish, or Scottish, the existence or nonexistence of ethnic bonds could play a central role in relations between men and women. The next chapter examines the various ways in which ethnic identifications affected cross-gender strikes.

101. See, for example, David R. Roediger, *The Wages of Whiteness: Race and the Making of the American Working Class* (London: Verso, 1991).
102. Perlman and Taft, *History of Labor in the United States*, p. 9.

4   Ethnicity, Race, and Strikes

Regardless of language or race
—*American Wool and Cotton Reporter*, April 30, 1903

On the day the 1902 strike at the Oregon City Woolen Mills ended, a political pundit wrote to one of the town's newspapers reminding voters in the upcoming state election of the time "when the Chinamen left the Oregon City woolen mills." Caught up in the excitement of the 1902 election, the man seemed oblivious to the fact that few of the mills' workers were likely to recall events of some twenty-five years earlier. Out of 163 workers, half were less than twenty-five years old in 1900. Fully two-thirds of the female workers fell under that age.[1] This writer's ability to refer to the Chinese exodus as though it had just happened attests to the enduring vision of the Chinese phantasm in the U.S. labor movement at the turn of the last century.[2]

The Oregon City invocation of the "Chinese menace" is not surprising. The last chapter mentioned how without any special comment the cigar makers' union in 1891 inserted "Chinese coolie" labor into their constitutional clause limiting membership. San Francisco cigar makers in particular consistently worried about competition, and not from women but from Chinese workers.[3] Cigar makers in San Francisco touted their own "white label" not the national union's "Blue Label." During an 1889 strike over a manufacturer's use of a "bogus label" in that city, rumors even appeared that Chinese-made cigars were being shipped to Key West and then back to the West Coast, where they were sold as "genuine Key West cigars."[4] These

---

1. *Oregon City Courier-Herald*, May 23, 1902, p. 8. See Alfred L. Lomax, *Pioneer Woolen Mills in Oregon: History of Wool and the Woolen Textile Industry in Oregon, 1811–1875* (Portland, Ore.: Binfords & Mart, 1941), pp. 237–45, for a brief discussion of Chinese labor in the Oregon City mills. Information on the ages of workers comes from the 1900 Federal Manuscript Census for Clackamas County for Oregon City, Oregon; see appendix 2. This strike is discussed further in chapter 6.

2. See Alexander Saxton, *The Indispensable Enemy: Labor and the Anti-Chinese Movement in California* (Berkeley and Los Angeles: University of California Press, 1971); Gwendolyn Mink, *Old Labor and New Immigrants in American Political Development: Union, Party, and State, 1875–1920* (Ithaca: Cornell University Press, 1986); and Andrew Gyory, *Closing the Gate: Race, Politics, and the Chinese Exclusion Act* (Chapel Hill: University of North Carolina Press, 1998).

3. See Saxton, *Indispensable Enemy*, and Ping Chiu, *Chinese Labor in California: An Economic Study* (Madison: State Historical Society of Wisconsin, 1963), pp. 119–26.

4. *San Francisco Examiner*, April 3, 1889, p. 2; March 27, 1889, p. 8.

tidbits of information on reactions to Chinese workers bring issues of race and ethnicity to the fore in cross-gender strikes.

Ethnicity or race might divide workers on strike, but they could also bring workers together. Through the twists and the turns of each strike's events, workers often chose at one moment to act as members of a particular gender and at others as members of a particular ethnic group. This chapter examines the strength of race and ethnicity in either bringing workers together despite gender divisions or creating even wider chasms along gender lines.

A note is needed here on the use of the terms "ethnicity" and "race." I use "ethnicity" when I am talking primarily about cultural ties among workers. This means that "ethnicity" will refer at times to African American workers' sense of group identity built on such cultural ties. I do not deny the power of that construct labeled "race" in the formation of these "ethnic" cultural ties. In fact, it is quite telling that the term "race" as used at the turn of the twentieth century had a much broader meaning than it does today, applying to Jews and Italians as well as to Cubans, Chinese, and those of African descent. In what follows, however, I save the term "race" for situations in which "ethnicity" is not strong enough. In the post–Civil War South in particular, the distinction between the black and white races easily could overcome all other possible identities. When I discuss below, for example, strikes that began over the employment of black workers, I use the term "race" to denote this particular (one might even say, "peculiar") form of ethnicity laden with the weight of slavery's legacy.

The strike of Jewish garment workers in 1892 Baltimore, already discussed in chapters 1 and 2, demonstrates the ways in which cross-class ethnic ties could be torn asunder by cross-gender class consciousness, which was then further reinforced by the actions of an ethnic "other."[5] The strikers in this case, mostly recent Jewish immigrants from Poland, labored in the sweatshops of Jewish coat tailors, most of whom were also from the Polish areas of the Pale. What historian Susan Glenn has called "the familial tone of the workroom life in these ghetto shops"[6] complicated this strike from its start. Sharing religious, ethnic, and geographic ties with their immigrant employers inhibited workers from taking the firm action required at the very beginning of the strike in order to make their demands stick. As the employers assured workers that they would discuss the demands at the end of the week, workers' identifications as union members battled with the ethnicity they shared with their employers.

The arrival in town of Charles Reichers, from the United Garment Workers of America (UGW), began to change this paralysis. Since Reichers did not share workers' ethnic identification with the coat contractors, he could move

5. Unless otherwise noted, the stories of this strike and the next are taken from the *Baltimore Sun* [hereafter cited as *Sun*].

6. Susan A. Glenn, *Daughters of the Shtetl: Life and Labor in the Immigrant Generation* (Ithaca: Cornell University Press, 1990), p. 134.

more easily to put the strike on a formal footing. Acting on the advice of Reichers, members of the two union locals involved preempted their employers' offers of negotiations and voted to strike. At the end of the strike's first month, the coat contractors attempted to divide the strikers along gender lines, suggesting that women employees not be required to belong to the union. Male union representatives rejected this suggestion, arguing that "the girls had stood by them during the strike and the male members of the union would look after them."[7] Ethnic ties among men and women helped reinforce their sense of class identity as employers' appeals to gender identification failed; neither the men nor the women allowed themselves to be used against the other.

The organizational issues of the strike also underscored how common ethnic bonds among the men and women on strike contributed to ensuring their continued solidarity. Just two weeks into the strike, the Knights of Labor District Master Workman was claiming that all the clothing cutters in Baltimore belonged to the Knights Clothing Cutters' and Trimmers' Assembly No. 7507, and using that information to urge the wholesalers to pressure contractors *not* to sign the UGW agreement. Several divisions other than the organizational one between garment workers (in the UGW) and clothing cutters (in the Knights of Labor) contributed to the salience of this continuing distinction. Not only did clothing cutters work in the shops of the contracting wholesalers, rather than in the sweatshops of the coat tailors, but the cutters organized by the Knights also were mostly Lithuanians, so they had no ethnic bonds with the Polish Jewish garment workers. These distinctions underlay the division of workers in the Baltimore industry into opposing union organizations.

Over the ensuing months, the conflicts brought to light by the initial actions of the strikers in Baltimore were played out on the organizational level, telling us much more about the dying Knights of Labor and the growing American Federation of Labor than about the identifications of the workers themselves. Before becoming bogged down in these organizational battles, though, the Baltimore strike demonstrated one way in which bonds and divisions of gender, ethnicity, and class might be played out in a volatile strike situation. While Baltimore garment workers refused to let their bosses divide them along gender lines, the organizations of the workers divided them along ethnic lines. The mixed responses of the boss "sweaters" to the strike demands may well have resulted also from the conflicting ethnic and economic pulls on the employers. While the ethnicity they held in common with the strikers encouraged some to sign the garment workers' agreement, economic necessity motivated others to do whatever was necessary to stay in the good favor of the wholesalers who kept them in business but with whom they had few direct ethnic ties.

7. *Sun*, July 28, 1892, p. 8.

These potential class and ethnic divisions played out again in another strike of Baltimore garment workers just four years later.[8] In 1896 some four to five thousand workers struck, this time against the wholesalers rather than against their subcontractors. The garment workers took advantage of ethnic, gender, and occupational identifications in this strike. Ten separate local unions represented the strikers, dividing them along both ethnic and gender lines. Locals 26 (men) and 33 (women) of Polish Jews from the 1892 strike participated, as did "Lithuanian tailors" Locals 96 (men) and 90 (women), German tailors' Local 44 (men), vest makers' Local 34 (men), pants makers' Local 38 (men), buttonhole workers' Local 97 (probably women), Bohemians' Local 69 of home workers, and Local 6, of male clothing cutters and trimmers.[9] The UGW even asked its former opponent, the Monumental Coat Contractors' Association, to join the strike. After due deliberation, the association announced that it would not formally join the strike but instead would "remain impartial."[10] Even if the coat contractors did not join the strike, others among the small subcontractors did, once again attesting to the ethnic bonds among these "boss sweaters" and their putative employees.

The strikers, demanding pay increases and union shops, remained on strike for almost a month, finally giving up the struggle a few days after the beginning of Passover. Strikers explained that they had not given up the long-term struggle but that the strike had "been handicapped by the unfavorable state of trade and the almost similar struggles on the part of our brothers in Chicago and Cincinnati, which have cut off the necessary financial support."[11] Promising to return to the fight in the future, strikers pledged loyalty to the union cause. The Clothiers' Board of Trade argued that the strike had been yet another fight between the AFL and the Knights, though newspaper coverage shows little evidence of 1892-style organizational conflicts.

Throughout the 1890s, New York City garment workers undertook a number of strikes that show considerable similarity to the strikes of the Baltimore workers. The series of strikes by cloak makers in the winter of 1890 provides just one example.[12] The strikes began on Wednesday, January 29 against the A. Friedlander & Company garment factory, whose workers included 150 "inside" employees working directly for Friedlander and some 650 subcontractors and their operatives. The issue for all was a reduction in piece-rate wages by as much as 50 percent. Once again, we see Glenn's "familial tone" of work in the fact that both workers and their immediate

8. Unless otherwise noted, the story of this strike is also taken from the *Baltimore Sun*. See also chapter 7.

9. The accounting of unions is taken from *Sun*, February 27, 1896, p. 8, and Maryland Bureau of Industrial Statistics, *Fifth Annual Report for 1896* (Baltimore: King Brothers, 1897), p. 150.

10. *Sun*, March 3, 1896, p. 6.

11. *Sun*, March 31, 1896, p. 10.

12. Unless otherwise noted, the story of this strike comes from coverage in the *New York Tribune* and the *New York World*. The more detailed story of this strike appears in chapter 7.

employers, the subcontractors, went on strike against their mutual employer. The ethnic dimensions are also clear, as papers alternately call the union involved the "United Cloak Makers' Union" and the "Jewish Cloak Makers' Union." Within days, Friedlander allegedly agreed to rescind the wage reduction and grant workers increases on some garments as well. With this example of union success before them, New York City's cloak makers began a string of strikes that ultimately involved some 2,500 men and women and in many ways began what would eventually become the International Ladies' Garment Workers' Union.

Though not yet displaying the finely honed organizational distinctions seen in the later strikes of the Baltimore workers, New York's 1890 cloak makers did display a similar fire. As in the Baltimore strikes, strikers were mostly Jews from eastern Europe, and the wholesale firms against which they struck tended to be owned by earlier immigrant German and German American Jews.[13] Also as in the 1892 Baltimore strike, New York's workers ultimately took on the entire production system of "sweating" in their strikes. Ultimately, more than 2,500 workers took part in the strikes that winter. Throughout, both male and female workers remained solidly loyal to the union cause. The contractors, however, soon abandoned that cause completely, so that by late February and early March wholesalers began to wipe their hands of responsibility, claiming that the furor was simply over how subcontractors were treating workers. One wholesaler pointed out that "it was only since the strike that he realized that the 'boss sweaters' had been systematically robbing their operators for years of $2 or $3 a week."[14] Once again, class divided operatives from contractors despite their shared ethnicity. Neither group enjoyed a shared ethnicity with the wholesalers.

The strikes of southern African American tobacco workers provide even more blatant examples of ethnicity shared by strikers but not with employers. In both an 1890 strike of chewing tobacco workers in Petersburg, Virginia, and a one-day-long strike of tobacco workers in Winston, North Carolina, in 1898, male and female co-workers provided a solid phalanx against their employers. Both strikes ended in success for the strikers. In the longer of the two strikes, the strike in Petersburg, lump makers, or "lumpers," and their "helpers" at the plug tobacco factory of Wm. Cameron & Brother in Petersburg, Virginia, struck for a 25 percent wage increase on Monday morning, May 5, 1890. "Mr. Cameron told the strikers that he was paying as much as any other factory for like work, and that he was not willing to pay any more."[15] By the end of the week, the work stoppage by the lump makers had halted work in the factory's press room as well. Though

13. New York Bureau of Statistics of Labor, *Eighth Annual Report for the Year 1890*, part 2: *Strikes and Boycotts* (Albany: James B. Lyon, 1891), p. 1033.

14. *New York Tribune*, March 2, 1890, p. 8.

15. *Daily Index Appeal*, May 6, 1890, p. 4. Unless otherwise cited, the story of this strike comes from coverage in the *Daily Index Appeal*.

Officers of the Tobacco Trade Union, Petersburg, Virginia [1899?] (courtesy of Library of Congress).

Cameron remained confident that work would resume in a matter of days, the strike continued for a month before ending with a 12.5 percent increase for the workers.[16]

The division of labor in plants like Cameron's reinforced acknowledgment of racial ethnicity while diminishing that of gender. Virtually all plug and chewing tobacco workers in southern plants at the time were African American; their supervisors were white.[17] The most skilled and experienced of the male lumpers "rarely found it necessary to test their work on the scales provided for that purpose."[18] Their "helpers" in both their work and their strike were probably the female "wrapper stemmers," who prepared the wrapping leaf for the plugs of chewing tobacco. The Cameron factory, one of the largest in Petersburg at the time, had probably begun to use some of the new lump machines to make the plugs of tobacco, though wrapping the plugs still would have been done by hand.[19] In addition to working together

16. U.S. Bureau of Labor, *Tenth Annual Report: Strikes and Lockouts* (Washington, D.C.: Government Printing Office, 1896) [hereafter cited as U.S. BLS, *10th AR*], pp. 1190–91.

17. See Nannie May Tilley, *The Bright-Tobacco Industry, 1860–1929* (Chapel Hill: University of North Carolina Press, 1948), pp. 491, 515; Stuart Bruce Kaufman, *Challenge and Change: The History of the Tobacco Workers' International Union* (Kensington, Md.: Bakery, Confectionery, and Tobacco Workers' International Union, 1986), p. 39.

18. Tilley, *Bright-Tobacco Industry*, pp. 517, 491.

19. See U.S. Bureau of Labor, *Thirteenth Annual Report: Hand and Machine Labor*, vol. 1 (Washington, D.C.: Government Printing Office, 1898), p. 396.

African American tobacco "lumpers," Richmond, Virginia [1899?] (courtesy of Library of Congress).

so closely, the men and women of the factory probably lived together in the same households and neighborhoods as well, as confirmed in the next strike.

On Saturday evening, January 22, 1898, the three hundred African American employees of Brown & Williamson's tobacco factory in Winston, North Carolina, received their pay for the two previous weeks.[20] Upon opening the envelopes, workers discovered that their pay was less than it had been for their last pay period, so over the following weekend they resolved to hold the first strike in years at the company. On Monday morning, the workers, both male and female, only had to strike for a few hours before their employer agreed to rescind the wage cut. The workers returned to their workbenches, and production resumed. At some point during the weekend, however, the workers also joined the tobacco workers' union, becoming the only union members in Forsyth County.[21]

The total ethnic solidarity of this group of workers played a large role in the rapid settlement of the strike. The manufacturers' strategy of hiring all

20. Unless otherwise noted, the story of this strike comes from the *Southern Tobacconist and Manufacturers' Record*, February 1, 1898 (10:5), n.p.

21. North Carolina Bureau of Labor and Printing, *Twelfth Annual Report* (Raleigh: Josephus Daniels, 1899), p. 200.

African American women "assorting" tobacco, Richmond, Virginia [1899?] (courtesy of Library of Congress).

African American workforces in southern tobacco production backfired here. In 1900 almost 80 percent of Winston-Salem's African American women tobacco workers and more than 70 percent of the men lived with at least one other tobacco worker in their household. Twenty-two percent of African American female tobacco workers lived with husbands also working in tobacco plants, and 18 percent of the men had wives employed in the same industry. Approximately one-third of the women and 30 percent of the men lived with siblings working in the industry; about 20 percent of each gender had parents employed in tobacco production.[22] Even in the rare cases in which African American tobacco workers lived in households in which they were the only tobacco worker, they still lived in African American neighborhoods, probably close by others of their race. In effect, these workers carried the "familial tone of the workshop" discussed in the case of the Baltimore garment workers one step further. While their family members might very well be in the same workshop, their employers and supervisors were overwhelmingly white. Both the community and the work process here were close

22. All figures are from data collected from the 1900 Federal Manuscript Census for Forsyth County, Winston-Salem, North Carolina. See appendix 2.

and familial, but the workplace itself was not. The result was the ideal situation for easy union organizing; workers could "talk union" all night long. In the segregated South of the time, identification as a black worker was recognized almost without saying it.

At other times and in other places, ethnic identification had to be provoked by further events. In the Auburn, Maine, shoe strike introduced in chapter 3, the use of immigrant strikebreakers reinforced strikers' shared ethnicity, though in this case that "ethnicity" was their sense of American identity.[23] Though this strike began in August 1893 as a strike of female stitchers only, it spread slowly to the more skilled male workers in the plant. First the cutters and then ultimately the lasters as well joined the strike against Auburn shoe manufacturers. This strike thus began with the realization of ever-broader gendered and occupational identities, only later incorporating ethnicity into the workers' sense of class.

On August 1, 1893, already feeling the pinch of economic downturn, management at the Pray, Small & Company shoe factory in Auburn, Maine, posted new wages for its employees. For almost two weeks after the posting of new wages on August 1, Pray, Small's female stitchers presumably discussed the proposed changes. It is easy to imagine the groans at the initial announcement of wage cuts, followed by increasingly animated discussion of the burdens the cuts would place on them and their families. On Saturday, August 12, stitchers at Pray, Small walked off their jobs, refusing to work for the lower wages. The union representing the stitchers, Local 12 of the Boot and Shoe Workers' International Union (BSWIU), then convened meetings of both the striking stitchers and the nonstriking male union workers in the factory. For the first week of the strike, male workers continued at their jobs even though only a handful of women remained in the stitching room. Without the labor of the stitchers, however, shoes remained unfinished. As negotiations with the company ground to a halt, the shoe workers' union declared the shop nonunion and announced that all workers would join the stitchers' strike.

Though more workers joined the strike on Monday, August 21, neither the lasters belonging to the Lasters' Protective Union nor the shoe cutters of the Boot and Shoe Cutters' Union (BSCU) responded to strikers' appeals for solidarity. The cutters had already reached agreement with Pray, Small on the new wages, and the lasters were still negotiating with the company. For both these groups of skilled male workers, their skills still precluded joining with their co-workers. That soon changed, however, for the cutters, who on Friday, August 25, despite their prior agreement with management on wages, "packed their traps and left the shop." Company officials rightly "supposed

---

23. Unless otherwise noted, the story of this strike comes from coverage in the *Lewiston Evening Journal* [hereafter cited as *LEJ*], the *Boston Globe* [hereafter cited as *Globe*], and the *Shoe and Leather Reporter* [hereafter cited as *S&LR*].

[that the cutters' walkout] was because of the trouble in the stitching room."[24] Cutters now joined the strike at Pray, Small.

The following Monday, August 28, the Auburn Manufacturers' Association, with which the management of Pray, Small & Company had been conferring throughout the past two weeks, escalated the stakes. The seven shoe companies belonging to the association told their cutters and stitchers that they would not be needed after the following Saturday. By this action, the shoe companies announced their "intention . . . to run free shops in the future," in other words, to not recognize union contracts.[25] This action by the manufacturers crystallized the Auburn shoe workers' awareness of their common situation. In light of the manufacturers' actions, Auburn shoe workers held a mass meeting featuring a two-hour-long speech by Henry J. Skeffington, national secretary of the shoe workers' union. The meeting ended with an "enthusiastic" vote for arbitration of the dispute.[26]

The following Monday was Labor Day, and Auburn shoe workers participated in city and state parades. In both, they acknowledged the industry's division of labor and their own understanding of their identifications as members of gendered occupations: cutters, lasters, and other male shoe workers marched separately, while "lady" shoe workers regardless of occupation rode in carriages. After Labor Day, the seven shoe employers of the Auburn Manufacturers' Association announced that all their workers—except lasters—would now sign individual contracts and that agreements with the workers' unions would no longer be recognized. Manufacturers gave workers until noon on Tuesday, September 19, to sign the individual contracts.

The workers responded by declaring through their unions (BSWIU Local 12 and BSCU Local 164):

> Believing in our right to organize for our mutual benefit, and having taken the solemn obligations of our respective unions, we firmly declare that we will fight this issue to the bitter end, at all times ready to hold to our agreements, submit to arbitration all difficulties arising between our employers and ourselves, and that is what we most desire to do on the question of adjusting prices in the stitching room of the Pray, Small Company.[27]

All the female stitchers and most of the town's male shoe workers were now united in their fight against the employers.

Auburn lasters, in the meantime, had thus far declined to join the job actions, claiming that they had no need to go against their union's contract with employers. Just before Labor Day, union lasters at the Pray, Small company had agreed to the company's proposed wages for the next year. By

---

24. *LEJ*, August 25, 1893, p. 7.
25. *S&LR*, August 31, 1893 (56:9), p. 493.
26. *LEJ*, August 29, 1893, p. 5.
27. *LEJ*, September 16, 1893, p. 16.

the following week, the same lasters also had no reason to work in the shops of Auburn Manufacturers' Association members, because of the reduced workforces. On Saturday, September 22, one shop told its lasters to return to work, but the lasters refused, calling it "an unreasonable demand . . . done simply as a test." Declaring that "for them to last shoes which are turned out by non-union men they would be false to their fellow workmen," the lasters met later that afternoon and voted to stop work and "remove their jacks from the shops" on Monday morning.[28]

At noon on Monday, September 25, some three hundred to four hundred lasters gathered at their union hall in Auburn. After an hour and a half of discussion and debate, they "came out and marched in squads to their respective shops after their kits." Other shoe workers cheered that decision, and an officer of the BSWIU asserted: "We have feared that the lasters were going to let us fight on single handed. Their action has given us both strength and courage."[29] The manufacturers retorted that the lasters had now broken their contract; the lasters responded that they had not broken their contract and "that the manufacturers intended to haul them over the coals from the very beginning." A prominent lasters' union member said, "Their aim was to break our union along with the rest."[30]

The action of the lasters signaled a new phase of the strike. The most-skilled male workers in the shoe shops, the lasters had remained carefully aloof to this point. Their decision to walk out meant that any continuing work in the shops ground to a halt, whatever the employers might say. The manufacturers, for their part, vowed to continue production. The *Shoe and Leather Reporter* now predicted a "long and bitter" conflict and stated, "The manufacturers feel that they must carry their point or there will be no peace for them in the future."[31]

Less than a week after the lasters entered the fray, reports reached strikers that the shoe companies were planning to bring in immigrant labor—either Italian or Armenian—to replace the now-striking lasters. When a dozen Armenian lasters arrived in town and began working in the factories on Saturday, September 30, all hell broke loose. Ethnicity now became salient in the strike. Nonimmigrant strikebreakers brought into town that day were met by union members who took them out to dinner and then to the local union hall. The Armenians, arriving at the same time, were greeted by crowds of stone-throwing strikers and their supporters, and the strikers accused them of responding with firearms and knives. Over the following week, physical conflict between the Armenian strikebreakers (said to number two dozen by week's end) and crowds including "hundreds of women and children" con-

28. *LEJ*, September 23, 1893, p. 7; *Globe*, September 24, 1893, p. 7.
29. *LEJ*, September 25, 1893, p. 7.
30. *LEJ*, September 26, 1893, p. 7.
31. *S&LR*, September 28, 1893 (56:13), p. 745.

tinued whenever the Armenians ventured outside their hotels or boarding-houses. For a brief time, ethnic identifications superseded all others, both among the self-styled "Yankee" strikers (many of whom were themselves immigrants from both French and British Canada) and among the Armenians, who were reminded of their ethnicity and status, that of "Armenians" and that of "scabs," every time they poked their noses out of the door and met the shouts, bricks, and bats of the strikers. At this point, gender virtually disappeared from the strike scene; both male and female strikers battled Armenian strikebreakers in Auburn's streets.

In addition to their direct action against the Armenian strikebreakers, the Auburn strikers and their unions appealed to their Congressional representatives for relief from immigrant competition. Union leader Skeffington accused Auburn manufacturers of trying "to fill the places of their Yankee employees with the imported offscouring of Europe." Within a week, Armenian communities in Massachusetts had become concerned enough about the situation to send representatives to Auburn to attempt to quiet the situation. The goal of the Armenian "Hentchakist" (or "Hentsharkist") party of Lynn in doing this was clearly stated as being "to assist the union with their utmost efforts."[32] A Boston paper quoted one of the representatives as saying that the approximately seven thousand Armenians in the United States "believe in unions, and think their countrymen should keep away from places where strikes are on."[33]

The arrival of the Armenian Hentchakists seems to have quieted the anti-Armenian hysteria in Auburn. By Sunday, October 8, rumor had it that "the Armenian shoemakers were leaving the shops and going back where they came from" (presumably in the United States, not Armenia).[34] By this time too, strikers in Auburn had new worries. On October 5 the first of several injunctions was granted by the state supreme court against leaders and activists of the shoe workers' unions. Though the strikers remained suspicious of the national origins of later strikebreakers, in general the legal battles now took precedence.

Once the injunctions moved the Auburn struggle from the streets into the courtroom, two things happened. First, the national unions and their leaders took over the legal battles. As control of events slipped out of the hands of local workers, enthusiasm for the strike waned. Second, manufacturing began to resume, albeit slowly, in the city's shoe factories. By February 1894, though the strike was still officially in place, some five hundred of the original two

32. *LEJ*, October 5, 1893, p. 5. Spelling aside, this may be a reference to the Social-Democratic Hnchagian Party, founded in 1887. See Robert Mirak, *Torn between Two Lands: Armenians in America, 1890 to World War I* (Cambridge: Harvard University Press, 1983), pp. 207–9, 88–89.

33. *Globe*, October 7, 1893 (a.m.), p. 7.

34. *Globe*, October 8, 1893, p. 1.

to three thousand strikers had returned to work.[35] By this point, many more workers had been replaced, and most of the original strikers had joined the swelling ranks of the unemployed at the beginning of the 1890s depression. The strike that women stitchers had begun so enthusiastically in August dwindled away, remaining a reality only in the boycott lists of the AFL and in the continued unemployment of many of the strikers.[36]

The narrative of the Auburn strike suggests yet another role ethnicity might play in a strike situation. The Pray, Small workers began their strike with adherence to their gendered occupational lines. Only when Auburn's manufacturers escalated the stakes did all shoe workers unite. The shoe companies then compounded the strikers' unity by introducing strikebreakers of a markedly different ethnicity. Strikers' identification of the strikebreakers as ethnic "others" provoked the rowdiest incidents of the strike. It also congealed a new identity for strikers, both male and female, as "Yankee employees."

The story of the New Jersey thread strike, told in chapter 3, highlights the ways in which ethnicity and gender could at times overlie and reinforce each other.[37] Within the sexual division of labor at the thread mills, workers in the Clark mills found themselves divided along ethnic lines as well. While the male workers in the mills were mainly Protestants from North Country England and Scotland, the young female workers were overwhelmingly Irish and first-generation Irish American Catholics.[38] Furthermore, the history of the male mule spinners' union, the National Cotton Mule Spinners' Association, was also firmly tied to the migration of Lancashire immigrants to New England.[39] Both occupationally and organizationally, ethnicity and gender operated in tandem in the New Jersey mills. This dual functioning of gender and ethnicity played a key role in the strike, almost overdetermining the divisions between the proud mule spinners and their female co-workers.

35. Samuel Gompers to AFL Executive Council, February 5, 1894, in *The Samuel Gompers Papers*, vol. 3: *Unrest and Depression, 1891–94*, ed. Stuart B. Kaufman and Peter J. Albert (Urbana: University of Illinois Press, 1989), p. 460. The *LEJ* reported Auburn shoe factories to be operating at two-thirds of their capacity as of early January 1894. U.S. BLS, *10th AR*, pp. 340–41, reported 1,106 new workers in the factories as of January 1, 1894.

36. Pray, Small & Company was still on the "We Don't Patronize" list in the *American Federationist ?*, no. 6 (August 1895): 111.

37. Unless otherwise noted, this strike story is taken from the *New York Times* [hereafter cited as *NYTimes*] and the *Newark Daily Advertiser*.

38. U.S. Department of the Interior, Census Office, *Report on Population of the United States at the Eleventh Census: 1890*, part 2 (Washington, D.C.: Government Printing Office, 1897), pp. 698–99; U.S. Bureau of Labor, *Fourth Annual Report: Working Women in Large Cities* (Washington, D.C.: Government Printing Office, 1889), pp. 236, 274–75. The statistics in these sources also indicate a large number of German male workers among the "cotton, woolen, and other textile mill operatives," but the Clark company was known for hiring "Scotch or North Country Englishmen." See *New York Daily Graphic*, January 25, 1888, p. 617.

39. See Mary H. Blewett, "Deference and Defiance: Labor Politics and the Meaning of Masculinity in the Mid-Nineteenth-Century New England Textile Industry," *Gender and History* 5 (Autumn 1993): 398–415; and Mary H. Blewett, *Constant Turmoil: The Politics of Industrial Life in Nineteenth-Century New England* (Amherst: University of Massachusetts Press, 2000), pp. 264–65.

By the end of December 1890 the Clarks began to import yarn from their Scottish mills, justifying this by citing public attention to the women workers who had been thrown out of work by the mule spinners' strike. These young women were telling newspaper reporters that they could not afford to live on the "scanty assistance" received from the relief funds. They would be forced to return to work, even if, as rumored, they would be working with imported strikebreakers.[40]

Through the first week of January, the Clark company did in fact begin to recruit strikebreakers aggressively. News reports said that the Clarks especially sought Canadian spinners from other textile centers. The company also began to stock the mills with food and sleeping supplies. Striking spinners scoffed at the idea of the mill hiring Canadian spinners, pointing out that "on a former occasion Superintendent Walmsley had said he would never again employ a down-east spinner, as there had always been trouble with those who came from Canada. He said that the Canadian spinners are not competent men and are little, if any, better than the piecers who are employed in the Clark mills."[41]

Despite strikers' disdain and picketers' efforts to prevent the introduction of strikebreakers, production in some mill departments resumed in January. The Clarks announced that once the initial spinning was under way, other workers would be reemployed and more departments would reopen. The introduction of strikebreakers escalated the strike, as mill management had apparently known that it would. The weekend before the mills reopened, management had requested further police protection for its property, though the mule spinners scoffed at the company's fears, stating: "They neither contemplate violence nor will countenance it if it be attempted."[42] Nevertheless, intermittent violence marked the strike throughout the rest of January and February. Striking spinners continued to deny any participation in violent outbreaks, largely by claiming their heritage as responsible employees and union men.

In this strike, gender and ethnicity were so closely identified with each other that it is virtually impossible to untangle the identifications out of which workers acted. It was apparently also impossible for the workers themselves to untangle these, for attempts to join together in any sort of class-based action failed repeatedly. With the mule spinners' union so deeply embedded in both male pride and traditions of immigration from Scotland and North England, the spinners repeatedly dismissed the concerns of the mostly Irish and Catholic female workers laid off by the cessation of production in the mills. The displayed identifications of women workers as women workers, as laid-off workers, as nonunion members, or as Irish Catholics

40. *Newark Daily Advertiser*, January 5, 1891, p. 1.
41. Ibid.
42. *NYTimes*, January 12, 1891, p. 2.

would congeal at points, only to be ripped apart by the crush of financial need or by the stronger organization of the mule spinners.

Ethnic discord might be expected in the next two strikes as well, because many ethnic as well as gender and organizational differences divided the workforce. However, both in the 1902 Wilkes-Barre, Pennsylvania, lace workers' strike and in the 1903 strike in Lowell, Massachusetts, little discord between ethnic groups appeared. How could the ethnically diverse workers in these strikes maintain their solidarity? The answers here can be found in the particularities of each strike.

The several hundred employees of the Wilkes-Barre Lace Manufacturing Company in 1902 belonged to five separate craft unions and encompassed (in descending order of representation) workers of Irish, German, English, native-born American, Welsh, Scottish, Polish, Austrian, French, Swedish, Swiss, Danish, British Canadian, French Canadian, and Hungarian descent.[43] (See appendix 2, table A2.2.) Here too a sexual division of labor ensured that occupational distinctions separated most men and women at the workplace. Though this strike ultimately ended in failure (workers returned to work on management's terms), it illustrates the type of situation in which incipient ethnic rivalries could be overcome by shared family ties within the context of larger events.

The famous anthracite coal strike of 1902 was just over a month old when it propelled men and women employed by the Wilkes-Barre Lace Company into a strike of their own.[44] In the midst of the fiercely fought coal strike, the lace strike began when members of the lace workers' unions approached five young workers who had relatives still at work in local coal mines. Union representatives then told these co-workers either to quit their jobs or have their relatives leave the mines. When two women refused—or were unable—to do either, the lace unions approached mill management and asked that they be fired. On Tuesday, June 17, mill manager J. W. Doran announced that he would not fire the girls. In response, the lace workers' union voted to strike. At a joint meeting of the cotton workers' Local 8957, the lace finishers' Local 8948, the lace menders Local 8151, the brass bobbin workers' Local 8628, and the lace weavers' Branch 2, workers voted to remain on strike until the issue was resolved.

The family ties of the lace workers appear to have both initiated their strike and overcome their ethnic differences. Almost one-third (32 percent)

43. Unless otherwise noted, the story of this strike is taken from the *American Wool and Cotton Reporter*, vol. 16, and the *Wilkes-Barre Times* [hereafter cited as *WBT*]. Information on the ethnicity and households of workers comes from the 1900 Federal Manuscript Census for Luzerne County for Wilkes-Barre, Pennsylvania. The list of ethnicities includes both immigrants from the country indicated and those who could be identified as having parents or grandparents from the given country. See appendix 2. (This strike is also discussed in chapter 6.)

44. Ronald L. Fillipelli, ed., *Labor Conflict in the United States: An Encyclopedia* (New York: Garland, 1990), pp. 17–19.

of the lace workers lived with at least one coal-mine worker in their household. Women were more likely than men to live with a coal miner; 41 percent of the women and only 18 percent of the men did. (See appendix 2, table A2.8.) Younger lace workers resided with coal miners more often than older lace workers did. It is not surprising that most of the miners were the fathers or brothers of these lace workers, which helps explain why the lace workers would have found it difficult to convince the miners in their families to change their strategies regarding the coal strike.[45] Ethnic differences in the presence or absence of miners in the households of lace workers appear to have been insignificant. The lace workers' comprehension of coal miners' solidarity and the symbolic reach of that solidarity into their own work lives therefore grew out of very personal familial ties.

Lace mill management must have found it difficult to understand why their workers felt so strongly about an issue that seemed to have nothing to do with their own work. At the same time, the workers' demand that the "girls" be fired went against all concepts of management's right to make hiring and firing decisions. Two unmovable parties to the situation resulted: lace workers would not relinquish their support of the coal strike, and management would not give up their control of the workplace. The third party to the situation, the workers' national union, had its own views of the strike. One can only imagine the consternation of the executive board of the National Amalgamated Association of Lace Workers when they heard about the Wilkes-Barre strike. The board, based in Philadelphia, disapproved of the strike, believing both in arbitration and in prior strike approval by the board.

The resulting mixed feelings of the executive board were apparently communicated when Manager Doran met with the board on July 5 in a conference that officially ended without any agreement. Within a week, mill management announced that they would reopen the mills, reserving for themselves the right to "employ or discharge" employees and to make decisions on promotions and mill rules. They further required that workers acknowledge overseers' judgments on the allocation of work and submit any complaints only to the mill management. Striking mill workers met over the weekend, voted not to accept management's conditions, and therefore continued their strike. Without workers, production could not resume. The Wilkes-Barre paper reported: "It is now likely that this fight between the management and the strikers will be one to a finish."[46]

At the beginning of August, Pennsylvania governor William Stone ordered National Guard troops into the anthracite region in response to increasing

45. Of the women who lived with miners, 47 percent lived with a coal-mining brother and 57 percent had coal-mining fathers. See chapter 6.
46. *WBT*, July 15, 1902, p. 8.

coal strike violence.[47] Perhaps because of the pressures of the escalating coal strike, lace mill strikers met with Doran once again and settled their strike. Under pressure from their national union, the strikers agreed to virtually all Doran's conditions, with the addition of the union's preferred arbitration procedure. On Monday, August 11, work resumed in the mill. The Wilkes-Barre paper reported: "Apparently the strikers were pleased that the difficulty is settled and naturally all were in good humor."[48] The historical record is unclear on whether the young people whose fathers' actions had sparked the strike returned to the lace mill or not, though the mother of one claimed that on his return from his first day of work "there was a lump on the side of his face, it was all black and blue, and his both eyes was blackened."[49] "Good humor," it appears, was relative.

This strike provides few of the identification shifts seen in many other strikes. Despite the consternation of their national union, the Wilkes-Barre lace workers remained unwavering in their support of the coal miners' strike. Neither their ethnicity nor their gender rose to supplant this identification. Instead, workers' familial connections to the massive 1902 anthracite coal strike remained paramount throughout the lace strike. In this case, strikers' loyalties arose more from workers' experiences beyond the workplace than from those within the workplace.

In the Lowell textile strike of 1903, first discussed in chapter 1, workers' identities did come precisely from workplace experiences, despite the extreme ethnic diversity of the workforce.[50] Even the industry's journal, the *American Wool and Cotton Reporter*, noted that in years past "the mill managements played one race against another, both industrially and politically," but the journal argued that the injustice of operatives' treatment in the mills led them to understand the usefulness of unions in the mills.[51] In the 1903 strike, Greek, Portuguese, Armenian, and Polish immigrants joined the largely French Canadian and Irish strikers and their unions. The Lowell Textile Council helped in this process by allowing workers to organize in either of two ways: by occupation or by ethnicity. Local unions of loom fixers and ring spinners, then, coexisted with those of Greeks and Portuguese. Again, the industry was explicit in its description of how this could happen:

47. Fillipelli, *Labor Conflict*, p. 18.
48. *WBT*, August 11, 1902, p. 6.
49. Testimony of Lillie Richardson, in U.S. Anthracite Coal Strike Commission, *Proceedings of the Anthracite Coal Strike Commission* (Washington, D.C.: Hanna & Budlong, 1902–3), p. 3536.
50. Unless otherwise noted, the story of this strike comes from coverage in the *Boston Globe*, the *Lowell Courier*, and the *American Wool and Cotton Reporter*. See also chapter 1.
51. *American Wool and Cotton Reporter*, April 30, 1903 (17:18), p. 522.

It matters not whether a man or woman comes from Canada, Poland, Ireland, England or Italy, it does not take him long to learn the value of the American dollar, and although interested persons may caution him to avoid this man or that man and not to give away his independence or hamper his freedom of action by joining a union, he will naturally affiliate with the men and women whose methods result in increasing his material well-being and that affiliation will take place regardless of language or race. This fact is illustrated in the case of the Greek, Polander and Portuguese operatives who are non-English speaking and live in communities of their own. They have, much to the surprise of the mill manager, learned the value of organizing as a means of self-protection.[52]

Workers learned this lesson both in the Lowell mills and in the streets and shops of the town. Though Lowell's immigrants established separate ethnic communities, the town remained small enough for members of these communities to share considerable opportunities for interaction. Very much a nineteenth-century "walking city" even in the early twentieth century, immigrant neighborhoods coexisted cheek-by-jowl in the shadow of the mills. All the mill workers heard the lapping of water in the mill canals inside their tenements at night. Inside the mills, ethnicity at times coincided with occupational segregation, as in the case of the overwhelmingly French Canadian loom fixers. In most of the unskilled jobs, however, members of various ethnic groups found themselves working side by side. Though few of the Greek, Armenian, Polish, or Portuguese operatives belonged to the unions of the Textile Council before the strike began in late March, they certainly recognized their larger, class identities as Lowell textile workers.

They also shared many issues in common with the other groups employed in the city's mills. Although in early March the members of the Textile Council expressed doubts about whether the newer immigrants would join the strike, they soon found that these groups, with overlapping identities as textile workers, union members, and ethnic group members, became the strike's staunchest supporters. In fact, over the course of the strike, the council experienced many more problems with French Canadian workers (much longer residents in Lowell) than with either Greeks or Portuguese.[53] Though French Canadian men formed the core of the loom fixers' union, and French Canadian women became the backbone of the ring spinners' union during the strike, many French Canadian families left Lowell completely for the strike's duration. With the Quebec-Vermont border less than three hundred miles from Lowell, and extended family members and farms waiting there, this policy of removal was a viable one for these textile workers. That

52. Ibid.

53. Though newspaper reports repeat "Greek, Armenian, and Portuguese" as a single phrase, there is little specific information on Armenian workers as a separate group. More such material exists for Greek and Portuguese workers.

Ethnic textile workers in Lowell strike of 1903 (*Boston Globe*, April 2, 1903, p. 1).

their decisions were family decisions is clear from the descriptions of family gatherings to make them, in which workers from several mills would contribute their input. While their exit relieved the Textile Council of responsibility for supporting them during the strike, it also weakened French Canadian ties to the city's union movement. Often during the course of the strike, strikebreakers causing a flare-up of violence turned out to be French Canadian. The relatively easy mobility of Lowell's French Canadian community thus had contradictory impacts of the strike itself. On the one hand, French Canadian strike supporters would not strain union coffers if they returned to the border. On the other hand, the diminution of the ethnic community would leave few strike supporters in town to indoctrinate fellow ethnics into the Massachusetts Labor movement.

Greek immigrants took a different tack. Pledging their loyalty to the union cause, these most-recent immigrants to Lowell also promised to provide their own financial support during the strike. Many observers attributed the

Family of Felix Chenour meets to discuss options during Lowell strike of 1903 (*Boston Globe*, April 6, 1903, p. 1).

Greeks' ability to do this to their goals in immigrating to the United States. As one put it, "The Greeks come over to this country determined to save their money, and they spend money for the necessities of life only."[54] Because the Greeks were a largely single and male community in Lowell, both unionists and city authorities initially looked askance at them. In the weeks leading up to the actual strike, union officials repeatedly expressed their surprise when Greeks showed up at union meetings. Once the strike began, the first "trouble" of the strike was attributed to the actions of Greeks celebrating "the Greek national holiday," though the "trouble" in question appears to be attributable to police actions in attempting to disperse the consistently peaceable crowd.[55]

Both Greeks and French Canadians in Lowell persisted in their courses of action throughout the strike, returning to work only when the strike was called off in June. Though we see slightly different strategies for coping with the strike, these and other immigrant workers in the town joined with Yankee and Irish American unionists in the strike cause. Initially surprised, those unionists soon came to appreciate the solidarity given to them. In the Lowell strike the commonalities of work and life created multiethnic strike solidarity.

In the strikes examined this far, several different roles of ethnicity have appeared. Ethnicity sometimes united strikers, even against employers of the

54. *Lowell Courier*, March 28, 1903, p. 3.
55. See *Globe*, April 8, 1903, p. 1.

Meeting of nonunion Greek operatives in Lowell, 1903 (*Boston Globe*, March 31, 1903, p. 2).

same background, as in Baltimore, and even more so when employers did not share the same ethnicity, as in Petersburg and Winston-Salem. It could also divide strikers, at times along the same lines as gender, as seen in the New Jersey thread strike. In some cases, ethnicity complicated issues of strikebreaking, as in the Maine shoe strike. But at other times, ethnic differences became negligible as strike circumstances blurred these differences as in Wilkes-Barre and Lowell.

Only in one situation did "ethnicity" itself cause cross-gender strikes: that in which race trumped ethnicity. Examples of this come from two strikes, one of shoe workers in Charleston, South Carolina, and one of textile workers in Atlanta, Georgia. In both these cases located in the segregated southeastern states, the strict distinction between black and white drew the lines of racialized ethnicity starkly.

The strike of virtually the entire workforce of the Fulton Bag & Cotton mills of Atlanta, Georgia, at the beginning of August 1897 provides the first example of race as cause for a cross-gender strike.[56] On Tuesday, August 3, the owner of the mill, Jacob Elsas, informed the white women employed in his folding department that they would be joined by black women the next day. The following day, in order to avoid trouble, he had the new workers

---

56. Unless otherwise noted, the story of this strike comes from coverage in the *Atlanta Constitution* [hereafter cited as *Constitution*].

The Greeks and their band in the Lowell strike parade, April 12, 1903 (*Boston Globe*, April 14, 1903, p. 2).

arrive before anyone else, but when the white women arrived at 6:00 a.m. and found black women already at work, they refused to work. It took the mills' other white women until 11:00 a.m. to discover what had happened, at which point they followed the women of the folding department off their jobs. By noon, the action Elsas took had created solidarity among all his white workers, both male and female. A crowd of some fourteen hundred strikers filled the streets around the factory. Rocks began to fly and police arrived, driving the strikers back by early afternoon. By 3:00 p.m., men, women, and children had crowded a meeting hall, where they signed up as members of the textile workers' union.

Faced with this racial solidarity, Elsas backed down within days, saying that he would return to the pre-strike status of white employment in the mills. While he would not remove all black workers, as strikers now requested ("We wanted all the niggers out," strike leader J. R. Owens explained),[57] he did agree to fire the black women in the folding department whose presence had been the cause for the strike. He also said he would transfer one black male machinist in the repair department to another department. Black workers would remain on the janitorial staff of the mills. Also put in place

57. *Constitution*, August 6, 1897, p. 2.

was a grievance system of sorts under which "if any other work done by other colored men or colored women is of a character to be offensive to the white operatives in contiguous work" the cases would be handled and acted on individually.[58] With this pseudo-guarantee of protection for white operatives, the strikers returned to work. While Elsas thus regained production in his mills, thwarting the immediate twin threats of lessened production and possible riot, the new awareness the workers had achieved led them to seek out union representation. The Fulton Bag & Cotton Mills workers subsequently became some of Atlanta's most ardent unionists.[59] In this case, both strikers and their union reinforced the company's original racial division of labor.

The strike of white workers in Charleston, South Carolina, later in the fall of 1897 had a slightly different genesis as well as a different ending.[60] At the beginning of October, the Charleston Shoe Manufacturing Company installed new machinery in its plant. On Saturday, October 9, the management informed workers that, as of Monday, a new piece-rate schedule of payment would go into effect. (Up to this point, all workers had been paid weekly wages.) When workers began to arrive at the factory early Monday morning, the superintendent confirmed the new wages, upon which fifteen young women quit and returned home. The company president was called to the scene, where he expressed his surprise at the complaints. Stating that shoe plants in New England paid all their workers by the piece, he argued that his offered rates were quite fair. He then compounded the situation by informing the male workers that "he would throw open the doors to any good operative who might apply." Asked if this meant that "negroes" would be hired, he replied that it did. Male workers in the plant then held a brief meeting, at which they decided to walk off their jobs as well. One explained to the local paper, "We were making a living, as it was, and that was all, and the company was treating us the best it could on the money, but we are white men and we will not work in the shoe factory or any other factory with negroes." The company president initially responded with pique, declaring that he would now hire only black workers, but he later took that back and announced that "he would open the doors to whites and blacks togeth-

58. *The Tradesman*, August 15, 1897 (37:11), p. 58.

59. Samuel Gompers to Mr. H. S. Hills, New Bedford, Mass., August 7, 1897, AFL Letterpress Copybooks of Samuel Gompers and William Green, 1883–1925, microfilm of originals at Library of Congress [hereafter cited as SG Letterbooks], 20:926; letter from Samuel Gompers to M. J. Williams, Atlanta, Georgia, August 7, 1897, SG Letterbooks, 20:925. The only criticism of the racism of textile workers appeared in the form of a resolution from the (apparently black) Lithonia, Georgia, quarrymen's union, which called the actions of the textile workers "detrimental to the progress of organized labor in the south" (*Constitution*, August 7, 1897, p. 2; August 8, 1897, p. 17). See also Clifford M. Kuhn, *Contesting the New South Order: The 1914–1915 Strike at Atlanta's Fulton Mills* (Chapel Hill: University of North Carolina Press, 2001) pp. 21–32.

60. Unless otherwise noted, the story of this strike comes from coverage in *The News and Courier* [hereafter cited as *TNC*] and the SL&R.

er."[61] He had already contacted several local black ministers in his search for new workers, and several black women stopped by the factory on the first day of the strike and gained employment.

It is interesting that the strike continued to be focused on the new piece rates for the factory's women workers, one of whom said, "It is utterly impossible for a girl to make over forty cents a day. That was why we struck. If these are not starvation prices I don't know what else they are. If the factory can get negroes to work for these wages it is at liberty to do it. We will not."[62] While the women did not take up the issue of racial replacement, both their male co-workers and the company's management laid blame for the entire strike on the racial issue. When a few operatives began to ask for their old jobs back later in October, the company responded that "they would have colored co-laborers."[63] All jobs in the factory were now opened to workers of either race.

Both these strikes echo southern white workers' understanding of race in the workplace. As Dolores Janiewski shows, strict segregation was the rule both between and within southern factories. This was particularly true in factories hiring white women.[64] In such cases, white men considered it part of their distinctively southern manhood to "protect" white women from the sexualized taint of black labor. When the Charleston striker said "We are white men and we will not work . . . with negroes," he spoke of precisely this southern white manhood; he was not a white *person* but an explicitly white *man*. Though the women he "protected" may have believed this strike was about their wages, to him the strike was about a much larger issue, one involving his entire social standing. While we do not know exactly how the Charleston strike ended or whether the factory continued with a biracial workforce, we do know that such a workforce was highly contested throughout the South.[65] Southern industrialists almost always listed the "presence of negroes" as their first reason that the South enjoyed greater labor peace than did the northern states. Industry understood what only a few in the labor movement did at the time: that the refusal of unions to admit black workers to their ranks weakened the entire labor movement. One industry commentator put it this way: "Racial antipathy and social ostracism prevents admission of the negro to white labor organizations. Unsystematic, and not being an organizer himself, the negro is a free lance in the labor field, and stands as what the labor unions designate a 'scab,' an irreconcilable and

61. *TNC*, October 12, 1897, n.p.
62. *TNC*, October 14, 1897, n.p.
63. *S&LR*, October 28, 1897 (64:18), p. 1271.
64. Dolores Janiewski, "Southern Honor, Southern Dishonor: Managerial Ideology and the Construction of Gender, Race, and Class Relations in Southern Industry," in *Work Engendered: Toward a New History of American Labor*, ed., Ava Baron (Ithaca: Cornell University Press, 1991), pp. 70–91.
65. No further information on the shoe factory and its workforce was found in either *The Tradesman* or the *S&LR*.

constant menace to the trade unions."[66] While certainly true to a large extent, as demonstrated in the Charleston and Atlanta strikes, race did not always create this type of menace to the union movement, even in southern industries employing women.

On the eve of the twentieth century, black and white workers of both sexes joined together in Louisville, Kentucky, to demand a wage increase from the Continental Tobacco Company.[67] On Friday, December 28, 1900, some fifteen hundred stemmers at the factory went on strike for twenty-five cents more per one hundred pounds of tobacco processed. This first day, white workers and black workers gathered on opposite sides of the factory. By the next day, however, all joined together in a mass meeting to decide on the strike's exact demands. The local paper reported that at the meeting "the white people jostl[ed] with the negroes."[68] The local AFL organizer reported that the strikers "presented a truly pitiful scene. Wearing thin calico dresses, with threadbare shawls around their shoulders, they stood around in groups shivering in the biting cold."[69] The president of the Tobacco Workers' International Union (TWIU), Henry Fischer, stepped into the strike at this point, encouraging the workers to stick together and to join the union. The stemmers' forewoman, Sallie Carmody, similarly warned the strikers to remain united, lest the managers replace "colored strippers by putting white girl strippers in their places." The tobacco workers' union then encouraged strikers to join one of the two racially segregated local unions in Louisville.[70]

After compiling their list of demands, strikers elected a committee of four, two white and two black, to meet with factory officials along with Fischer and two other representatives of organized labor. This committee named a black man, Lewis Washington, as their spokesperson. When they met with the company, they demanded a 3.25-cent-per-pound wage increase, a half-hour dinner break and permission to leave the factory to eat, elimination of the "docking" or fines system, abolition of the custom of having to pick stems out of the rubbish, and reemployment of all strikers. The following day, the company gave in on all demands except that for a wage increase. The strikers' committee met for several hours to consider the company's offer before agreeing to the terms. On January 4, all workers returned to work except a few "girls" who allegedly "did not understand that all the strikers were coming back."[71]

Though the tobacco workers' union paid considerable attention to black male workers during this strike, it paid much less to women workers of either

---

66. *The Tradesman*, April 15, 1903 (49:4), p. 73.
67. Unless otherwise noted, the story of this strike comes from coverage in the *Louisville Courier-Journal* and the *Louisville Times*.
68. *Louisville Courier-Journal*, January 1, 1901, p. 1.
69. *American Federationist* 8 (February 1901): 59.
70. Ibid.
71. *Louisville Times*, January 4, 1901.

race. That some of the women felt this slight can be seen in women's reactions to the settlement of the strike. Though union members argued that some women did not return to work as scheduled on Friday because of a misunderstanding, one of the only times we hear the women workers' voices in the strike comes in response to questions about returning to work. The local paper quoted one "girl" on the issue: "You boys want the docking board to come down, and you want your dinner hour. We want that extra quarter of a cent a pound."[72] Begun as a strike of women workers, this one quickly moved beyond the women's control. Though both black and white workers belonged to the appropriate union by the end of the strike, women workers like this one felt that their original demands had been lost in the shuffle.

The strikes narrated in this chapter highlight the myriad ways in which ethnicity and race could function in cross-gender strikes. Ethnicity could overdetermine gender divisions, as in the Newark strike, ripping apart strikers' solidarity. At other times, such as in the Baltimore and Petersburg strikes, ethnicity reinforced workers' common bonds across the sexual division of labor. In still other situations, such as that of Lowell, workers discovered similarities beyond ethnicities and overcame both ethnicity and gender. Always, though, the particularities of each strike's narrative determined the exact role played by ethnicity. While unions could use gender as a device to pull together workers across the nation, ethnicity could rarely be used in that manner.

Even when a strike succeeded in partially overcoming both racial-ethnic and gender divisions, such as the strike in Louisville, it often remained in the peripheral vision of the nation's union leaders. The main labor action was still in the Northeast, and to an increasing degree in the industrializing midwestern states. Strikes occurring elsewhere in the nation, in what I call the industrial periphery, can illustrate some of the most interesting contradictions in the strict craft unionism of the American Federation of Labor. That is the topic of the next chapter.

72. Ibid.

5 Strikes in the Industrial Periphery

Using up the sunshine of their lives
—*Galveston Daily News*, March 27, 1895

In February 1891, at the peak of tobacco deliveries to the sorting and packing warehouses of Edgerton, Wisconsin, some five hundred workers in Edgerton and then another three hundred or more in nearby Stoughton went out on strike, demanding that their wages be increased by one-third.[1] Within a week, strikers in both towns returned to work at higher wages. A small town of fewer than two thousand inhabitants in 1890, Edgerton was known as the "geographical center of the [state's] tobacco district."[2] Each year from January through April, farmers brought the previous summer's tobacco crop, dried in their own drying barns, to Edgerton's twenty-five packing houses to be sorted, packed, and sold to the highest bidder. The slightly larger town of Stoughton boasted only fifteen packing houses, but in both towns tobacco packing provided a "fairly remunerative winter occupation" for women and men from the surrounding farms.[3]

The Edgerton newspaper deplored the two strikes, pointing out: "If the tobacco business is worth anything to the packing towns, every citizen ought to discourage strikes and disaffection among the laborers."[4] The newspaper's concern about the strikes mirrors that of the packing-house operators, who must have felt frustrated when their "hands" walked off their jobs at the peak of the season. To the extent that these workers came from farm families, they would know as well—or perhaps even better—than their bosses just when that peak would arrive. The week before the Edgerton strike began, for example, deliveries of tobacco to the Edgerton warehouses were "the largest of the season," and Stoughton reported: "Every local packer is running full blast, and employing all the hands he can get."[5] In addition, the new

1. Unless otherwise noted, the story of these strikes comes from coverage in *Wisconsin Tobacco Reporter* [hereafter cited as *WTR*], and U.S. Bureau of Labor, *Tenth Annual Report: Strikes and Lockouts* (Washington, D.C.: Government Printing Office, 1896), pp. 1238–41.
2. U.S. Department of the Interior, Census Office, *Report on Population of the United States at the Eleventh Census, 1890* (Washington, D.C.: Government Printing Office, 1895), p. 381; Wisconsin Bureau of Labor and Industrial Statistics, *First Biennial Report* (Madison: Democrat Printing Company, 1884) [hereafter cited as Wis. BLIS, *1st BR*], p. 220.
3. Wis. BLIS, *1st BR*, p. 159.
4. *WTR*, February 27, 1891, p. 1.
5. *WTR*, February 13, 1891, p. 1.

McKinley tariffs had already pushed the prices fetched by tobacco leaf higher than in the past.[6] As the editor of the *Wisconsin Tobacco Reporter* pointed out, "Because a larger number of hands are needed at the packing points this season, ought not to be construed as a license to demand unusual wages or embarras [*sic*] the employers."[7] The workers' inside knowledge of the tobacco market allowed them to wield the economic clout of striking at the most propitious moment.

Though few details of these strikes have survived for historians, even this brief story highlights characteristics that the Wisconsin strikes had in common with other strikes occurring in the "industrial periphery" of the time. U.S. labor historians have generally borrowed the terms "core" and "periphery" from geographers to describe the relationships between core industrialized countries such as the United States, Great Britain, and Germany, and periphery countries of eastern and southern Europe or Mexico.[8] However, the concepts of core and periphery are also meaningful in describing workers' experiences solely within the United States. Although by the end of the nineteenth century the United States was the premier industrial power in the world, much of the population still lived in areas distant from the nation's industrial centers. Some industries, however, had already established a toehold in what were still basically nonindustrial areas of the nation. Though most strikes at the turn of the century occurred in the industrial core, workers on the periphery of that core, such as those in the Wisconsin tobacco-packing houses, often took action when difficulties at the workplace combined with other facets of their lives. Often acting without formal union intervention, these workers went on strike, just as union members did elsewhere.

Between 1887 and 1903, 75 percent of all strikes in the United States took place in the nation's industrial core, defined here as the states of Massachusetts, Rhode Island, Connecticut, New York, New Jersey, Pennsylvania, Ohio, Indiana, Illinois, and Missouri. These ten states also contributed just over 75 percent of the nation's value added in 1900. The dominance of these states in the four industries under consideration here is even greater, contributing more than 85 percent of the nation's value added in clothing, 78 percent of that in textiles, 78 percent of that in leather products, including boots and shoes, and almost 62 percent of that in tobacco. The states of New York, Massachusetts, and Pennsylvania alone accounted for almost half (47.5

6. *Tobacco (New York)*, June 1, 1891 (11:129), p. 224.
7. *WTR*, February 27, 1891, p. 1.
8. See David Montgomery, *The Fall of the House of Labor* (Cambridge: Cambridge University Press, 1987), pp. 70–71, for a nineteenth-century example; and Jefferson Cowie, *Capital Moves: RCA's 70-Year Quest for Cheap Labor* (Ithaca: Cornell University Press, 1999), pp. 61–62, 185–99, for a problematized twentieth-century one.

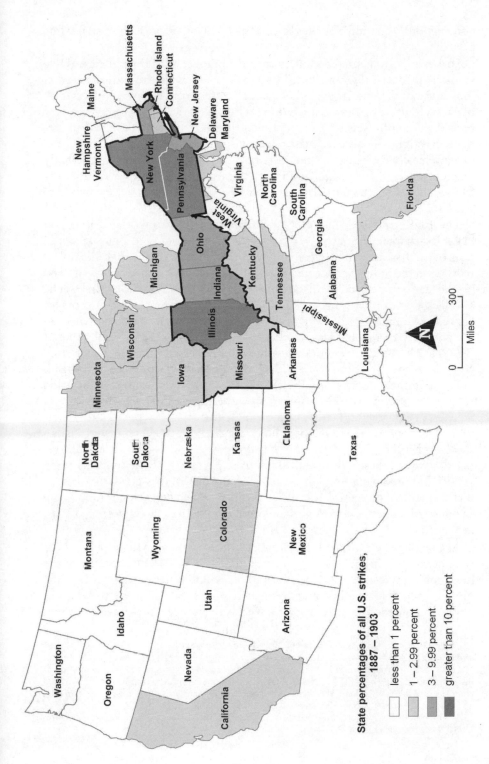

State percentages of all U.S. strikes, 1887 – 1903

- less than 1 percent
- 1 – 2.99 percent
- 3 – 9.99 percent
- greater than 10 percent

N

0   300

Miles

Incidence of strikes in the United States, 1887–1903 (Syracuse University Cartography Laboratory).

percent) of the nation's strikes and 43 percent of its 1900 industry value added.[9]

Strikes in the industrial periphery shared a number of characteristics. While some involved workers affiliated at least loosely with the national union movement of the time, many others, like the Wisconsin tobacco strikes, took place without any union recognition. While local activists often expressed considerable enthusiasm for such periphery strikes, these actions usually remained peripheral to the business of unionism as a whole in the nation. Often geographically distant from union control and almost always emotionally distant from it, these strikes could open up new arenas of behavior not only for women workers but also for African American and other minority workers.

The 1898 strike of Winston, North Carolina, tobacco workers described in the last chapter demonstrates the possible militance and pro-union qualities of groups of strikers who were new to the labor movement. Just like other workers in the industrial periphery, these African American workers showed no inclination to divide themselves along gender or occupational lines. The all-black workforce in this strike instead formed the first union in Forsyth County, one made up of both male and female workers. This activism on the part of African American workers was also seen in the biracial strike of the Louisville, Kentucky, workers, who not only elected a biracial negotiating committee but also then placed a black man, Lewis Washington, at its head.

Without the "benefit" of the AFL's model of craft unionism nearby, workers in the industrial periphery saw themselves first and foremost as workers in a particular factory or industry, rather than having to battle their self-perceptions as doughty mule spinners or skilled garment cutters or "lady" shoe stitchers in order to work in harmony with wider groups of workers. In other words, these strikes tended not to display the types of divisions along gender and/or occupational lines seen in many other cross-gender strikes. In fact, in many of the peripheral strikes women played key roles in mobilizing fellow workers for action. A strike of textile operatives in Galveston, Texas, in the winter of 1895 illustrates this.[10]

The management of the Galveston Cotton & Woolen Mill experimented with new looms in the weave room in January 1895. Perhaps because of the new looms, the weave room began running behind other departments of the mill. To make up for this, management required only weavers to work an hour overtime each day. After several weeks, the weavers presented a petition

---

9. Strike statistics are taken from U.S. Bureau of Labor, *Sixteenth Annual Report: Strikes and Lockouts* (Washington, D.C.: Government Printing Office, 1901), pp. 136–76; U.S. Bureau of Labor, *Twenty-first Annual Report: Strikes and Lockouts* (Washington, D.C.: Government Printing Office, 1907), pp. 15, 120–423. State contributions to national industry value added come from Albert W. Niemi Jr., *State and Regional Patterns in American Manufacturing, 1860–1900* (Westport, Conn.: Greenwood Press, 1974), table 13, pp. 50–54.

10. Unless otherwise noted, the story of this strike comes from coverage in the *Galveston Daily News* [hereafter cited as *GDN*].

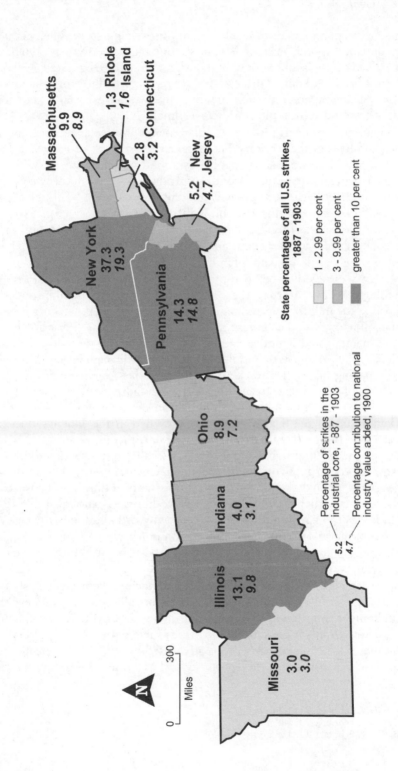

The industrial core of the United States, c. 1900 (Syracuse University Cartography Laboratory).

to management on January 21, asking that the overtime stop. When management did not respond, a group of weavers took matters into their own hands and walked off their jobs at 6:30 p.m. rather than at the requested 7:30 p.m. After this brief but pointed protest, the weavers returned to work the following day. Strike leaders recounted later that "the women especially were being overworked and suffering from [the overtime]."[11]

The question of overtime in the mills remained unresolved, rankling the minds and lives of the workers. Finally, during the week of February 11, a cold snap hit Galveston, accompanied by an unusual snowstorm. While the mill management attempted to continue production through this week, they finally admitted defeat at noon on Thursday, February 14. "Though the engine and heating apparatus was run night and day at a very large extra expense for fuel, it was found impossible to keep the mill comfortably warm. The younger help was very cold and the mill had to be shut down."[12] The day after the shutdown, snow rendered Galveston's streets impassable, so only a few workers showed up at the mill and production could not resume. The following day, Saturday, the mill still could not open. In all, production stopped in the mill for approximately twenty-four normal working hours.

The following Monday, in response to this weather-related shutdown, mill management posted a notice calling for five hours of overtime from all workers, to be worked as one additional hour a day through Friday. However, despite having lost half a week's pay the week before, virtually the entire workforce of the plant, between four and five hundred workers, walked out in protest against this additional imposition of extra work. When these workers returned the next morning, as they had in the January overtime protest, they found the mill doors locked against them.

During the ensuing strike and lockout, a small group of women acted as spokespersons for the workers before management, city officials, and local trade unions. Though they added other complaints over time, they consistently explained that "they simply thought twelve hours . . . enough for a day's work. It was too hard on the women, especially, who had in many cases to do the cooking before and after work, and thus depriving them of sleep, they not being able to get through their housework at night before 10 o'clock, and having to be up again at 4 o'clock."[13] During a particularly testy exchange with members of the Galveston city council on February 22, spokeswoman Mrs. E. W. Ormond, responding to one alderman's comment that the mill might shut down, snapped, "Let them shut down. We lived before the Galveston mills were started and we can live without them." She also noted that one of the key provisions advertised to workers in getting them to come to Galveston was the "promise of eleven hours for a day's work."

11. *GDN*, February 21, 1895, p. 10.
12. *GDN*, February 22, 1895, p. 10.
13. *GDN*, February 21, 1895, p. 10.

She then heaped several more complaints onto that of overtime, claiming, "These people in these mills are really treated no better than slaves. If there isn't a law in the matter there should be." Ormond ended in exasperation: "Why didn't the superintendents meet us face to face before you? That was what we wanted. We wanted to say to them what we are saying to you."[14] Mrs. Ormond and her followers clearly voiced their sense of being over-worked, put-upon employees. If their employer would not take their concerns seriously, they would do so themselves.

The gutsy women of the Galveston mill spoke unusually bluntly about the contradictions between their roles as housewives and wage earners, but they were not the only women to take such active roles in periphery strikes. When the Maginnis Cotton Mills of New Orleans announced a 10 percent wage cut in early July 1894, four "girls" from the factory took on the task of speaking to the mill's owner about its unfairness.[15] These young women also took the first steps of striking and then organizing themselves into what they called the "Cotton Mill Operatives' Union." The women's leader, Annie O'Leary, even opened up her home to fellow strikers as the strike headquarters.

Though the local labor movement of New Orleans, dominated by men, quickly took over negotiations for this strike, the initial actions by the mill's women workers illustrates the possibilities for women's militance that strikes in the industrial periphery opened up. The rapid intrusion of male AFL-affiliated union leadership may also prove that organization's inability to comprehend fully female activism. Despite some rumblings about a possible repetition of the general strike of the city's workers two years earlier, this time on behalf of the Maginnis strikers, within six weeks the Maginnis strike fizzled out. The newspaper's statement—"Some of [the strikers] have gone to work in other places and others expect to. One girl has gotten married since the strike began and will not return to work at all. She is regarded with envy by the rest of the girls"—probably reflects the gendered assumptions of the city's United Labor Council as well as that of the paper.[16] In return for placing their trust in the men of the labor council, Annie O'Leary and her co-workers ultimately received little except faint praise for "their grit."[17]

But the lessons (or lack thereof) for the labor movement of women's potential militance do not encompass all that the historian learns from these strikes. One of the only men in the Galveston strike to speak before the city's aldermen, a Mr. Murdock, referred to the experiences his family had working in six other mills as well: "The hands are human, the same as your wives and daughters. . . . They have no right to require us to work overtime for

---

14. *GDN*, February 23, 1895, p. 8.
15. Unless otherwise noted, the story of this strike comes from coverage in the *New Orleans Picayune* [hereafter cited as *NOP*].
16. *NOP*, July 22, 1894, p. 2.
17. *NOP*, July 20, 1894, p. 3.

time lost in cold weather any more than in case of sickness. The same hand that makes sickness made the cold weather."[18] Murdock, Mrs. Ormond, and New Orleans' Annie O'Leary all spoke and acted out of what can be called a "culture of complaint" seen throughout periphery strikes. In textile strikes, this culture developed out of the labor recruitment policies of the managements of periphery mills. Often located in areas without obvious available labor pools, these mills turned to preexisting textile centers for labor recruitment, where they looked for workers who would be cheap, competent, and compliant. This entailed avoiding the older New England textile centers in Massachusetts and Rhode Island and instead recruiting from those in the New South, itself part of the industrial periphery.

This attempt to transplant a southern family system of labor to other locations ultimately reinforced the workers' growing "culture of complaint," which is described further in the next chapter. In the Galveston strike, for example, strikers added to their complaints that they had been brought to Texas under false pretenses; though promised nine to ten dollars a week, they were making only between four and eight dollars a week. After the mill began running with replacement workers, a group of now-idle workers petitioned the city council for assistance. The Galveston paper described the scene:

> Ranged around the room were forty or fifty women and children, some of the women with babes at their breasts. Outside, with their faces pressed close against the partition which divides the council chamber from the rest of the world, were the men folks. There were several kinds of people among this throng. Some were listless and shiftless in appearance, some were bright-eyed and eager, some were haggard and worn—all looking what they were, people who had been using up the sunshine of their lives among the spindles and looms and noise and dust of a huge factory.

"We are idle and in a destitute condition," these factory workers argued, asking "for immediate assistance for between 500 and 600 people who are starving, or transportation back to our homes." Their supporters on the city council attempted to appropriate one thousand dollars from city funds "to send the cotton operatives back to North Carolina," only to be thwarted by the city attorney's ruling that such was an improper use of the city's "unforeseen contingency fund." Instead, the council took up a collection among themselves, netting $175 to assist the former workers.[19]

Strikes other than the one in Galveston also bring this issue to the fore. On Monday, May 8, 1893, the management of the Overland Cotton Company of South Denver, Colorado, posted notices announcing that on the following Monday the mill would increase hours, without any corresponding

---

18. *GDN*, February 23, 1895, p. 8.
19. *GDN*, March 27, 1895, p. 8.

wage increase.[20] Although the company claimed that it planned to lower rents in company housing to compensate for the lower wages, workers remained unconvinced. Previously working sixty hours a week, the new work schedule called for eleven-and-a-quarter hours on weekdays and nine and three-quarters hours on Saturdays, totaling sixty-six hours a week. Workers began grumbling in untold numbers of casual conversations and numerous small-group meetings.

By Friday, almost all the mill's workers met at Odd Fellows' Hall, formed a Cotton Mill Operatives' Union, and announced plans to affiliate with the American Federation of Labor. The president of the newly formed union announced that its purpose was "to take direct action in the impending crisis and to induce the managers of the mills to pay the men [*sic*] the same wages as they now receive." They elected a committee of six to meet with the mill's general manager and report back the following day. State senator and labor activist Hamilton Armstrong addressed the crowd with a mixture of encouragement and admonition:

> This question of organization you are to consider tonight is a very serious one and should have been thought of some time ago. If you intend to strike let everyone in the mill join hands, and if you intend to go out Monday tie the old mill up and tie it up good. . . . If you had organized before this and affiliated with the trades assembly we could have offered you financial as well as moral support. But now we can offer only our moral support. . . . From what I have heard of this affair you have all to gain and nothing to lose, and you will have the public sympathy.[21]

In response to the workers' actions, General Manager Choate reminded readers of the Denver newspaper that when the mills had opened just a few years earlier, they operated with some of the shortest hours in the nation. Their competitors in the Midwest and the South, Choate claimed, all operated sixty-six to seventy-two hours a week, while paying 35 to 40 percent less in wages. Furthermore, the company had "built for the employes a boarding house said to be superior to anything connected with any manufactory in the country and established their help in new houses, principally brick, at rents scarcely 50 per cent of those current in Denver." There would be no strike, Choate opined, and if there was, the mills would either run on schedule or be closed down. "If the latter course should be found neccessary it will be a blow to the manufacturing interests of Denver which it will take years to recover from."[22]

---

20. Unless otherwise cited, the story of this strike comes from coverage in the *Rocky Mountain News* [hereafter cited as *RMN*].

21. *RMN*, May 13, 1893, p. 3.

22. Ibid.

The Overland Cotton Mill, South Denver, Colorado, c. 1892 (photo by William Henry Jackson, courtesy of Denver Public Library, Western History Collection, WHJ-643).

The following evening, workers gathered once again in Odd Fellows' Hall and voted unanimously to demand that their hours and wages remain the same. The next day, workers posted notices at the mills and boardinghouses announcing their plans to strike on Monday, May 15. Throughout the ensuing month-long strike, both sides constantly raised comparisons with other textile mill locations throughout the nation. The management would repeat claims of high wages and short hours, while workers argued that their counterparts in New York and Massachusetts earned higher wages and that those in southern mills faced a much lower cost of living. The knowledge of national cotton mill wage rates and conditions evinced in such arguments came from two sources. The first was Denver's general rapid growth and in-migration of workers from all over the United States during the 1870s and 1880s.[23] The comparisons with southern mills in particular grew from the recruiting strategies of the Overland Cotton Mill. In relatively labor-scarce Denver, the company had turned to the southern states to recruit workers. Ads such as that published in the *Atlanta Journal* the year before brought southern cotton mill workers to Denver: "WANTED—HELP 5 or 6 good white families, cotton mill hands, weavers and spinners, to go to Denver, Colorado; cheap tickets; cotton mills advance railroad fare."[24] In other words, the company sought

23. Robert M. Tank, "Mobility and Occupational Structure on the Late Nineteenth-Century Urban Frontier: The Case of Denver, Colorado," *Pacific Historical Review* 47, no. 2 (May 1978): 191.

24. *Atlanta Journal*, November 24, 1892, p. 6.

to re-create a particularly southern type of family wage economy in their western mill.[25] By doing so, they unwittingly ensured that their workers would be well aware of wages and working conditions elsewhere.

The textile industry of the New South had developed only in the past decade or so in the southeastern states. Though these states had traditionally grown the bulk of the nation's cotton crop, feeding the antebellum cotton textile industries of both New England and old England, before the end of the Civil War they had rarely participated in the transformation of this raw material into finished products. After the end of Reconstruction in 1877, though, the rise of the southern boosters' "New South" relied on the growth of the region's textile industry. While the southeastern states contributed only 4.9 percent of the nation's value added in textiles in 1860, by 1900 they contributed 10.6 percent of it.[26] Put in other terms, in 1880 the South had only half a million cotton spindles in operation, but by 1905 they had almost nine million spindles, and by 1910 they had more than eleven million. The number of establishments had also grown, with the eight southeastern states having only 164 mills in 1880 but 731 by 1910.[27]

Although the southern textile industry did not grow to dominate the national industry until later in the twentieth century, its rapid growth in the late nineteenth century drew considerable attention from northern textile industrialists and workers alike. The final decades of that century brought almost constant comment from industry sources on southern mills, their possibilities and their problems. Chief among both possibilities and problems was that of labor. The new textile mills of the South provided almost ideal employment for the families of former tenant farmers, Confederate war widows, and other white denizens of the southern Piedmont. Though textile industry advocates argued vociferously both for and against these workers, textile magnates, like other southern manufacturers, found no other workforce available to them. Attempts to draw textile workers from New England or Europe invariably failed. However, the textile companies soon found compensating factors as they learned to utilize the native white workers of the South.[28]

25. See Jacquelyn Dowd Hall et al., *Like a Family: The Making of a Southern Cotton Mill World* (Chapel Hill: University of North Carolina Press, 1987), for the now-classic description of the southern family mill labor system.

26. Niemi, *State and Regional Patterns*, pp. 14–15.

27. Melvin Thomas Copeland, *The Cotton Manufacturing Industry of the United States* (New York: A. M. Kelly, 1966), pp. 34–35.

28. Many historians have studied the growth of the southern textile industry. These include, among others, Bess Beatty, *Alamance: The Holt Family and Industrialization in a North Carolina County, 1837–1900* (Baton Rouge: Louisiana State University Press, 1999); Hall et al., *Like a Family*; Douglas Flamming, *Creating the Modern South: Millhands and Managers in Dalton, Georgia, 1884–1984* (Chapel Hill: University of North Carolina Press, 1992); Dolores E. Janiewski, *Sisterhood Denied: Race, Gender, and Class in a New South Community* (Philadelphia: Temple University Press, 1985); Clifford M. Kuhn, *Contesting the New South Order: The*

Migrating from situations of often desperate poverty in tenant farming in particular, these families would put virtually all family members to work in the new textile mills. One observer in 1891 noted:

> The farmers' families in North Carolina and Virginia, as a rule, have more branches and buds attached to or blossoming out from the parent stem then are found in the native born families of New England. Here are neither Irish, French nor Negro. The native born of the South are taking to the factory business, as ducks take to water, and now are credited as being very smart and proficient in all departments.[29]

This tendency to hire workers in family groups had a number of consequences for the southern mills. First, the incidence of child labor in the South was much greater than it was in any other sector of the nation. In 1900, for example, fully one-quarter of southern textile mill workers were under the age of sixteen, while less than 7 percent of those in New England were.[30] Most southern mill owners, in fact, held out the possibility of employment for a family's children as one of their main inducements to textile employment. There were also other inducements, though: southern mill owners quickly came to be known for a paternalistic style of management, under which they would provide housing, rudimentary education, and other such perquisites.

For southern textile workers, wages were much lower and hours of work much longer than for textile workers in New England. While all observers agreed on this, its meaning in terms of southern workers' standard of living was often disputed. The paternalistic offerings of mill owners, the more "genial" climate of the South, and the region's overall lower cost of living were all pointed to as explaining the difference between wages in the two regions.[31] And though many observers commented on the lax attendance of southern workers at the workplace, no one at the time seems to have considered that this might be related to the long hours of labor.

Commentators on the southern scene also agreed that southern workers showed little tendency to be influenced by union agitators. Said Benjamin F. Pierce in 1891, "There are certain large rewards in cotton spinning [in North Carolina]—no strikes, no anarchists and socialists to make disturbance."[32] The North Carolina labor commissioner, writing five years later, agreed, pointing out: "This labor comes almost entirely from the farms, and is conservative, and not spoiled by contact with anarchist or in fact any kind of agitators." As long as mill owners continued their benevolent, paternalistic

---

1914–1915 *Strike at Atlanta's Fulton Mills* (Chapel Hill: University of North Carolina Press, 2001).

29. *American Wool and Cotton Reporter* [*AW&CR*], April 9, 1891 (5:15), p. 514.

30. Copeland, *Cotton Manufacturing Industry*, p. 43.

31. See, for example, "The Labor in Southern Mills," in *The Tradesman*, April 15, 1895 (33:4), esp. p. 66.

32. "Manufacturing Advantages in the South," *AW&CR*, April 23, 1891 (5:17), p. 605.

ways, he continued, this would continue to be true. "She [the South] does not need missionaries, long haired men or short haired, bloomer attired women, nor a single agitator or walking delegate." Only if "greediness" came to rule the South would such foreign influences begin to play a role in southern labor.[33]

Textile manufacturers attempted to re-create these alleged characteristics of white southern labor—its relative cheapness, its compliance, and its hard work—throughout the mills of the southeastern and western states. This combination existed not only in Denver's Overland and Galveston's cotton mills, but also in many other mills of the industrial periphery. The same characteristics also operated in later strikes in Oregon City, Oregon, and on the Kentucky-Indiana border in Evansville, Indiana. Because of this, I count both strikes in the industrial periphery, even though Evansville was technically in the industrial core state of Indiana. Situated at the very southernmost tip of the state, wedged between Kentucky and Missouri, Evansville often took on a southern cast.[34] The companies in both cases took advantage of a family economy form of waged labor, recruiting workers from all over the nation and especially from southern textile centers. Both strikes also started with actions taken by women workers; in Oregon City the strike began with a group of fourteen women weavers refusing to accept a wage reduction and "stretch-out" of their work, while in Evansville all observers agreed that it was the women workers who showed the greatest interest in their strike for shorter hours. Both these strikes also evidence interesting relationships with the labor movements of their cities.

The strike in Evansville had roots in actions taken in the late spring of 1900 when a committee of workers asked that their daily hours be cut from eleven to ten without any corresponding wage decrease.[35] At some point in May or June, workers organized themselves as Local 214 of the National Textile Workers' Union of America. The union's regional organizer encouraged them to continue to negotiate their demands rather than to strike. After several more meetings with mill superintendent John Osborn, workers believed they would gain their request. On Saturday, June 30, the mill posted notices that, beginning the following Monday, ten hours would constitute the working day but that wages would be reduced accordingly. That Monday evening, workers voted unanimously to strike.

By the end of the strike's first week, the Evansville Central Labor Union had notified the state labor commission about the strike. The commission then began an investigation of the strike the following week. The company

33. "Labor Conditions in the South," *The Tradesman*, January 1, 1896 (33:9), pp. 88–89.

34. See Lawrence M. Lipin, *Producers, Proletarians, and Politicians: Workers and Party Politics in Evansville and New Albany, Indiana, 1850–1887* (Urbana: University of Illinois Press, 1994), pp. 80–81, for an early hint of this.

35. Unless otherwise noted, the story of this strike comes from coverage in the *Evansville Journal* [hereafter cited as *EJ*].

repeated its position, stating that, while willing to reduce workers' hours, it could not compete with mills elsewhere if it maintained eleven-hour wages. The state labor commission counseled moderation and urged strikers to return to work. The Evansville newspaper conjectured that the strike would be short, noting that the workers had not belonged to the national union long enough to receive strike benefits from it. However, the paper misjudged both the strikers' firmness and their ability to gain support from other city unionists.

Throughout the rest of the summer, strikers held a series of picnics to raise funds for their strike. Held at various parks around the city, the picnics usually featured some local band. Although admission was free, strikers sold tickets to each event. By Labor Day, "the striking employes of the cotton mill, women, girls, men and boys, making a total of several hundred . . . formed no little part of the parade," which ended in Garvin's Grove, where music, games, and food greeted Evansville's workers.[36]

Soon after, the Evansville Cotton Manufacturing Company, having spent the summer making various improvements in the mill, announced that workers had two weeks to return to work. At the end of that time, they would hire new workers if necessary and resume operations. The company's attempt to bring in strikebreakers led to outbreaks of violence, beginning with the crowd of women and children who chased four women hired to clean the mill home on September 14, crying out "Scab! scab!" and rattling tin cans at them.[37] When the plant reopened for full production, the city stationed six police officers at the mill to prevent trouble, though demonstrations in front of the mill continued, with more "tin-canning" as well as mud-throwing and other actions.

By the end of the week, the company gave up its attempt to restart production in the mill. On Sunday, Father P. H. Fitzpatrick of Sacred Heart Catholic Church, of which "many strikers are members," preached a sermon condemning the week's lawlessness. If many of the strikers belonged to Sacred Heart, most of them were probably German Catholics. Few Evansville textile workers shared Father Fitzpatrick's Irish heritage, and few of the strikers shared his abhorrence of strike activities.[38]

When Labor Commissioner B. F. Schmid returned to renew negotiations the next week, Father Fitzpatrick accompanied him to a meeting with Superintendent Osborn and representatives of the strikers. When the strikers noticed that Fitzpatrick was present, they refused to continue, ordering him to leave. Osborn then announced that he would not continue if Fitzpatrick was not

36. *EJ*, September 4, 1900, p. 1.
37. *EJ*, September 16, 1900, p. 16.
38. *EJ*, September 24, 1900, p. 1. Some 43 percent of Evansville cotton mill workers were of German descent, while just under 6 percent were Irish, and almost 12 percent came from southeastern states. See 1900 Federal Manuscript Census for Vanderburgh County for Evansville, Indiana. See also appendix 2, table A2.2

present. Negotiations ended, much to the disgust of Commissioner Schmid, who claimed, "The trouble is the strikers are listening to fire-eating politicians and insult those who have worked zealously and honestly on their behalf. So long as they do that, there can be no agreement."[39]

Evansville certainly had no shortage of "fire-eating politicians" for workers to listen to in the fall of 1900, a presidential and gubernatorial election year. Not only did presidential candidate Theodore Roosevelt visit Evansville in October, but near-local-boy and Social Democratic candidate Eugene Debs also paid a visit right before the election. More than fire-eating politicians, though, the cotton mill's workers listened to their local labor movement. Throughout the strike, both the Evansville Central Labor Union and local representatives of the AFL played important roles in the strike. Not unlike the labor movement of the Denver region, which was dominated by metal miners, that of Evansville was dominated by coal miners. Some of the cotton mill workers lived in families headed by coal miners, and more than 40 percent of them came from the types of German American families that dominated the local unions.[40] Evansville mill workers had begun their strike on their own, but the continued support from local unionists helped to sustain it.

Coal miners became more visible in the strike as it wore on. By December, they even quit their own work early one day in order to join a protest against conditions in the cotton mill. Miners promised continued financial support for the strike, reminding strikers that they "were not going to starve and that if they were it was just as good to 'starve not working as it was to starve working.' "[41] Only a few days later, on December 18, strikers voted unanimously to return to work under conditions offered by Osborn, but some workers left work again in January, claiming unfair treatment. The strike ultimately ended officially in February, when a special meeting of the Evansville Central Labor Union declared the strike over.

In Oregon City two years later, the local labor movement was just as present as it had been in Evansville, though it was also less sophisticated.[42] At the beginning of April 1902, employees at the Willamette Pulp & Paper mill in Oregon City formed a union affiliated with the "local AFL." Three weeks later, this union, apparently an AFL federal labor union, reported some seven hundred members, including two hundred from the Oregon City Woolen Mills. Though this textile subdivision of the local AFL appears to have affiliated itself as a branch of the United Textile Workers, it never becomes clear whether the textile workers negotiated for themselves or whether the larger paper and pulp workers' federal union took on this task.

---

39. *EJ*, September 26, 1900, p. 3.
40. From 1900 Manuscript Census data. See appendix 2.
41. *EJ*, December 9, 1900, p. 9.
42. Unless otherwise noted, the story of this strike comes from coverage in the *Oregon City Courier-Herald* and the *Oregon City Enterprise*.

Paper factories and woolen mill, Oregon City, Oregon, c. 1890s (courtesy of Oregon Historical Society, CN005567).

When strikers finally settled the strike on May 19, however, Oregon City's mayor and a committee from the federal union assisted members of the UTW Local 337 in the final negotiations. Strikers and the company compromised on wages and agreed to "partial" union recognition, for what might be called a "partial" union. An "indignation meeting" set for that evening became a "jollification" instead.[43]

In the Denver strike as well, a virtually all-male labor movement assisted the largely female textile mill strikers. Despite initial hesitancy about financial strike support, Denver's unions almost instantly offered both money and action on behalf of the Overland strikers. The Denver Trades and Labor Assembly clearly wanted to promote "responsible" unionism, as seen both in Hamilton Armstrong's bemoaning of the fact that operatives had not organized earlier and in the assembly's role in the arbitration process. Within days of the beginning of the strike, the trades assembly appointed a committee to "look after the matter" and met almost immediately with mill manager Choate.[44] Hoping to refute the company's claims of ideal working and living conditions, the trades assembly committee arranged for three local ministers to visit the Overland mills during the first week of the strike and later took two prominent Denver residents on a tour of the mill operatives' living conditions.

The Denver trades assembly also moved in other ways to assist the Overland strikers. Beginning during the second week of the strike, the assembly's

43. *Oregon City Courier-Herald*, May 23, 1902, p. 4.
44. *RMN*, May 15, 1893, p. 8.

committee began to make plans to help strikers return "to their southern homes."[45] It also compiled "a list of girls at the mills" in order to find "positions in private families" for them, though it is unclear how attractive such positions as domestic servants would have been to the cotton factory girls.[46] Individual unions and supporters, however, did not hesitate to offer support for the relatively spontaneous strike of cotton operatives. Denver's labor movement clearly understood and sympathized with militance.[47]

The role of the local labor movement in Denver, as well as in other locations, demonstrates the AFL version of the tendency Kim Voss found among members of the Knights of Labor in New Jersey: male Knights could assist women and other less-skilled workers more easily in their own communities than in their own industries.[48] In these later AFL examples from the industrial periphery, we find the same true of AFL union members. However, these strikes also demonstrate some of the difficulties members of AFL craft unions had in understanding the significance of strikes for these workers' lives. The Denver trades assembly committee probably thought they were doing a great thing when they attempted to match up striking girls with local families in need of servants, but the girls, many of whom lived and worked with their own biological families in the mill, would not have appreciated the effort. Similarly, when the trades assembly tried to evoke public sympathy by accusing the company of utilizing child labor, they must have been perplexed by the lukewarm reception the idea received from the strikers, most of whom had traveled to Denver precisely because the mill promised work for their children. In other words, male union activists could attempt to assist women and their male co-workers in such strikes, but their attempts to do so could go far astray without an understanding of the dynamics of the strikers' lives.

Despite such misunderstandings, the strike stories narrated here demonstrate that even strikes in the nation's industrial periphery could be accompanied by considerable militance. Perhaps the best examples of this come from strikes of South Florida cigar workers. While other strikes examined show ways in which local labor activists could misunderstand the goals of largely female groups of strikers, the strike of Key West cigar workers in the fall of 1889 illustrates even greater misreadings by the mainstream U.S. labor movement.[49] In the case of the Key West strike, both employers and the U.S. labor movement in general looked askance at the militance of the Cuban workers. One industry journal warned manufacturers in early October that

45. *RMN*, June 4, 1893, p. 13.

46. *RMN*, May 24, 1893, p. 5.

47. See David Brundage, *The Making of Western Labor Radicalism: Denver's Organized Workers, 1878–1905* (Urbana: University of Illinois Press, 1994).

48. Kim Voss, *The Making of American Exceptionalism: The Knights of Labor and Class Formation in the Nineteenth Century* (Ithaca: Cornell University Press, 1993), p. 182.

49. Unless otherwise noted, the story of this strike comes from L. Glenn Westfall, *Key West: Cigar City U.S.A.* (Key West, Fla.: Historic Key West Preservation Board, 1984), and from coverage in *Tobacco (New York)*.

cigar makers in both Havana and Key West were "backed by the apostles of socialism and anarchy."[50] Samuel Gompers and the AFL would have agreed, as the various revolutionary and Spanish-language unions of Key West's Cuban cigar makers operated, literally, beyond their comprehension.

The question of Key West's status as a location on the industrial periphery of the United States has a somewhat different twist than that of the other strikers under consideration in this chapter. While strikers in the industrial periphery tended to look to the labor movement of the nation's core for inspiration and guidance, the cigar makers of Key West had no interest whatsoever in the U.S. labor movement, let alone in Gompers's Cigar Makers' International Union. After the Key West strike ended in January 1890, a correspondent sent a report on the strike's aftermath to the *Cigar Makers' Official Journal*. After acknowledging that, after an almost three-month-long strike, manufacturers had given in to strikers' demands completely, he added in a postscript to his letter, "If you ever intend to organize a Union here you will have to send some one to do it. The boys here do not understand it."[51]

While the journal's correspondent was right that "the boys" of Key West did not understand the "it" of moderate American craft unionism, it is also true that American unionists did not understand Key West cigar makers and especially the fundamental social and political issues tearing at the very fabric of Cuban society at the time. The 1889 strike was deeply embroiled in tensions among Spanish colonialists, American annexationists, Cuban reformists, and Cuban revolutionaries. Though Cuban-made Key West "Clear Havana" cigars were sold in New York City, the workers who made them had participated for years in the Cuban revolutionary movement and looked almost exclusively toward the labor movement in Havana for direction and guidance during the 1889 strike. The proximity of Key West to Havana explains the logic of this orientation.

The strike in Key West virtually shut down the cigar industry in the town, as workers demanded a new payment schedule that would differentiate their pay according to the quality of the cigars they made. Almost five thousand workers, including some seven hundred women, walked off their jobs. Though little material exists on women's participation in the strike, we know from various literary and visual sources that women worked alongside men, probably as stemmers, preparing tobacco leaf for rolling. They also participated in the various political and social movements of the time alongside their male counterparts. While the women of the "Women's Patriot Club [Mariana Grajales de Maceo] of Key West" may have been the wives and daughters of the manufacturers, there is no reason to think that working-class women

50. *Tobacco (New York)*, October 4, 1889 (7:22), p. 4.
51. *Cigar Makers' Official Journal*, 15 (January 1890): 9.

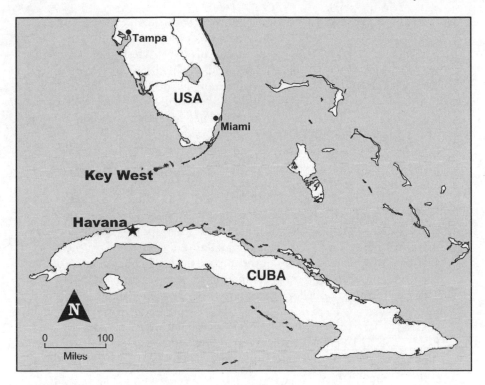

Key West, Florida, and its proximity to Havana, Cuba (Syracuse University Cartography Laboratory).

did not also participate in the same revolutionary activities as the men.[52] Though "the boys" in Key West neglected to mention their female co-workers explicitly, the women who worked side by side with the men struck just as militantly. Throughout the strike, both male and female workers in the Key West factories manifested their identities as members of the Cuban working class.

When the general strike and lockout of Key West factories began in October, two ships arrived within days to carry strikers and their families back to Havana. One was a Spanish gunboat, while the second was a merchant ship engaged by the anarchist Alianza Obrera. Enrique Messonier, a Cuban anarchist, had arrived in Key West the year before the strike and spent considerable time investigating cigar makers' complaints there. Messonier and other anarchists at this time argued that cigar makers should abandon the

52. See picture in Gerald Eugene Poyo, *With All, and for the Good of All: The Emergence of Popular Nationalism in the Cuban Communities of the United States, 1848–1898* (Durham, N.C.: Duke University Press, 1989), p. 79. Nancy Hewitt describes this phenomenon among Tampa's women as well, in *Southern Discomfort: Women's Activism in Tampa, Florida, 1880s–1920s* (Urbana: University of Illinois Press, 2001), chap. 7, pp. 200–221.

political struggle for Cuban independence because so many of the cigar manufacturers supported that movement. Workers in both Cuba and Florida faced more important social problems, according to Messonier. Throughout the strike, Messonier and the Alianza would helped strikers leave Key West. Though hundreds left for Tampa, many more headed back to Havana, where the returnees found that the island's Spanish rulers had instituted a new emigration ruling that once emigrants returned to Cuba they could not return to Florida for six months. Because Key West was acknowledged as a leading center of the Cuban independence movement, this ruling had the dual effect of bolstering the Havana cigar industry by providing it with a surplus labor force while undercutting the independence movement.

Meanwhile, the Key West Board of Trade, in an attempt to rid the city of the anarchist influence, banished Messonier to Tampa. The Spanish had exiled anarchists from Havana because their strikes disrupted that city's cigar industry, but many Key West cigar manufacturers wanted to rid their city of Messonier's influence because of the impact the strike had on the Cuban independence movement. The appearance of the Spanish gunboat in Key West's harbor confirmed the belief of many pro-independence manufacturers that the strike itself was part of a Spanish conspiracy. Because workers had provided considerable financial support to revolutionary forces since the late 1870s, strikes, whether in Key West, Havana, or the new cigar town of Tampa, would cut off financial donations to the Spanish government's most troublesome opposition.[53]

Wrapped up in their conspiracy theories, the Key's cigar manufacturers had a difficult time taking the workers' demands seriously. Throughout the strike, the manufacturers continued to believe that the strike would be settled rapidly, while strikers continued to maintain an extremely solid front. Even during December, when manufacturers had been convinced the workers would return and thereby save their pre-Christmas production, workers remained on strike. Whether Key West's cigar manufacturers were more upset because their trade had been disrupted or because their schemes for Cuban independence had been thwarted temporarily, they finally had to admit defeat. Most other strikes of this duration would have ended in defeat for the strikers, but this one in Key West ended in virtual victory for the anarchist-led workers. In early January, workers achieved the wage increases they had requested, though they agreed that if "the trade" rejected the resulting new cigar prices they would let the manufacturers rescind the increases. They also dropped an earlier demand to increase pickers' wages by twenty cents per thousand and agreed that in the future they would not have operatives'

53. Poyo, *With All*, pp. 86–94; Louis A. Perez, *Cuba: Between Reform and Revolution* (New York: Oxford University Press, 1988), pp. 144–48; Jean Stubbs, *Tobacco on the Periphery: A Case Study in Cuban Labour History, 1860–1958* (Cambridge: Cambridge University Press, 1985), esp. pp. 93, 100–107; C. Neale Ronning, *José Martí and the Emigré Colony in Key West: Leadership and State Formation* (New York: Praeger, 1990), pp. 29–34.

committees within the shops. This last point was key for manufacturers, who placed most of the blame for the strike on the "radical" committees feared by cigar factory owners.[54]

For the Cuban independence movement, the Key West strike of 1889 provided an important opening for José Martí to gain a greater audience for his vision of a more socialist independence movement. In the midst of the strike, Martí wrote to one compatriot: "The worker is not an inferior being, nor should he be isolated and governed by brute force, but rather by opening to him, in a brotherly way, the considerations and rights which assure peace and happiness among a people."[55] The politics of José Martí and the Cuban independence movement in general did not interest the cigar makers' union and the rest of the AFL at this time. For them, the Key West strike and its participants—both male and female—remained virtually unintelligible, seemingly opposed to the careful craft unionism of the Federation.

In January 1890 the *Cigar Makers' Official Journal* translated and published a statement the Key West strikers had made in which they sarcastically apologized for "ruining" the manufacturers' "fall and Christmas trade" and then promised to ruin the spring and summer trade as well unless their demands were met. The strikers continued with their threat: "It's now for the manufacturers to decide; if they can afford to sustain their rights as capitalists, we as men [*sic*] of principle, as disciplined and organized workmen, as citizens worthy of respect, will stick to our petition . . . rather than to submit to the manufacturers' will."[56] In this way, the strikers responded to their employers' charges of irresponsibility and capriciousness by pointing out that their refusals to arbitrate the dispute arose from the rightness of their cause.

Though members of the U.S. cigar makers' union may not have understood the tenacity of the strikers in Cayo Hueso, these strikers in fact showed many of the same qualities seen in the Wisconsin tobacco workers' strikes that opened this chapter. Though Edgerton tobacco sorters clearly were not entangled in a struggle against colonialism, both groups of workers evinced knowledge of the industry and its production cycles. Both groups maintained an impressive level of solidarity. Both groups won their demands, returning to work at higher wage levels. And neither group needed the assistance of workers in the nation's industrial core or the AFL in order to achieve this.[57]

The strikes of the industrial periphery described here suggest to the historian yet another way of thinking about the relationships among women, men,

54. *Tobacco (New York)*, November 15, 1889 (8:2), p. 6; January 10, 1890 (8:10), p. 3.

55. José Martí, *Obras completas de Martí*, 1st ed., vol. 2, ed. Gonzalade Quesada y Miranda (Lattabana: Editorial Tropico, 1936), p. 90: "El obrero no es un ser inferior, ni se ha de tender a tenerlo en corrales y gobernalo con la pica, sino en abrirle, de hermano a hermano, las consideraciones y derechos queaseguran en los pueblos la paz y la felicidad." Also cited in and translated by Ronning, *José Martí and the Emigré Colony*, p. 34.

56. *Cigar Makers' Official Journal* 15 (January 1890): 6.

57. Hewitt's description of the CMIU's experience in Tampa factories in 1988 and 1900 bears out this claim. See Hewitt, *Southern Discomfort*, pp. 125–31.

and unions as national institutions. As noted in chapter 3, a key goal of the AFL at this time was to bring together workers across the nation. While the unions of the AFL could at times use gender successfully to create this sense of literal union brotherhood, these cross-gender strikes suggest that calls to brotherhood might not always work in situations where women workers did not feel as tied to ideologies of ladylike behavior. Just as women in western states tended to gain suffrage decades ahead of those in the East, women workers in the industrial periphery also experienced greater scope of action than those in the industrial and union core states.[58]

Outside the direct influence of the AFL, the geographic marginalization of these strikes in the industrial periphery meant that the strikers' experiences were generally not incorporated into any of the more permanent organizations of the time. Gender combined with geographic distance translated into an almost psychological barrier that ensured that the unions of the AFL would not be able to hear these women's voices or incorporate their lessons. Allowing a wider scope of action for women and other groups marginalized by the mainstream labor movement, these strikes highlight the extent to which the gendered nature of craft unionism was attributable to the gender coding of the AFL as an organization. These strikes suggest that gendered workplaces alone did not create limited roles for women workers in the labor movement. Galveston's Mrs. Ormond, New Orleans' Annie O'Leary, Louisville's Lewis Washington, and even the unnamed women of Key West used their knowledge of their work and their industries to speak and act more forcefully than the labor movement of the industrial core would have allowed. The extensive family networks in which many of these individuals were embedded contributed to their actions, as did also the families of strikers in the industrial core.

58. See Eleanor Flexner, *Century of Struggle: The Woman's Rights Movement in the United States*, rev. ed. (1959; reprint, Cambridge: Harvard University Press, 1975), chap. 11, pp. 159–66; Elizabeth Jameson, *All That Glitters: Class, Conflict, and Community in Cripple Creek* (Urbana: University of Illinois Press, 1998), pp. 122–25.

6   Family Ties

"For the sake of the children and women"
—*Philadelphia Inquirer*, June 18, 1903

Anna Whitesell worked as a weaver in the Haw River mill of the T. M. Holt Company in North Carolina in 1900. On September 27, "boss weaver" Jim May threatened to fire Anna, claiming she made too many trips away from her looms for supplies. May then turned to Johnie Pope, an orphan working in the mill, and offered Whitesell's job to her.[1] When Pope turned down the offer, she too was threatened with discharge. One observer said, "Being an orphan and having to choose between giving up her job and incurring the frowns of her union friends, she did not know what to do and burst into tears."[2] That night, a meeting of the Haw River local of the National Union of Textile Workers (NUTW) listened to the two girls' stories and agreed to demand that the mill fire Foreman May. They would strike if their demand was denied.[3]

The following day, Holt management turned down the union demand, and by the following Thursday workers at all three mills in Haw River had gone on strike. That day, every mill in Alamance County posted a notice that henceforward only nonunion labor would be employed. In addition, all union members were required to vacate the company houses in which they lived by October 15. Many in the county, both workers and observers, viewed this action by mill owners as extreme. As the editor of the *Alamance Gleaner* put it, "There was trouble at no other mill, and why should the owners organize to stamp out the organization of their help—those who served them?"[4] Signs of trouble now began to appear in other Alamance County mills as well.

On Monday, October 15, hundreds of textile workers, union and nonunion alike, did not show up for work, and that evening the strikers were addressed by C. P. Davis, an AFL organizer from nearby High Point. The next morning,

1. Jerome Dowd, "Strikes and Lockouts in North Carolina," *Gunton's Magazine* 20 (February 1901): 136–41.
2. Ibid., p. 138.
3. Unless otherwise noted, the story of this strike comes from coverage in the *Alamance Gleaner* [hereafter cited as *Gleaner*], the *Charlotte Daily Observer*, and the *American Wool and Cotton Reporter* [hereafter cited as *AW&CR*].
4. *Gleaner*, October 11, 1900, p. 2.

some 250 union members marched from Haw River to Graham, a few miles away, where another five hundred textile workers joined them. Speakers at the ensuing rally counseled orderliness and "good behavior." By the middle of the week, hundreds of textile workers were idle. Most of the mills in the county either sat empty or operated with greatly reduced forces. Anticipating the evictions of union members, the union now focused on organizing food and shelter for strikers. By the end of the week, between five and eight thousand workers in Alamance County were out of work, either striking or locked out by their employers. One thousand workers attended a meeting in Burlington on Saturday, at which the union organizer told them to hold firm and suggested that a boycott of the goods of the various firms might be called.

What explains Johnie Pope's refusal of a better job, and the subsequent strike of some five thousand textile workers in Alamance County, North Carolina? Certainly part of the explanation lies in the union's heightened efforts the preceding summer to enlist the previously quiescent North Carolina textile workers into the union ranks. However, even more of the explanation comes from the way in which even orphans like Johnie Pope were embedded in communities based on a family system of textile labor. The last two chapters have already hinted at the interactions of different forms of community with workers' families. Family connections reinforced the ethnic and racial communities described in chapter 4. Families also aided and abetted in the development of the "culture of complaint" seen in the industrial periphery, as workers would discuss workplaces with co-workers both on the job and at home.

Cross-gender strikes reveal some of the ways an employer's use of family systems of labor could lead to workers developing family strike strategies. We see this in the textile industry in both the South and the Northeast, in the Massachusetts shoe industry, and in the tobacco industry in the South. Several strike stories also suggest ways in which family connections might reinforce commitments to striking even when family members did not share the same workplaces. Family issues could also inform and inflame strike demands, though sometimes in contradictory ways. Across a range of industries and locations, such issues as child labor could create conflict among strikers, at worst, and ambivalence at best. In addition, fictive families and familial ideologies might warp relations among cross-gendered strikers. Whether the families examined are biological or imagined, the resonance of "family" in cross-gender strikes was marked. The experiences of Johnie Pope and Anna Whitesell in sparking the Alamance strike provide one such example.

Alamance County, "with her 19 cotton, 1 woolen and 1 knitting mill, operating 84,808 spindles and 4,599 looms, manufactur[ing] ginghams plaids, colored cottons, domestics, cheviots, shirtings, stripes, jeans, blankets, warps, yarns and hosiery," stood at the productive center of the North Carolina textile industry. Only Gaston County to the southwest, with twenty-three mills, contributed more to the state's industry.[5] As Jacquelyn Dowd Hall and others have shown, Alamance and Gaston counties remained crucial to the growing southern textile industry throughout the twentieth century.[6] In the late nineteenth century these counties also contained the most developed version of the southern family labor system and wage economy described in chapter 5. Family ties among the textile workers of Alamance County played a role in propelling these workers to strike action in 1900, just as they were crucial to their daily work lives.

Anna Whitesell's family illustrates these family ties.[7] Anna's mother, Malinda, headed the family, and herself worked as a weaver, probably in the Holt factory. Anna herself was only fifteen years old in 1900. Her younger sister, Agnes, only eleven years old, also worked as a weaver. Two younger brothers, Mac (age nine) and Harley (age six), remained at home, looked after by the family's black servant, Fannie Henry. Though the census listed Malinda as married, no husband appears in the Whitesell household's enumeration. Thirty-eight-year-old Malinda Whitesell had to make do on the three weavers' salaries to survive. Eighteen percent of Alamance textile worker families contained three textile workers, while more than two-thirds contained more. (See appendix 2, table A2.3.) The family with whom Johnie Pope lived also reflects the Alamance family system of labor. Nancy and Holloway Sipes no longer worked, but five of their six children between the ages of thirty-two and twenty-one worked in the mills, as did one daughter-in-law residing with them. All but one of the Sipes daughters as well as one son worked as weavers, while the remaining son worked as a quiller. The oldest daughter listed no occupation. A thirteen-year-old adopted son was in school, and twenty-year-old Johnie, the family's boarder, worked as a weaver. While less than 6 percent of the county's textile-working families had as many textile workers in them as the Sipeses did, this type of household linkage to work was quite common.

Only 4.7 percent of all Alamance textile workers lived in households in which no other textile worker resided; for female textile workers, this number was even smaller, with only one percent living as the sole textile worker in the household. The extreme youth of the workers in the Whitesell family was also common in Alamance, with 18 percent of all textile workers and 24 percent of female textile workers under the age of fifteen. (See appendix 2, table A2.4.) Though doffers in the mills were most likely to be under the

5. North Carolina Bureau of Labor and Printing, *Thirteenth Annual Report for the Year 1899* (Raleigh, N.C.: Edwards & Broughton and E. M. Uzzell, 1900), pp. 212–13.

6. Jacquelyn Dowd Hall et al., *Like a Family: The Making of a Southern Cotton Mill World* (Chapel Hill: University of North Carolina Press, 1987); Bess Beatty, *Alamance: The Holt Family and Industrialization in a North Carolina County, 1837–1900* (Baton Rouge: Louisiana State University Press, 1999).

7. Information on Alamance cotton mill workers comes from a sample of every fifth cotton mill worker in the county collected from the 1900 Federal Manuscript Census for Alamance County. See appendix 2.

age of fifteen (75 percent), 8 percent of weavers were as young, and one-third of all weavers were between the ages of fifteen and nineteen. Both the Sipes and the Whitesell families shared with other Alamance textile workers the presence of siblings in the workplace. While 84 percent of the county's textile workers lived in households containing other textile workers, more than half (54.2 percent) of these had siblings working along with them.

Virtually every historian of textile factory production has dealt in some way with the implications of family systems of labor. As historian Patrick Joyce put it in his work on textile-factory culture in late nineteenth-century England, "it was the phenomenon of the family in work that made the connection between the factory and the community such an intimate one."[8] A number of the strike stories told earlier have already hinted at this intimate connection, from the Baltimore sweatshops of 1892 to the Lowell textile workers of 1903. While Joyce goes on to argue that "the mythology of the family sanctioned the fiction of unity and interdependence that enabled poverty and inequality to be borne," the Alamance strike of 1900 suggests that a different story about the family in work can also be told.[9]

Though the orphaned Johnie Pope technically stood outside the family system of labor so common in the South, her experience of that family system both at work and in the family with which she boarded fueled her refusal to take another girl's job. Though Anna Whitesell allegedly belonged to the nascent textile union while Johnie did not, it was the girls' embeddedness in their community and families that led Johnie to react to what she viewed as arbitrary behavior on the part of boss weaver May and refuse her own promotion. By firing Anna, May had overstepped the bounds of his authority. Textile workers countywide would soon join young Johnie Pope in her resistance to what they all viewed as May's capriciousness. The "culture of complaint" described in the last chapter had deep roots in the very family system of labor that southern industrialists had hoped to use to create a passive labor force. Workers might begin talking about their grievances in the mill, but the discussion quickly spilled into their family lives.

At the same time that family ties contributed to the initial strength of the strike, the intertwining of families with the virtually total control of textile communities by mill owners ultimately led to the downfall of both the strike and the union in Alamance. While mill owners had announced their intention

8. Patrick Joyce, *Work, Society, and Politics: The Culture of the Factory in Later Victorian England* (New Brunswick, N.J.: Rutgers University Press, 1980), p. 111. Historians from Tamara K. Hareven (*Family Time and Industrial Time: The Relationship between the Family and Work in a New England Industrial Community* [Cambridge: Cambridge University Press, 1982]) to Hall et al. (*Like a Family*), Bess Beatty (*Alamance*), Douglas Flamming (*Creating the Modern South: Millhands and Managers in Dalton, Georgia, 1884–1984* [Chapel Hill: University of North Carolina Press, 1992]), and Clifford M. Kuhn (*Contesting the New South Order: The 1914–1915 Strike at Atlanta's Fulton Mills* [Chapel Hill: University of North Carolina Press, 2001]) have all considered the topic.

9. Joyce, *Work, Society, and Politics*, p. 115.

to evict strike supporters and union members from their homes at the start
of the strike, they did not begin to carry out evictions until November. The
November 15 *Alamance Gleaner* carried two stories side by side. The first
commented on the previous week's weather, noting: "The first real winter
weather came the latter part of last week, the first appearing Friday morning. . . . Since then there has been a little ice and heavy frosts nearly every
morning."[10] The second story noted the virtually simultaneous beginning of
legal eviction procedures. Once the county sheriff and his deputies began to
carry out the eviction orders, both strikers and union leaders panicked. The
union had obtained neither enough tents to house all the strikers nor enough
financial donations to feed them, and both in remote mill sites and in the
county's larger towns it was the mills that controlled all available housing.
By Monday, November 19, the textile workers' union representative in
Burlington allegedly advised strikers to apply for their positions once again.
He believed that "the determination of the mill owners was too pronounced
to be misunderstood and once they had filled their cottages with new hands,
the strikers could not have secured work at all . . . even after surrendering."[11]
The large and fecund families of the textile workers could no longer afford
to survive without the paternalistic assistance of the mill owners.

Many of the Alamance workers searched for other employment,
"prefer[ring] to go elsewhere rather than surrender rights and privileges
which they as citizens deem their own and should enjoy."[12] However, when
most shuffled back to work and promised to eschew all union sympathies
in the future, they embodied "the need for certainty and coherence that the
acceptance of caste and hierarchy meant."[13] The "caste and hierarchy" accepted by the Alamance workers was expressed early in the strike by a
"conservative and well-posted gentleman, interested in the business." In the
industry's lead journal this gentleman discussed the differences between
northern and southern mill labor. Southern workers are "as law-abiding and
law-respecting as any class of people," he said, and continued, "They are,
for the most part, the friends and neighbors of their employers; in most cases
their parents and grandparents and our 'forebears' held similar relations with
each other; they do not as a rule dislike a man because he is rich or better
off financially than themselves."[14] In that observer's eyes, southern workers
knew their place relative to their employers.

The unspoken glue binding centuries of white North Carolinians together
was race. While even a poorly paid and struggling weaver like Malinda
Whitesell could afford to employ a black servant to care for her youngest
children, blacks would not work in the mills next to Malinda's descendants

10. *Gleaner*, November 15, 1900, p. 3.
11. *AW&CR*, November 29, 1901 (14:48), p. 1450.
12. *Gleaner*, November 29, 1900, p. 3.
13. Joyce, *Work, Society, and Politics*, p. 98.
14. *AW&CR*, October 25, 1900 (14:43), p. 1283.

until the 1960s.[15] The ugly strikes over the hiring of southern blacks described in chapter 4 remind us of the strength and tenacity of southern racial glue. The *American Wool and Cotton Reporter* implicitly reminded its readers of this "glue" shortly after the demise of the Alamance strike. The Vesta cotton mills of South Carolina, one of the few southern mills to employ blacks, had decided to move to a new site in Georgia. The company's mistake, one correspondent reported, came in its not owning the workers' housing "and so having no control over them after working hours. . . . There can be no doubt but that, all things considered, the white laborer should be found in the mill and the negro upon the farm."[16] The Alamance mill owners certainly would have agreed on the crucial importance of controlling workers' housing, and thereby their lives. Black industrial workers received housing only rarely from southern employers after the Civil War, but those employers' "friends and neighbors" among white workers would receive housing and other paternalistic "benefits." All they had to do was give up any outward signs of independence, such as union membership.

If some dynamics of the Alamance strike were unique to the South, events in other textile-mill strike towns demonstrate surprising similarities. The town of New Bedford, Massachusetts, site of a huge textile strike in 1898, illustrates this. Along with Fall River, New Bedford was one of the Massachusetts textile towns most often compared with southern mills by industry commentators. If southern mill owners viewed New Bedford as a hotbed of unionism, anarchism, and socialism, New Bedford industrialists were equally conscious of the competition they faced from the southern mills. Both issues came alive in the strike that broke out in New Bedford in January 1898.[17]

Family dynamics in these two disparate settings shared intriguing parallels. (See appendix 2, table A2.5.) More than 80 percent of textile workers in both New Bedford and Alamance lived in households containing at least one other textile worker.[18] When compared with the households of Evansville, Indiana, and Oregon City textile workers, workers in New Bedford and Alamance appear to have much in common. As in Alamance, the work lives of the New Bedford workers were embedded in complex family economies. Though substantially fewer child laborers worked in the Massachusetts town (5 percent or less, compared with almost 18 percent in Alamance; see appendix 2, table A2.4), New Bedford textile workers living with others working in the same industry included almost 45 percent who lived and

15. See Timothy J. Minchin, *Hiring the Black Worker: The Racial Integration of the Southern Textile Industry, 1960–1980* (Chapel Hill: University of North Carolina Press, 1999), pp. 7–42.

16. *AW&CR*, February 7, 1901 (15:6), p. 154; January 31, 1901 (15:5), p. 129.

17. Unless otherwise noted, the story of this strike comes from coverage in the *Boston Globe* and the *New Bedford Morning Mercury*. This strike is recounted in more detail in chapter 7.

18. Information on New Bedford cotton mill workers comes from a sample of every tenth cotton mill worker collected from the 1900 Federal Manuscript Census for Bristol County, Massachusetts. See appendix 2.

worked with siblings, nearly 25 percent living and working with parents, and fully 15 percent with spouses. (See appendix 2, table A2.6.) Just as in the allegedly quiescent southern mills, New Bedford workers responded to perceived injustice from within tightly knit communities that linked family life and work life.

The New Bedford strike began after New England mill owners announced an impending 10 percent wage cut on December 31, 1897, that would go into effect on Monday, January 17, in cotton mills throughout the region. The strongest textile union at the time, the National Cotton Mule Spinners' Association, decided that its efforts and energy should be focused on a single location. With several smaller strikes already going on in a number of places, the union chose New Bedford as the focal point.

On January 17, 1898, strikes shut down twenty-two mills belonging to nine separate companies in New Bedford. The mule spinners had requested support from the other local textile unions, in particular those of weavers and loom fixers. Well before January 17 they knew that members of those unions would support the strike. For union leaders, however, the main surprise on January 17 was the response of nonunion workers to the strike call. In the opening days of the strike, virtually everyone stayed away from the mills. However, New Bedford's weavers soon foiled the spinners' attempts to keep the strike tightly focused on the wage cut alone.

The Friday before the strike began, a mass meeting of weavers, including both weavers' union members and nonmembers, had voted to add a second issue to the strike: the docking of pay for imperfect and supposedly inferior work. "The fines issue," as it came to be called, had rankled New Bedford weavers for some time; months before the wage cut was announced, they had voted to consider striking over this issue in April 1898. The January 14 weavers' meeting voted to add this issue to the impending strike's grievances. When union members among the weavers met alone on the second day of the strike, they voted 383–153 in favor of including the fines issue in the strike. Many observers later argued that including this issue led to both the strike's long duration and its ultimate defeat in April. Mill owners would have compromised on the size of the wage reduction, the argument went, but they would not relinquish managerial control over work processes and products by giving up their system of fines.

Both the wage issue and the fines issue affected New Bedford's textile workers in fundamental ways. A 10 percent wage cut meant that the collective income of an entire family would be slashed. Despite multiple wage earners in many families, textile workers still lived close to the margin, and a deduction for less-than-perfect work could easily wreak havoc on a family's budget. Many weavers argued that the perniciousness of this practice could be seen clearly when manufacturers fined the weaver but then retained and sold the cloth he or she had made.

Mentions of family connections—borne out by the statistical data—run through the newspaper coverage of the strike. On January 20 the New Bedford paper expressed astonishment that two textile-worker couples had announced their intentions to marry despite the strike. In addition, journalists often noted the conversations of married couples in weavers' strike meetings, most likely weavers like Thomas and Sophia Kimball, James and Ester Swallow, and Frank and Mary Sylvia, all in their twenties or thirties, all childless, and most fairly recent immigrants from French Canada, England, or elsewhere.[19] While only 15 percent of New Bedford's textile workers lived with spouses employed in the industry, 20 percent of the city's weavers (and more than 30 percent of female weavers) did. The rigid sexual division of labor in other textile occupations obviated opportunities for intra-occupational marriages in other jobs. In contrast to weavers' situations, less than 8 percent of female ring spinners and just over 8 percent of male mule spinners had spouses employed in textiles. Married women made up almost half of all the city's women weavers.

Firmly embedded in the mills' family systems of labor, New Bedford strikers often adopted strategies as families for dealing with the strike. Just as in the later Lowell strike, one of the most common of these was the decision by French Canadian families to return to their Canadian homes. Joseph Belgin, a fifty-two-year-old weaver, might have taken his family of six back to Quebec, because all four of his children, one son and three daughters, also worked as weavers, and all were born in Canada. The decision would have been slightly more difficult for Alexander Mounette's family of eleven, because his wife and children had all been born in the United States. At the same time, the fact that his four oldest children all worked in New Bedford's mills might have encouraged the family to move elsewhere for the duration of the strike. For those who had arrived from more distant shores, family strategies varied. Early in the strike, one reporter noted, single men living in boardinghouses before the strike now planned to return to their parental homes. These moves came less because of reduced incomes, according to this observer, and more because the young men's mothers, released from waged work by the strike, now had the time to care for their sons. Other families reportedly simply doubled up, combining meager household furnishings and presumably meager strike benefits as well.

Family-linked hiring practices meant that massive strikes, such as that of 1898, could very well leave textile families without any means of support other than union strike benefits. The John Flood family illustrates the potential impact. Though thirty-seven-year-old Flood worked as a loom fixer and therefore earned a fairly high wage and received strike benefits as well, neither

19. These individual examples are all taken from the 1900 Federal Manuscript Census; there is no evidence that any of these particular individuals did or did not participate in the 1898 strike.

salaries nor benefits were as high for other family members. Flood's wife, Margaret, his sister, Mary, and his fourteen-year-old daughter, Rose, all worked as weavers. The family's fifteen-year-old son, Bartholomay, worked as a backboy in the mule-spinning department of one of the mills. The seventeen-year-old daughter, Mary, remained at home as the family's housekeeper under normal circumstances, along with her eighty-two-year-old grandmother, and three siblings under the age of fourteen. Even combining union benefits, the strike spelled severe hardship for a family like this. The laborers' wages that Flood's seventy-eight-year-old father earned hardly made up the difference.

The types of family ties seen operating in both New Bedford and Alamance also functioned in other textile strike situations, though to a slightly lesser extent. (See appendix 2, tables A2.4, A2.5, and A2.6.) The surprisingly stubborn strikers of Evansville, Indiana, for example, tended to have more siblings working together than the other strike cities. Even in Oregon City, where only half the workers lived with other textile workers, most of those worked alongside siblings or parents.[20]

Though historians have paid the most attention to family systems of labor in the textile industry, familial hiring patterns show up in other industries as well. Shoe factory workers in Marlboro, Massachusetts, for example, lived in families quite similar to those of New Bedford's textile workers. Though about 12 percent of workers in each situation lived with children employed in the same industry, only 3 percent of Marlboro's shoe workers lived with spouses, and fully 55 percent lived with siblings employed in the industry.[21] More of the shoe-working women remained single into their thirties (see appendix 2, table A2.7), mirroring the patterns Mary Blewett found in her study of Lynn shoe workers.[22] Some of these older single women in Marlboro formed households with their siblings, while others remained living with unemployed and widowed mothers. The four daughters of Mary Flynn, for example, all worked as shoe stitchers or vampers. Marriage, however, appears to have ended the employment of these women. The wife of French Canadian shoe cutter Joseph Levigne listed no employment in 1900, while a daughter worked as a stitcher and two sons were employed as a cutter and a laster. The Irish family of shoe finisher Callahan McCarthy followed the same pattern, with wife Margaret unemployed and the three oldest daughters employed as shoe stitchers while two younger ones attended school.

20. 1900 Federal Manuscript Census data for Vanderburgh County, Indiana, and Clackamas County, Oregon. See appendix 2.

21. Information on Marlboro shoe workers comes from a sample of every fifth shoe worker in Marlboro collected from the 1900 Federal Manuscript Census for Middlesex County (and the city of Marlboro[ugh]), Massachusetts. See appendix 2.

22. Mary H. Blewett, *Men, Women, and Work: Class, Gender, and Protest* (Urbana: University of Illinois Press, 1988), pp. 346–47.

A strike of shoe workers in the seven largest factories in Marlboro in the fall of 1898 demonstrates many similarities to the textile strikes.[23] On November 10, 1898, the three great shoe companies in the town posted notices announcing that after Wednesday, November 23, they would not follow the current price lists. The companies would negotiate new price lists with individual employees and committees, but not with "the agents of the labor organizations."[24] The shoe workers of Marlboro did not wait. Before the new price lists could go into effect, and with the cooperation and support of the Boot and Shoe Workers' Union, workers struck on Tuesday, November 15. Though the town's employers consistently expressed amazement at the outbreak of the strike, the shoe workers felt quite differently. The ensuing strike lasted almost six months, ending with the virtual annihilation of the union in Marlboro, previously one of its strongholds.

Over the course of the strike, familiar family strategies appeared among the strikers. Because more than 40 percent of Marlboro's shoe workers were French Canadian, families like that of Joseph Levigne might return to Quebec, while others remained in town. In the opening weeks of the strike, at least two factory owners actually reduced rents in their tenement houses; at the tenth week, they were serving eviction notices. By the middle of February, merchants began to refuse credit both to families and to the shoe unions. By the time the union called the strike off in early May 1899, about one-third of the original 3,500 strikers had left town, many returning to Quebec. Another one-third had already returned to work, while the rest remained on strike.[25]

These striking shoe workers survived the same ways that textile workers did; in families where all wage earners worked in the struck industry, living off the wages of nonindustry members was simply impossible. Many families resorted to requesting municipal relief, which increased from assisting approximately 50 families a week before the strike to granting aid to 131 families during one week in January.[26] Marlboro's manufacturers managed in this strike to destroy not only the shoe workers' unions in the town but also many of their families. One group of observers noted in the aftermath of the strike: "Some of the workers will lose their homes by foreclosure. Others will lose most of their savings. . . . Families will be broken up, as in some cases the individual members of families will be obliged to take situ-

23. Unless otherwise noted, the story of this strike comes from coverage in the *Boston Globe*. See also chapter 7.

24. *Boston Globe*, November 15, 1898, p. 1.

25. Fay Spencer Baldwin et al., *The Strike of the Shoe Workers in Marlboro, Mass., Nov. 14, 1898–May 5, 1899: A Report, Prepared for the Civic Department of the Twentieth Century Club of Boston* (Boston: Boston Co-operative, [1899?]), microfiche edition, *Pamphlets in American History: Labor*, L815 (Sanford, N.C.: Microfilming Corporation of America 1979)], p. 14.

26. Ibid., p. 13.

ations in different places."[27] Family patterns of employment in this case ultimately led to family patterns of unemployment and further migration.

The black tobacco strikers of Winston, North Carolina, exhibited household patterns similar to those seen in families of white workers in both Massachusetts and North Carolina.[28] While only 30 percent of Winston-Salem's black tobacco workers lived with siblings employed in the town's tobacco factories, fully 20 percent lived with spouses so employed. (See appendix 2, table A2.6.) Families like those of Floyd and Nettie Neale, and William and Sallie Price, in both of which the husband worked as a tobacco roller and the wife as a stemmer, were almost as common as families like the Bitting family, where farm laborer Jacob Bitting's wife and two oldest children all worked as tobacco-factory stemmers. Though tobacco factory owners rarely discussed explicitly their use of black family labor, the census demonstrates that family linkages to the workplace certainly existed.

When the *Southern Tobacconist* complained that "the colored people cannot be taught . . . gratitude or justice, whatever the whites may do," they reflected the flip side of the refusal of southern tobacco factory owners' refusal to take on the paternalistic views of workers' families enjoyed by southern textile workers, all white.[29] Claiming that stemmers in southern plants "are mostly shiftless and unreliable, negro women and children, who crowd the stemming factories and plug plants in winter to get warmth and shelter and a little money, who in summer desert their work for sunshine and cheap living on what the genial sunny South affords as an easy living," southern tobacco manufacturers neglected to mention that in many sites, such as Winston, work generally ceased in June and July anyway.[30] The alleged "shiftlessness" on the part of these workers may have been in fact a reaction to the insecurity of the work itself.

The unreliability of waged labor for these workers, and the rigid racial assumptions of the South, combined with the close family connections to the workplace, came together for these workers to make the connection between workplace and family a potentially volatile one. When the workers at Brown & Williamson in Winston struck against a pay reduction in January 1898, they acted in a solidarity that had grown out of workplace-family connections.[31] Once again, family ties reinforced the workers' workplace "culture of complaint." Household solidarity quickly became community solidarity and forced their employer to rescind the wage cut.

27. Ibid., pp. 13–14.
28. Information on Winston tobacco workers comes from data on tobacco workers collected from the 1900 Federal Manuscript Census for Forsyth County, North Carolina. See appendix 2.
29. *Southern Tobacconist and Manufacturers' Record*, December 18, 1900 (12:45), p. 1.
30. *Southern Tobacconist and Manufacturers' Record*, April 16, 1901 (13:9), p. 6. See also Dolores E. Janiewski, *Sisterhood Denied: Race, Gender, and Class in a New South Community* (Philadelphia: Temple University Press, 1985).
31. See chapter 4 for a more complete story of this strike.

If household solidarity could transmute itself into community support for strikes and strikers, family solidarity could lead to several distinctive types of strategies for strike survival. We have already seen how particular families might choose to leave town during a strike, especially if their original home was not too distant. Whether French Canadian families in Massachusetts or Cuban cigar makers' families in Key West, returning to one's original home—and country—provided one way for families to deal with the hardships experienced during strikes. Family members could also bring pressure on other family members to toe the picket line, and family pressures often determined whether participants remained on strike or returned to work. These latter family pressures did not always need to come from family members working within the same industry. Family connections across industry lines could also become crucial in strikes.

In Evansville, Indiana, for example, there were relatively few intrafamily connections, compared with other locations within the textile industry. Only 63 percent of Evansville's cotton workers lived in households with other textile employees in them. (See appendix 2, table A2.5.) In this case, however, this may have contributed to the surprising duration of the strike there in 1900.[32] While strikers' families lost the wages of striking cotton workers within their households, other family members continued to bring money into the household coffers. In two Evansville families headed by females, for example, daughters worked as weavers in the cotton mill while sons worked as coal miners and "machine hands." While the occupations of these cotton workers' siblings may or may not have contributed to beliefs about the strike itself, in either case they allowed the striking mill workers a degree of freedom in their strike decisions.

In other strikes, family ties beyond the industry under examination could be crucial in an even more direct manner, as demonstrated by the strikes in both Oregon City, Oregon, and Wilkes-Barre, Pennsylvania, in 1902. In both cases, the strikes appear to have started at least in part because workers had knowledge of unions within their families yet outside their industry. In the case of Oregon City, for example, workers at the Willamette Pulp & Paper Company organized in early April what local papers termed the "local union of the American Federation of Labor."[33] Though workers at the Oregon City Woolen Mill formed their own union, a branch of the United Textile Workers, the day their strike began, the line separating the two unions from each other often blurred. On April 25, four days after the woolen mill strike began, the *Courier-Herald* reported that one hundred new members had

32. Unless otherwise noted, the story of this strike comes from coverage in the *Evansville Journal*. Information on Evansville cotton mill workers comes from data collected from the 1900 Federal Manuscript Census for Vanderburgh County, Indiana. See appendix 2.

33. *Oregon City Courier-Herald* [hereafter cited as OCC-H], April 25, 1902, p. 3, for example. Unless otherwise noted, the story of this strike comes from the *OCC-H* and the *Oregon City Enterprise*. The story of this strike is told in more detail in chapter 5.

joined the AFL's federal labor union, while more than two hundred belonged to the textile union. The paper claimed that "some of the men belong to both organizations."[34] Later in the strike, paper mill workers provided financial support for strikers as well as assistance in negotiating the strike's end.

To some extent, the family ties of Oregon City workers contributed to the solidaristic bonds expressed in the two unions.[35] While only about half of Oregon City workers lived in households with other woolen mill workers, the lowest percentage of any of the selected data sets, almost 20 percent of the woolen mill workers lived in households containing paper mill workers. (See appendix 2, table A2.8.) Furthermore, almost 25 percent of woolen mill workers' households contained both more than one woolen mill worker and at least one paper mill worker. The nature of the relationships among these workers differed by the sex of the woolen mill worker. Women workers most often had siblings working in the paper mills (77.7 percent), though one-third had both siblings and fathers employed in the town's paper mills. Male workers were most likely (55 percent) to live with unrelated paper mill workers, though 22 percent of them had siblings and 22 percent had fathers in the paper mills. With fewer than 3,500 residents in Oregon City in 1900, both direct family ties and other close associations with union members played important roles in the strike.[36]

The story in Wilkes-Barre, Pennsylvania, is somewhat different.[37] The Wilkes-Barre strike demonstrates how the family, embedded in the community, could amplify resistance to both employers and inequality. When the lace workers of Wilkes-Barre struck in 1902, it was not for reasons of their own but in support of the coal miners' strike going on at the time. As recounted in chapter 4, the lace workers' strike began when union members discovered that five young workers had relatives scabbing in local struck coal mines. Union members gave these co-workers the choice of either quitting their jobs or having their relatives quit working in the mines. With two women refusing to do either, the lace unions demanded that mill management fire them. When the mill's manager refused, the lace unions voted to strike.

The federal commission empaneled to investigate the 1902 coal strike ended up addressing the lace mill strike as well. The wife of one strikebreaker described the trials suffered by her fifteen-year-old lace-working son:

---

34. *OCC-H*, April 25, 1902, p. 3.

35. Information on Oregon City woolen mill workers comes from data collected from the 1900 Federal Manuscript Census for Clackamas County, Oregon. See appendix 2.

36. U.S. Bureau of the Census, *Population at the Twelfth Census, 1900*, vol. 1, part 1 (Washington, D.C.: Government Printing Office, 1901), p. 324.

37. Unless otherwise noted, the story of this strike comes from the *AW&CR*, vol. 16, and the *Wilkes-Barre Times* [hereafter cited as *WBT*]. See chapter 4.

> About two o'clock my son came home. . . . From the Lace Mill, and he had a note and it said, "Mr. Richardson, as long as you are an unfair worker, you must either quit your work, or we can't work with your son." Signed, "The Brass Bobbin Winders of the Lace Mill." He was to come back the next morning and tell them what he said. So the next morning I sent him [the boy] back. . . . I told him to tell them his father didn't give up his position for his.[38]

The Richardson boy was paid by the mill throughout the ensuing strike, as were the other young folks whose continued employment provoked the strike.[39] Mrs. Richardson's testimony before the commission spelled out the difficult situation in which children on both sides of both strikes found themselves during the lace strike. Instructions from parents or siblings carried great weight for the young lace workers. Other testimony by both coal miners and their daughters spelled out the varied reasons behind child labor in the textile mills of the Pennsylvania anthracite region, describing injured fathers, ill mothers, and general family indebtedness.[40]

The family ties of the lace workers explain the importance of the coal strike issue to the workers. While almost one-third (32 percent) of all lace workers lived with at least one coal mine worker in their household, 41 percent of the women did.[41] (See appendix 2, table A2.8.) Younger lace workers were also more likely than older lace workers to reside with coal miners. (Some 44 percent of women between fifteen and nineteen years old, and 29 percent of men in that age-group lived with a miner.) Most of the miners these young women lived with were either their fathers (56 percent) or their brothers (46 percent). This explains both why the coal strike was so important to the young lace workers and why they would have found it difficult to convince the miners in their families to change their minds about the coal strike. Lace workers comprehended coal miners' solidarity and brought that solidarity into their own work lives precisely because they shared such personal family ties with miners.

Demonstrating the fierce outrage common to coal strikes in isolated regions, miners' solidarity often included violent tactics to enforce strike discipline. Local newspapers during the strike were filled with references to "effigies of unfair workers" and other "outrages."[42] The final report of the President's Anthracite Coal Strike Commission noted: "Men who chose to be employed,

38. Testimony of Lillie Richardson, in U.S. Anthracite Coal Strike Commission, *Proceedings of the Anthracite Coal Strike Commission* (Washington, D.C.: Hanna & Budlong, 1902–3), pp. 3534–35.

39. Ibid., p. 3536; see also the testimony of J. W. Doran, p. 3558, and Samuel Scott, p. 4435.

40. Ibid., pp. 2846–69, 2923–3184. None of these involved workers in the Wilkes-Barre lace mill, but instead focused on child labor in area silk mills.

41. Information on the Wilkes-Barre lace workers comes from data collected from the 1900 Federal Manuscript Census for Luzerne County, Pennsylvania. See appendix 2.

42. See, for example, *WBT*, June 9, 1902, p. 6, and June 12, 1902, p. 2.

or who remained at work, were assailed and threatened, and they and their families terrorized and intimidated. In several instances the houses of such workmen were dynamited, or otherwise assaulted, and the lives of unoffending women and children put in jeopardy."[43] Speaking on behalf of the coal mine operators, John T. Lenahan proclaimed, "Let me ask you, in God's name, what shadow of an excuse can there be found in the exercise in [the boycott] against the women, against the girl, against the poor babe that has done naught in this world to wrong a soul."[44]

Coal operators, lace mill owners, even the lace workers' union leaders in Philadelphia—none of these understood the import to miners' relatives of employing girls and boys whose family members scabbed during the coal strike. The union call to "brothers and sisters" for solidarity was taken quite literally in Wilkes-Barre.

If the Wilkes-Barre lace workers' strike provides one extreme example of family issues leading to a strike, other strikes provide different examples of how such family issues might arise. Two specific types of strikes illustrate this. Both strikes against the location of employment and strikes against child labor illustrate just how complex such family issues could become.

Struggles by the cigar makers' union to stamp out tenement-house production provide one such example. Throughout the final decades of the nineteenth century, the union repeatedly attempted to rid its industry of this system in which employers provided housing in exchange for the products produced by workers' families therein. The young Samuel Gompers achieved his first fame beyond the union through his efforts to establish New York State's first laws against tenement-house cigar production in the 1870s.[45] By the late 1880s, scofflaw producers brought the issue to the attention of the union again.

The 1888 strike against a resumption of tenement-house cigar production in New York City, described in chapter 3 was one such effort.[46] Complaining that declining prices and competition with machine-made cigars necessitated revival of cheaper tenement-house production, manufacturers announced wage cuts in early 1888. As one striker put it, "Three years ago I earned from $10 to $12 per week regularly. My husband would earn $18. Now we

43. *Report of the Anthracite Coal Strike Commission, 1902* (Philadelphia: Anthracite Bureau of Information, 1920), p. 73.

44. *WBT*, February 10, 1903, p. 9.

45. *The Samuel Gompers Papers*, vol. 2: *The Early Years of the American Federation of Labor, 1887–90*, ed. Stuart Kaufman (Urbana: University of Illinois Press, 1987), pp. 169–210; Patricia A. Cooper, *Once a Cigar Maker: Men, Women, and Work Culture* (Urbana: University of Illinois Press, 1987), p. 22; Eileen Boris, *Home to Work: Motherhood and the Politics of Industrial Homework in the United States* (Cambridge: Cambridge University Press, 1994), pp. 21–47; Dorothee Schneider, *Trade Unions and Community: The German Working Class in New York City, 1870–1900* (Urbana: University of Illinois Press, 1994), pp. 98–100.

46. Unless otherwise noted, the story of this strike comes from coverage in the *New York Sun*.

find it hard work between us to earn $12. Before we struck the price for rolling was $5 and $5.25 per 1,000. He reduced the rate all round $1.75. That would make it difficult to earn $3.50 per week."[47] That husband and wife clearly shared responsibility for earning their family's income.

Seven years later, the New York State Bureau of Labor Statistics carried out a study of tenement-house cigar production. The examination included an inspection of tenement houses on East Thirty-eighth Street, perhaps the same ones owned by the firm of Jacoby & Bookman that experienced evictions during the 1888 strike. During the 1888 evictions, reporters had commented on the prevalence of young children among the tenement cigar workers.[48] The 1895 state inspecting team took the same notice, bemoaning that in at least one case "the mother has laid aside her work for a moment and taken her child from its cradle to comfort it."[49] The inspectors went on to complain that the children in such families worked from infancy and, even when attending school, returned home in the evenings to work alongside their parents. They then quoted a former member of the state assembly, who claimed that manufacturers argued "that the cigar makers now employed in tenement-house shops prefer this system of work."[50]

The tenement production issue erupted once again in the huge strike and lockout of cigar makers in 1900 recounted in chapter 1.[51] The three tenement houses served with eviction papers by Homan & Harburger during that strike provide insight into the living and working conditions of Bohemian tenement-house workers at the turn of the twentieth century.[52] More than 85 percent of the residents in the three buildings lived with at least one person listed by the census as being a cigar worker. Those who did not live with cigar workers included a clerk, a grocer, and several families who had immigrated less than a month before the census count and did not yet have jobs. Furthermore, these tended to be young families. Fully 43 percent of the 179 individuals in the three buildings were under the age of fifteen; almost half of those (thirty-five) were under the age of six.

With so many young children in the families of Bohemian tenement-house cigar makers, many of the young immigrant families would have been quite glad to have the opportunity for "the mother [to lay] aside her work for a

47. "Cigarmaker Strikers and Pickets," *New York Daily Graphic*, February 15, 1888, p. 774.

48. *New York Sun*, February 15, 1888, p. 3.

49. New York Bureau of Labor Statistics, *Twelfth Annual Report* (Albany: Bureau of Statistics of Labor, 1895) [hereafter cited as N.Y. BLS, *12th AR*], "Tenement-House Cigarmaking in New York City," p. 547.

50. Ibid., p. 553.

51. Unless otherwise noted, the story of this strike comes from coverage in the *New York World* and *New York Tribune*. See also chapter 1.

52. Information on Homan & Harburger tenements comes from the 1900 Federal Manuscript Census for New York County, Borough of Manhattan, Enumeration District 759, Sheets 16B–18B. See appendix 2.

Inspecting tenement cigar production, East 38th Street, New York City, 1895, perhaps in tenements of Jacoby & Bookman (New York Bureau of Labor Statistics, *Twelfth Annual Report*).

moment and taken her child from its cradle to comfort it."[53] While higher wages in factory production would have made up some of the difference once some family members could no longer contribute to production, the end of the tenement-house system certainly would have spelled disaster for some of the families among the tenement residents. Union cigar makers did not have mixed feelings about the end of tenement production, but the tenement-house workers themselves certainly did.

The same type of ambivalence was reflected in the Omaha tailors' strike of 1889, in which tailors battled among themselves over the issue of working in their homes.[54] Though that strike was fought at first against an attempted price reduction for the tailors' work, it also demanded that all work be done in employers' shops rather than in the homes of the tailors. August Beerman, a supporter of the Journeymen Tailors' Union in Omaha, had gathered enough votes during a recent revision of the union's bylaws to insert a clause requiring "that all new comers must do the work in the bosses back shop."[55] Beerman thus followed the lead of the 1887 convention of the tailors' union, when it resolved "that we unequivocally condemn the system in our trade of having the work done in our homes; and while we recognize the system

53. N.Y. BLS, *12th AR*, p. 547.
54. Unless otherwise cited, the story of this strike comes from coverage in the *Omaha Daily Bee*.
55. Letter from Beerman in *The Tailor* 3 (June 1893): 5.

to be deep-rooted, we would recommend the gradual substitution of the system of workshops provided by the employers of trades."[56] Though all the Omaha tailors supported restoring wages, some could not support the attack on home work. The result was that "the men working at home, and who had the assistance of members of their family and others, withdrew from the national association and formed another union, which, meeting with the views of the home workers, was incorporated as the Omaha Tailors' Union."[57]

As described in chapter 3, the tailors' union battle against home work met with resistance that was both fierce and at times covert. Because these tailors wanted to project the image of highly skilled and independent craftsmen, they could hardly acknowledge openly the labor of their allegedly unskilled wives and children that went into their products. At the same time, the money earned through those family members' labor contributed to the tailors' standard of living, a standard the tailors wanted to claim as equivalent to that of any other highly skilled male worker. In other words, custom tailors attempted to pass off what was really a family's earnings as an individual's wages. Neither the custom tailor himself nor his employer openly acknowledged the other laborers working in the tailor's home.

In this way, the tailors' "back shop" issue was quite similar to the issue of child labor in general. In the 1893 Overland cotton strike in Denver, for example, local labor activists quickly seized on the issue of child labor in the mill.[58] One of their earliest strike strategy proposals was to gain public sympathy by accusing the company of breaking Colorado's child labor laws. Workers gave the local newspaper stories of children as young as seven years old employed in the mills even before the strike officially began. Responding in kind, the mill's manager denied all child labor allegations, arguing that "if there are any in the mill under age, it is because their parents have preferred to bring them there, and their age is so near 14 as to be not within the knowledge of the management."[59] The issue soon died, however, as the strikers themselves seemed unwilling to confront the issue. While the manager's statement about parental preference might not have been completely true, economic decisions that parents made did sometimes entail having children work alongside their parents.

Even if the child labor issue per se died out in the Denver strike, the power of strikers' family relationships is evident throughout the strike. As workers

56. Constitution and By-laws of the Journeymen Tailors' National Union, Adopted August 1887, "American Labor Unions' Constitutions and Proceedings," pp. 19–20, microform edition (Ann Arbor: University Microforms, 1980s–).

57. Nebraska Bureau of Labor and Industrial Statistics, *Second Biennial Report for 1889 and 1890* (Lincoln: Lincoln Paper House, 1890), p. 337.

58. Unless otherwise cited, the story of this strike comes from coverage in the *Rocky Mountain News* [hereafter cited as *RMN*].

59. *RMN*, May 13, 1893, p. 3.

began to return to work, continuing strikers tended to apply pressure along family lines. For example, it was reported that when a striking family of four by the name of Stuart returned to work, they "were induced to leave" again as a group, not as individuals. Similarly, a "committee from the strikers" visited a Mrs. Fisk to convince her to take her son, Dan, out of the mills.[60] In other words, operatives in the Denver mills functioned very much as members of families rather than as individuals. In this setting, charges of child labor came loaded with a raft of assumptions about family obligations.

Similar ambivalence appeared in the strike best known as the "children's strike" of Philadelphia textile workers. During May 1903, leaders of the Central Union of Textile Workers in the city of Philadelphia announced that they would strike on June 1 in order to gain a fifty-five-hour workweek.[61] Many manufacturers claimed that the strike would never be successful, but quite a few plants gave in to workers' demands for shorter hours even before the strike began. Somewhere between 50,000 and 100,000 workers particip-ated in the strike. Unlike in the city of Lowell, where textile workers were striking at the same time, the Philadelphia strikers worked in a number of discreet specialty industries. Most of the firms making up the city's textile industry made some sort of specialty product. Woolen ingrain carpets, cotton upholstery, and hosiery and other knit goods made up some of the city's products. Most individual firms were small; the 1900 Manufacturing Census reveals an average of sixty-six employees in each individual establishment.[62] Melvin Copeland, in his history of cotton manufacturing in the United States, attributed Philadelphia's preeminence in such specialty production to the early presence of skilled immigrants in the city.[63] These skilled workers brought their own brand of craft unionism to the city's textile industry (see chapter 7). Employed in the "fancy" branches of industry, these workers viewed themselves as special too.

The city of brotherly love also had a high rate of child labor in its mills, compared with other Northeastern locations. Boys and girls between the ages of ten and fifteen made up more than 12 percent of the workforce in Philadelphia industry in 1900.[64] The initial statement by the "working committee" of the Central Textile Union stressed the effects of long hours of work on women and children in particular:

60. *RMN*, May 18, 1893, p. 8.

61. Unless otherwise noted, the story of this strike comes from coverage in the *Philadelphia Inquirer* [hereafter cited as *Inquirer*] and the *Philadelphia Public Ledger*.

62. U.S. Census Bureau, *Twelfth Census of the United States, 1900*, vol. 3: *Manufactures*, part 2: *States and Territories* (Washington, D.C.: Government Printing Office, 1902), pp. 784–91.

63. Melvin Thomas Copeland, *The Cotton Manufacturing Industry of the United States* (New York: A. M. Kelley, 1966), p. 31.

64. U.S. Bureau of the Census, *Occupations at the Twelfth Census* (Washington, D.C.: Government Printing Office, 1904), pp. 676–77. Some 17 percent of all women in textiles were under sixteen years old, while only 8 percent of men were that young.

The request for shorter working hours is made principally for the sake of the children and women and for these reasons:

To improve health.

To increase the opportunity for education.

To gain time for enjoying some of life's pleasures.

To get some of the benefits from the use of machinery.

To enable the bread winners to spend more time with their families.

To give the workers more than a bare half hour in which to eat their noon meals.

For six years the organized textile workers of Philadelphia have been trying in vain to persuade the politician-controlled Legislature . . . to pass a law which would reduce the working hours of children and women and stop them from doing any night work. It is the women and children workers who are the most disorganized and who can least resist poverty on one hand and a few extra pennies on the other. The unions have, therefore, decided to make a supreme effort at this time on their own account for the sake of humanity.[65]

Even in the early days of the strike, however, workers evinced conflicting views on child labor. The hosiery section of the industry tended to employ the most women and children of any of the specific industries in Philadelphia. In at least one instance, members of a hosiery workers' union voted against striking for the shorter workweek. As the newspaper explained it, "The children, who did not belong [to the union], wanted the shorter work week, and walked out of the mills. There was nothing left for the grown-up workers to do but to follow them."[66] When strike leaders held a mass meeting specifically for hosiery workers the next day, however, the relative lack of women and children in the audience drew attention from the speakers, one of whom charged that "the little ones had been kept away purposely by their parents, to prevent the public from learning how their fathers and mothers were violating the factory act."[67] Much like the Denver strikers more than a decade earlier, the adult workers themselves appeared to be shying away from the issue of child labor. In Philadelphia, even the strikers' leaders tended to blame parents rather than employers for its prevalence.

Less than two weeks later, the issue regained prominence in the strike when famous labor activist "Mother" Mary Jones arrived in the city. On the second day of her visit, the strikers organized a mass march led by child laborers. The *Philadelpia Inquirer* described the scene:

65. *Inquirer*, June 1, 1903, p. 16.
66. *Inquirer*, June 5, 1903, p. 1.
67. *Inquirer*, June 6, 1903, p. 4.

Many of the small paraders seemed to be not yet in their teens. They carried small American flags over their shoulders, and some of the more stalwart boys marched with banners above their heads, bearing terse epigrams. . . .

"We Want to Go to School."

"More Time to Eat Our Meals."

"More Schools and Less Hospitals."

"Fifty-five Hours or Nothing."

"A Full Dinner Pail and an Hour to Empty It."

Along the line of march the youthful toilers elicited expressions of pity and sympathy from the crowds that lined the sidewalks.[68]

Mother Jones well understood the emotional appeal such "youthful toilers" made. When she spoke to the gathered strikers and their supporters,

she lifted two small boys upon the table, and she began her address with her hands resting affectionately upon their heads. She said in part:

"One of these little boys has had his tongue taken out by the machinery; the other has had his head almost severed in the mills."[69]

Throughout Mother Jones's involvement in the strike, she staged these types of heartrending tableaus. At the beginning of July, she extended this tactic to what was perhaps its logical extreme. She organized a "Children's March" to speak with President Teddy Roosevelt about the plight of the Philadelphia strikers. Though the marchers' ranks were soon depleted, a few dozen men and six boys ultimately traveled to Oyster Bay, Long Island, where President Roosevelt declined to meet with them, citing lack of federal jurisdiction over the issue.[70]

While Mother Jones eventually faded from the strike scene, the issue of child labor remained around a bit longer, though at some distance. Toward the end of July, for example, one of Pennsylvania's factory inspectors wrote to the strikers' executive committee thanking them for their information on enforcement of child labor law. He then asked them to assist him by letting him know of all further violations. In the end, perhaps the most telling comment on child labor came in that very early comment about "mothers and fathers violating the child labor act," for here as elsewhere, children participated in waged labor not because they wanted to mimic their parents or avoid school, but because their families needed their wages in order to survive. Ending child labor thus evoked mixed emotions among parents. A shorter workweek was a more obvious benefit, allowing all members of textile families to spend more time in other activities while still providing

68. *Inquirer*, June 18, 1903, p. 1.

69. Ibid., p. 2.

70. Letter from B. F. Barnes to Mother Jones, August 1, 1903, from *The Correspondence of Mother Jones*, ed. Edward M. Steel (Pittsburgh: University of Pittsburgh Press, 1985), p. 48.

Philadelphia textile boys, ready for Mother Jones's "Children's March," 1903 (*Philadelphia Inquirer*, July 8, 1903, p. 2).

for their sustenance. The grand Philadelphia strike, however, would attain neither. By early October, most strikers had returned to work. The shorter hours many of them now faced had more to do with seasonal slowness in their product markets than with any employer concessions.

One strike displayed a different type of ambivalence over the issue of child labor. Cigar makers in Detroit, Michigan, struck at noon on June 4, 1895.[71] Members of the Cigar Makers' International Union were striking specifically against the practice of companies' setting up what the union referred to as "angel shops." Union members believed that the depression of the 1890s had encouraged employers to set up such separate workshops in order to avoid paying high wages to the city's unionized hand cigar rollers. Instead, "underpaid women and child labor" toiled in these annex shops.[72] The union's struggle, which dragged on for more than a year, consistently held up the use of child labor as the ultimate evil against which they battled. Samuel Gompers compared the Detroit battle to the union's earlier battles to fight tenement-house cigar making and similar fights against sweatshop

71. Unless otherwise noted, the story of this strike comes from coverage in the *Detroit Free Press* [hereafter cited as *DFP*].

72. Michigan Bureau of Labor and Industrial Statistics, *Thirteenth Annual Report* (Lansing: Robert Smith & Company, 1896), p. 350.

clothing manufacture.[73] By September, strikers were meeting with state factory inspectors to pass along information on child labor in the cigar factories' shops. Photographers hired by the union took pictures of "girl labor" in the factories, both for the use of the factory inspectors and for distribution as publicity for the strike.

The union met some fifty "Cubans, Spaniards, and Mexicans" brought to the city by one employer at the end of August, and explained the situation to them. At least a dozen of these men immediately refused to work as strikebreakers, announcing that "they would not work with girls."[74] Wording the issue this way helps clarify the connection between the "illy paid women" and the "child labor" in this struggle. A federal study of child labor based largely on the 1900 census found that in that year Detroit had some 29 boys and 534 girls between the ages of ten and fifteen working in tobacco and cigar factories.[75] The strike carried on in Detroit, in other words, was a strike against the employment of girls. In 1890 some 93 percent of females employed in the city's tobacco and cigar factories were between the ages of ten and twenty-four.[76] At least half of these were under the age of fifteen. As one Detroit minister put it in his comments on a state report on child labor, of the more than five thousand women employed in Michigan in 1895, "more than half the number set down as women are simply half-developed girls still in their teens."[77]

Did Detroit's cigar makers make a distinction between the child labor of "girls" under the age of fifteen and those sixteen to twenty-four years old? The union made attempts at various points in the strike to try to bring the women workers into the union, and during such attempts, no mention was made of the age of the workers. Female as well as male members of the unions were fined for strikebreaking activities. As in other situations, as discussed in chapter 3, the cigar makers' union upheld the strictest craft unionism only when that unionism did not threaten the union's strength. Otherwise their membership qualifications could become remarkably flexible. In Detroit this meant that union members simultaneously fought against child labor and attempted to recruit the factories' "girls" into their organization. Perhaps this overlap of the categories of "child" and "female" explains why the rallying cry of this strike could remain that of "no child labor." The "children"

---

73. Samuel Gompers to N. Jackson, September 4, 1895, in American Federation of Labor Letterpress Copybooks of Samuel Gompers and William Green, 1883–1925, microfilm of originals at Library of Congress, 11/12:385.

74. *DFP*, August 28, 1895, p. 5.

75. U.S. Census Bureau, *Child Labor in the United States, Based on Unpublished Information Derived from the Schedules of the Twelfth Census, 1900* (Washington, D.C.: Government Printing Office, 1904–7), p. 96.

76. U.S. Department of the Interior, Census Office, *Report on the Population of the United States at the Eleventh Census: 1890, Part 1* (Washington, D.C.: Government Printing Office, 1894–1895), pp. 664–65.

77. *DFP*, November 18, 1895, p. 8.

in Detroit's angel shops were not young men serving some sort of apprenticeship, as might be argued by textile workers about the employment of "back boys" in mule spinning, for example. In the eyes of Detroit cigar makers, the young women of the angel shops had two strikes against them: they were both young and female.

The potentially scabbing Cubans did not state that they were returning to Chicago because they did not believe in breaking the strike, or because they believed that child labor was evil. Rather, they objected to working "with girls." Similarly, when cigar makers marched in Detroit's 1895 Labor Day parade, one sign carried asked, "Shall the father support the child or the child the father?"[78] The question was not whether parents should support their children or not, but rather a statement of working-class male duty. Despite their flexibility in expanding union membership when necessary, cigar makers, in Detroit as elsewhere, continued to believe that men should receive union wages high enough to support families, rather than forcing wives and daughters into the workforce. This famed "family wage" was, for cigar makers, the union's ultimate goal.

Though in Detroit this issue of child and female labor was as "real" as it was rhetorical, in many other strike situations "the family" appeared more rhetorical than real. While most of this chapter has examined the various implications of actual families in the strikes under consideration, the very concept of "the family" also had intriguing manifestations in strikes. The most well-known ideological manifestation of families in unions today lies in union leaders' exhortations to union "brothers and sisters." At the turn of the twentieth century, however, they tended to address explicitly "brothers" alone. In addition, the relationships among male and female workers, if not linked by biological family ties, tended to look much more like the relationship of fathers to daughters than of brothers and sisters. As such, it could easily help reinforce extreme inequality of women and men on strike and in the workplace.

One of the best examples of this comes once again from the Kearney, New Jersey, thread mill strike of the 1890–91, first seen in chapter 3 as an example of untrammeled craft unionism and then examined again in chapter 4 as an example of ethnic tensions.[79] Compounding both, age differences between the male mule spinners who officially ran the strike, and the young female ring spinners who attempted to assist them, gave the entire strike an almost sinister cast. The mule spinners repeatedly called their young female co-workers "girls" and argued that the failure of these young women to organize before the strike's inception proved their unfitness for union consideration. This combination continued throughout the strike. The paternalistic mule

78. *DFP*, September 3, 1895, p. 1.
79. Unless otherwise noted, the story of this strike comes from coverage in the *Newark Daily Advertiser* and the *New York Times*.

spinners allowed the young women to help collect various donations, but then, the women charged, used the money so collected for their own purposes.

Even the AFL participated in this infantilization of the women, touting the men's heroism and using Superintendent Walmsley's abuse of women workers to demonstrate the "system of tyranny and persecution" at the Clark O. N. T. Thread mills.[80] This appeal to AFL members' sense of morality called on union members to sympathize as fathers with the strikers battling in order to improve the conditions of helpless girl workers.

In fact, the official Kearney strikers battled only for their own benefit. The mule spinners' young co-workers, who were not really their daughters but women of a different ethnicity and religion though of the appropriate age, could be used to gain public sympathy. They were on their own, however, when it came to addressing their own issues or answering their own financial needs.

From Johnie Pope to Mother Jones to the doughty mule spinners of Kearney, the "families" examined in this chapter include both biological families and the ideological manifestations of sex and age. Actual family and household ties most often increased solidarity in cross-gender strikes. Family issues such as child labor or the location of work had mixed effects, often provoking public sympathy for strikers' plights, but equally often dividing the strikers themselves according to their own self-interests. More ideological expressions of family could diminish strike solidarity, as the paternalism of male strikers toward female co-workers could undercut attempts of women to achieve—or even vocalize—their own demands. How this happened even in situations in which craft unions attempted to develop more inclusive styles of unionism is the focus of the following chapter.

80. See *The Tailor*, 2 (April 1891): 6; and *Seattle Post-Intelligencer*, March 16, 1891, p. 8. Most of these comments referred back to the 1888 strike of women workers when Walmsley had first begun working in the Kearney mills. See *New York Daily Graphic*, January 25, 1888, p. 614.

7   *Industrial Unions in the AFL?*

"We stood united, but we fell divided."
—*Philadelphia Public Ledger*, September 2, 1903

In December 1897, members of the Arkwright Club, a group of Massachusetts and other northern New England cotton manufacturers, announced that competition with southern mills forced them to equalize wages by instituting a regional wage cut of at least 10 percent. Though the manufacturers of New Bedford initially refused to join in the club's report, explaining that they did not see direct competition with mills in the South, they soon gave in to peer pressure and announced that they too would institute a wage cut. Ironically, the mills of New Bedford became the focal point of the ensuing strike.[1]

When the wage cut went into effect on Monday, January 17, 1898, pickets surrounded virtually all the city's mills. The management of the Bristol mill, which manufactured prints in competition with nearby Fall River's mills, attempted to run its plant that Monday. While pickets had shown up outside the gates as early as 5:00 a.m., someone had removed two planks from the back of the mill's fence, allowing some fifty strikebreakers to enter surreptitiously. Strikers soon discovered the breach and attempted to block it with a combination of telephone wire and a discarded Christmas tree. That evening, more than one thousand strikers gathered to greet the small squad of strikebreakers as they left the mill. Soon the crowd began to throw rocks through the mill's windows. Police called to the scene had difficulty seeing the culprits in the darkness of the winter evening, so they made no arrests. Strikers managed to make enough trouble and cause enough damage to the mill to discourage the city's manufacturers from attempting to operate their mills. The following day, none of the city's mills even tried to open. They would remain closed until the beginning of April.

The strongest and oldest of the textile workers' unions, that of the mule spinners, strove to keep the strike focused on the wage issue, but the mills' less-well-organized weavers had other ideas (see chapter 6). Having already

1. Unless otherwise noted, the story of this strike comes from coverage in the *Boston Globe* [hereafter cited as *Globe*] and the *New Bedford Morning Mercury* [hereafter cited as *MM*], as well as the description of the strike in Mary H. Blewett, *Constant Turmoil: The Politics of Industrial Life in Nineteenth-Century New England* (Amherst: University of Massachusetts Press, 2000), chap. 10, pp. 338–87.

decided to struggle against the practice of fining prevalent in some of the city's mills, New Bedford's weavers—both unionized and not—voted repeatedly to include the fines issue in the strike's demands. Both gender and ethnicity overlay and were intertwined with occupational, organizational, and political differences. Throughout the strike of 1898, such divisions complicated the management of the strike and ultimately undermined the New Bedford strikers.

The New Bedford strike illustrates many of the problems textile workers faced as they attempted to address the new developments of the industry at the turn of the twentieth century. As the Philadelphia Central Union of Textile Workers stated in its 1903 constitution: "The days when single unions were able to secure for themselves better conditions are fast going past. The time for united action by all branches of the same industry has come."[2] Though garment and textile unions provide the most explicit examples of this trend, all four of the industries examined in this book displayed some movement away from pure and simple craft unionism and into the new realm of what would eventually come to be known as industrial unionism. In all four industries, the expansionist moves began with the amalgamation of pre-existing individual craft unions. Only in locations where no unions had existed previously did the amalgamated unions begin to act like industrial unions, bringing all workers in a factory into a single local union. At times the amalgamation of craft unions could function to provide space and voice for women workers. At other times, male craft unionists simply ignored their female co-workers' demands. The ways in which the 1898 strike forced New Bedford's workers to confront these issues appear particularly convoluted, but they also illuminate trends seen in other, more straightforward strikes as well.

In some ways, the New Bedford strike can be seen as an early example of the great benefits gained through the amalgamation of unions. The New Bedford strike committee consisted of five delegates from each of the city's five preexisting textile unions: the mule spinners', weavers', carders', loom fixers', and slasher-tenders' unions. Within days of the strike's inception, however, this committee faced serious disagreements, the primary one being over the strike's purpose. Four of the five unions wanted to fight solely against the proposed wage cut. The fifth union, that of the weavers, voted on the evening of the strike's second day to add to the demands their union's separate fight against the system of fines that was prevalent in some of the city's mills.

Weavers represented one of the only textile occupations that came close to containing equal numbers of men and women. They also represented the largest single occupation in New Bedford, making up almost 40 percent of

2. "Preamble," *Constitution of the Central Union of Textile Workers of Philadelphia and Vicinity* (Philadelphia: New Era Co-operative Press, 1903), microfiche edition, *Pamphlets in American History: Labor*, L2125 (Sanford, N.C.: Microfilming Corporation of America, 1979), n.p. (p. 1).

the city's textile workers.³ In the week before the strike began, both a mass meeting of all the mills' weavers, union and nonunion alike, and the meeting of union weavers only on January 18, voted overwhelmingly to add the fines issue to the strike. The other unions, in particular that of the mule spinners, complained vociferously, arguing that the fines issue simply muddled what would otherwise be a clear-cut fight. But weavers felt otherwise. As William Cunnane, president of the weavers' union, put it, if the battle were fought and won against the wage reduction alone, "victory will be but a shadow and a delusion, a thing without substance and without shape, something for which they have fought and suffered, and from which every one but [the weavers] themselves derive substantial benefits."⁴ Cunnane even argued early on that behind the announced wage reduction that had spurred the strike lay the New Bedford manufacturers' fears of a weavers' strike planned for spring 1898.

Cunnane's early defense of the fines issue demonstrates the difficulties inherent in having the various textile occupations work together. A major champion of the fines issue, weaver Harriet Pickering, pointed out in an interview with the *Boston Globe* that the causes of the "defects" for which weavers faced fines often came from the work of workers earlier in the production process: "If the spinner or the speeder tender makes a bad piecing of the yarn and it breaks out in the loom, the fine comes on the weaver. . . . It is quite customary for the warper, or slasher, or the overseer, or designer, to make a miscalculation and get too many ends on the beam. Then the weaver has to catch the extra threads."⁵ In other words, weavers were financially penalized for their co-workers' errors.

The fines issue, based as it was in production differences embedded in the division of labor at the mills, exacerbated divisions among the amalgamated unions during the strike. Even Cunnane, who later opposed Pickering on the issue, admitted that "viewed from the standpoint of the cotton operative who is not a weaver, . . . the raising of the 'fines system' at this time is considered, to put it mildly, extremely unwise. . . . [But] viewed from the standpoint of the great body of weavers, the fines system is a vital issue."⁶

Later in the strike, Pickering's consistent pushing of the fight against the fining system created severe divisions even within the weavers' union. Attempting to maintain unity among the strikers, the weavers' national secretary, Matthew Hart, blasted Pickering's constant "harping" on the fines issue. Refusing to use her name, he told a February meeting of the union:

3. Weavers make up 37.7 percent of the textile worker sample from the 1900 New Bedford census. See appendix 2.
   4. *Globe*, January 24, 1898 (p.m.), p. 1.
   5. *Globe*, January 20, 1898 (p.m.), p. 4.
   6. *Globe*, January 24, 1898 (p.m.), p. 1.

This party seems to be looking for notoriety. . . . When the strike is over something will be done toward reprimanding her. If the weavers have given the handling of the strike to the executive committee and they are not capable of handling it, let any 21 of them petition for a meeting of the union and fire the whole coboodle [*sic*] out. This woman carries nothing only a long tongue, and the tongue had better be shortened. I hope the lady members, when this woman talks of having meetings, will ignore her and give her to understand that the executive committee will attend to the business, or else elect her to be the executive committee and let her say "I'm the leader, the Joan of Arc just come down from the middle ages."[7]

What had Pickering done to deserve this acrimony? She had attempted to hold separate meetings of women weavers only, had met with several mill owners on her own early in the strike, and had testified before the state legislature in a hearing on the fines issue. She had also been singled out by Eva McDonald Valesh, correspondent for the Hearst paper, the *New York Journal*, as "New Bedford's Joan of Arc."[8] Hart's comments suggest that the official union stand on Pickering's actions had as much to do with her gender and her notoriety as with her refusal to toe the line and follow appropriate union protocol.

Socialist factionalism further divided New Bedford unionists. Pickering called herself a Christian Socialist, though she acknowledged, "There are not many of them here, but in England, where I was born and raised, they are many and strong."[9] In New Bedford, as elsewhere, socialists were deeply divided in 1898 among adherents of Daniel DeLeon's Socialist Labor Party, followers of Eugene V. Debs's Social Democracy of America, and various strands of socialism brought from England with Lancashire workers like Pickering. When Pickering finally managed to hold her meeting of women weavers on February 3, she invited several representatives from the Providence, Rhode Island, socialist "Abraham Lincoln Liberty League" to address the assembled group. The New Bedford paper's correspondent reported that his

attention was somewhat diverted from the socialist's speech by the argument which was going on behind me. A weaver and his wife had come to the meeting, the man somewhat reluctantly, apparently. He was anxious to go home.

"Wait awhile," said Mrs. Weaver. "Harriet will have something to say by and bye."

7. *MM*, February 12, 1898, p. 5.
8. Blewett, *Constant Turmoil*, p. 349; Elizabeth Faue, *Writing the Wrongs: Eva Valesh and the Rise of Labor Journalism* (Ithaca: Cornell University Press, 2002), p. 132.
9. *Globe*, January 20, 1898 (p.m.), p. 4.

"She will never get a chance," was the rejoinder. "That fellow will talk all night."[10]

This brief exchange suggests several things about the attachment, or lack thereof, of rank-and-file workers to socialism. The women weavers of New Bedford apparently trusted Harriet Pickering; she was one of their own. As in this example, they even sat through long-winded socialist speeches in order to hear what she had to say. Listening to speeches, however, did not necessarily mean believing the words. This held true for both socialists and trade unionists.

Samuel Gompers arrived in Massachusetts just a few days after Pickering's meeting. After speaking to textile strikers in Biddeford, Maine, on Monday, and to workers in Lowell on Tuesday, Gompers arrived in New Bedford on Wednesday, February 9. Challenged to a debate by local members of the Socialist Labor Party (SLP), Gompers refused, decrying divisiveness during the strike.

> I know you will win, if you will only be true to each other. You cannot but win if you stand true, but if you find men who, under the pretense of advocating labor, will throw into the fight an issue which breeds discord, they should be branded by the name of traitor to the cause of labor. . . . How dare a man, or any number of men, presumably in the conflict, attack the principles and policy and tactics involved in such an organization when it is engaged in conflict? Such things are permissible in times of peace, but any man or men who will divide the forces of labor which will result in taking the bread out of the mouths of the helpless women and children are the paid hirelings of the mill owners.[11]

Fighting back hecklers in the crowd, Gompers ended up largely discussing the dangers of disunity without offering the financial support strikers had wanted. Before dashing from the hall to catch a train for Pittsburgh, Gompers urged the crowd, "Be true to yourselves. Depend upon yourselves and you will win the fight which will make you free."[12]

Once Gompers left the hall, the rancor left too. The crowd voted its thanks to Gompers, apparently unanimously. Even members of the SLP, such as spinner Samuel Smith, expressed their gratitude to Gompers and their regrets that his speech had been disrupted. Smith commented that while "he was just as warm a socialist as anybody and was willing himself to argue on his belief at the proper time and place . . . he thought more respect should have been shown to so prominent a man as the leader of the American Federation

10. *MM*, February 4, 1898, p. 8.
11. *Globe*, February 10, 1898 (a.m.), pp. 1–2.
12. Ibid., p. 2.

of Labor."[13] Many others, however, questioned Gompers's sincerity, grumbling that he had not offered concrete assistance to the strikers.

Two days later, SLP leader Daniel DeLeon arrived in New Bedford. Speaking to a packed crowd in the city hall, he delivered what remains one of his most famous speeches, "What Means This Strike?" Local SLP organizer James Hancock described the scene: "The meeting at our City Hall was a splendid sight, every available inch was occupied window sills were filled and many went away could not get in."[14] Refusing, in his view, to talk down to the workers "with rosy promises and prophecies, funny anecdotes, bombastic recitations in prose and poetry," DeLeon instead gave a substantive "lesson" in the principles of socialism. Drawing many of his specific examples from the New Bedford mills, he worked his way from the source of wages and profits to the "principles of sound organization." Arguing that "pure and simple unionism" could never achieve workers' ultimate goal of attaining socialism, DeLeon urged workers to seek out "the shop organization that combines in its warfare the annually recurring class-conscious ballot."[15] Taking the New Bedford bull by the horns, DeLeon even used as his main example of the futility of non-class-conscious voting the uselessness of the Massachusetts anti-fines bill. This bill had been passed in 1891 and amended in 1892 by the state legislature, under the legislative guidance of Samuel Ross, Republican member of the legislature and national secretary of the mule spinners' union.[16] DeLeon concluded by calling on the strikers to organize into locals of the SLP's Socialist Trades and Labor Alliance.

DeLeon may have been talking more theory than practical advice, but he managed to address both low wages and the weavers' fines issue. Besides, no one in New Bedford had expected any financial assistance from DeLeon or the Socialist Labor Party. Gompers had mostly discussed divisions among the workers, barely acknowledging any issue for the strike at all while also not opening AFL coffers to the strikers. DeLeon reminded New Bedford workers of this throughout his visit as he repeatedly remarked, "The capitalist class . . . can not respect you so long as you submit yourselves to be led by the purple-faced and pimple-nosed brigade of labor fakirs."[17]

The most well-known of the "pimple-nosed labor fakirs," Samuel Gompers, returned once again to New Bedford a month later. Though Gompers had planned to dispel all lingering dissatisfaction with this second visit, he must have been discouraged when one of the textile unionists invited to a private

13. *MM*, February 10, 1898, p. 5; also in *Globe*, February 10, 1898 (a.m.), p. 2.

14. Letter from James Hancock to Henry Kuhn, February 10, 1898, *Records of the Socialist Labor Party [1877–1907]* (Madison: State Historical Society of Wisconsin, 1970), microfilm edition [hereafter cited as *SLP Records*], reel 18, frames 470–70a.

15. Daniel DeLeon, "What Means This Strike? An Address Delivered in the City Hall of New Bedford, Mass., February 11, 1898," in *Socialist Landmarks: Four Addresses* (New York: New York Labor News Company, 1952), pp. 81, 104, 111.

16. Ibid., p. 109; Blewett, *Constant Turmoil*, pp. 352–53.

17. *MM*, February 14, 1898, p. 1.

meeting, Thomas Connolly of the Lowell weavers' union, overtly snubbed him, refusing even to shake his hand. The speech Gompers made to the public barely went better, as he was challenged once again, this time on financial rather than political grounds. By the end of the speech, Gompers was probably literally "purple-faced" with frustration. Hancock reported back to SLP headquarters: "I cannot resist a smile as I note how fitfully the dying embers of such a fire as [Gompers] represents and under such a skilful [sic] manipulator of Fans and Bellows is miserably and feebly flickering away."[18]

The fire of the Socialist Trades and Labor Alliance, however, was burning no brighter. In all their public statements, neither DeLeon nor Gompers ever acknowledged fully the presence of women among the strikers. Though both made reference to strikers' wives, women workers seemed to remain invisible to the two men. When Eugene V. Debs arrived in town a week after Gompers's second trip, he took a different rhetorical stance, stating, "I have been from the beginning, am now, and always will be to the end in profound sympathy with the textile workers of this city in the strong defence they are putting up for their homes and their children." That Debs was referring to the children of both male and female strikers became clear when he stated that the strike "on the part of the men, women and children whose wage is but a meagre one . . . is a question of human endeavor."[19] Debs's recognition of women strikers helps explain why weaver Harriet Pickering joined Debs's social democracy after his visit.[20]

While the various splits among socialists may have contributed to the ultimate failure of the New Bedford strike, socialist schisms provide only one small part of the explanation. Pickering's weavers' union faced internal divisions as well as growing tensions with the other craft unions in town. While the mule spinners' union was spending most of its time on the issue of how strike benefits should be dispersed, the weavers' union was expending considerable energy on preventing Pickering from holding meetings of women weavers only. Pickering herself, however, argued that the disunity of the various unions was creating a fatal problem for the strikers.

> One of the things I am contending for is the thorough amalgamation of all trade unionism. If we are to fight a combine, we must do it with a combine. The manufacturers are all combined. And here in New Bedford, when we want to deal with them, we find them united and we deal with them in a body. Yet, on our side, they treat with us as the Weavers' union, and the Spinners' union and the Card room union. There is no one body of operatives, except when we have

18. James Hancock to H. Kuhn, March 1898, *SLP Records*, reel 18, frames 698–99.
19. *MM*, March 11, 1898, p. 5.
20. Blewett, *Constant Turmoil*, p. 365.

a strike on our hands and that is only for a temporary convention. What I hope to live to see is an amalgamated textile union, embodying everything.[21]

Such a union eventually developed, but it did not show itself during the New Bedford strike. As the strike began to collapse in early April with the reopening of the mills, first nonunion workers and then workers belonging to unions returned to work. Whatever problems the weavers' union and other strike leaders had with Harriet Pickering, she was right about the need for more unity among the various textile craft unions.

When the New Bedford strike broke out in early 1898, workers in the New England textile industry were still organizing into unions along a fairly narrow craft basis. Although, as in New Bedford, attempts were made at coordinating actions, such coordination entailed neither sharing of strike benefits nor even necessarily presenting uniform strike demands. The National Cotton Mule Spinners' Association (NCMSA), first established beyond Fall River in 1858, stands at the center of this story. Rooted both in British traditions brought from Lancashire and in the contingencies of the cotton industry in Fall River, the organization spread slowly from its original location, forming locals elsewhere in Massachusetts and other New England locations. After a short time in the 1880s when it affiliated itself with both the Knights of Labor and the American Federation of Labor, it became affiliated solely with the AFL in 1888.[22] Through all its transmutations, the mule spinners' union remained a strict craft union, reflecting the conviction of its members that they were the most skilled and necessary employees in the cotton industry.

By 1890, other occupationally based unions had also begun to organize in New England textile towns. Weavers formed local unions first in Massachusetts locations, such as Fall River and New Bedford, and these locals came together in 1895 in the Massachusetts State Federation of Weavers; two years later, weavers from other states were admitted, and the organization became the New England Federation of Weavers. In 1898 the name was changed to the National Federation of Textile Operatives, though membership remained limited to weavers. The highly skilled loom fixers also established their own craft union, setting up an apprenticeship program and helping manufacturers establish textile schools in several Massachusetts towns. By the 1890s, more tenuous craft unions of carders and slasher tenders had also popped up in New England textile towns. Young women dominated both those occupations.

21. *Globe*, January 20, 1898 (p.m.), p. 4.
22. The history below is taken largely from Herbert J. Lahne, *The Cotton Mill Worker* (New York: Farrar & Rinehart, 1944), chap. 13, pp. 175–88.

The various New England craft unions in the textile industry shared certain characteristics: they all defined membership by occupation, they established systems of dues payments and benefits, and they prized the autonomy of local unions and of each craft union. Though various local unions might cooperate enough to establish "textile councils" in different towns, they paid little attention to workers who had not formed their own craft unions. Thus, though several unions, including that of the arrogant mule spinners, noted at times the importance of organizing the increasing numbers of ring spinners, they rarely did much on behalf of those workers.

The American Federation of Labor, having already granted a charter to the mule spinners' union, first attempted to bring together the scattered craft unions of the textile industry in 1890. Beginning with locals in Lawrence, Lowell, Fall River, and New Bedford, Massachusetts, the International Union of Textile Workers (IUTW) soon ran into organizational difficulty. The strongest craft locals in New England saw no benefit in affiliating with the new "national" union, and the New England branches of the union soon ran into disagreements with branches elsewhere. Attempts by the Socialist Labor Party to gain control of the union later in the 1890s also led to several splits within the union. At the same time, the AFL pushed for the organization of southern textile workers. By 1898, control of the IUTW lay with the weak and scattered southern locals of the union. The craft unions of New England simply continued on their old paths of autonomy and virtually ignored the dictates of the southern-dominated national union. The result was the type of "temporary convention" bemoaned by Pickering in the New Bedford strike.

Samuel Gompers attempted to use the New Bedford strike to bring together the disparate local unions of the textile industry, but to no avail. For both his visits to New Bedford during the strike, his main goal was to heal divisions among the New Bedford workers. He wrote to one colleague:

> We realize that the mill owners are a unit in defense of their interests, no matter where they may be located. We should certainly learn that important lesson which they teach by their action, and instead of remaining isolated, unite worker with worker, union with union in the most compact and intelligent way to have the wage earners yet brought into existence under the banner of the A. F. of L.[23]

Throughout late 1900 and early 1901, the AFL continued to try to sort out the textile workers' difficulties. The southern-based IUTW was simply too weak to survive on its own, and the New England craft unions continued to barrel on down their own road.

23. Letter from Samuel Gompers to Thos. F. Tracy, American Federation of Labor Letterpress Copybooks of Samuel Gompers and William Green, 1883–1925, microfilm of originals at Library of Congress [hereafter cited as SG Letterbooks], February 21, 1898, 22:713–14.

The strike of workers at the Evansville, Indiana, Cotton Manufacturing Company in 1900 demonstrates some of the possible benefits of organizing all textile workers into a single union.[24] The committee that met with company officials in May to request that hours be cut from eleven to ten per day without any corresponding wage decrease had probably already been working to organize co-workers into the then-collapsing IUTW. Workers joined that union as Local 214 in June, when organizer Charles Spalding warned them not to strike. However, management posted notices announcing that both hours and wages would be cut, so the workers voted unanimously to strike on July 2.

Despite predictions of a short strike, strikers held out through the entire summer and fall. Because they had joined the national union only weeks before they struck, they received no strike benefits from the union. Instead, they had to rely on their own fund-raising efforts for financial support. When the company attempted to resume production with strikebreakers in September, strikers, along with their supporters from the local central labor union, responded with militance and "tin-can parades." By the end of September, mill management announced that it was closing the mills indefinitely. Only in mid-December did strikers propose arbitration, which the mill's superintendent rejected; instead, he set his own terms for settlement, including a refusal to sign a one-year contract with the union. Strikers finally accepted the company's terms and voted to end the strike on December 18.

This strike clearly demonstrates several differences from the earlier New Bedford strike. In Evansville, no hints of separate occupationally defined unions ever appeared. Without the long history of New England craft unions, cotton mill employees, both male and female, simply joined together under the auspices of the national union. Though newspaper coverage of the strike mentions several times that women workers showed more interest in the strike than men did, all the strikers appear to have participated in all strike activities, including fund-raising and the September anti-scab demonstrations.

The makeup of the final negotiating committee for the union reflects the unity of workers across gender and occupational lines. Utilizing the experience of Joseph Vogel from the Evansville Central Labor Union, the committee consisted of a twenty-eight-year-old male spinner, a fifty-year-old mill engineer whose fifteen-year-old daughter also worked in the mill, and a forty-four-year-old female weaver. This committee sent its proposal for a settlement of the strike to Superintendent Osborn. While the workers themselves appear to have made no distinctions along the potentially divisive lines of gender

24. Unless otherwise noted, the story of this strike comes from coverage in the *Evansville Journal*. See also chapters 5 and 6.

and occupation, Osborn took a more gendered view of the situation, addressing his reply only to the three men on the committee.[25]

Textile workers in the Alamance County, North Carolina, strike the same year appear to have followed the same occupation-blind and gender-blind approach to organizing workers into the national union. Their strike, described in the previous chapter, represented both the strength of the IUTW in the South and the problems involved in maintaining that strength without the assistance of the more-established New England textile unions. In 1901, Gompers and other national leaders of the AFL finally managed to convince New England textile unions once again to join other textile unions in a more cohesive national body. The United Textile Workers of America (UTW) held its founding convention in November 1901. The mule spinners' association (the NCMSA) was allowed to "affiliate" with the new national union without giving up its autonomy or its separate affiliation with the American Federation of Labor.[26]

The Alamance strike haunted the new organization, though, as southern representatives asked the new national textile union to help pay debts incurred during the strike. Disputes over the disbursement and use of funds donated for that purpose, as well as further such claims, led the UTW to repudiate "all debts and claims arising from the late International Union of Textile Workers."[27] By 1903 the general secretary reported that twenty of the forty-one local unions surrendering their charters in the previous year had been members of the earlier union.[28] The new national union quickly became dominated by the older New England unions, with their histories of strict craft jurisdictions. To the extent to which the United Textile Workers adhered to the model of craft unionism put forward by its strongest member unions, its vision of industry-wide unionism would retain many of the weaknesses found in single-occupation unions. In other cases, the union found itself free to expand on its possibilities as an industrial-type union, organizing all workers within the textile industry into a single union.

At its best, the post-1901 structure of the textile workers' union could lead to the cross-occupational, and therefore cross-gender, harmony and cooperation seen in the 1902 strike of Pawtucket thread workers described in chapter 3.[29] This strike typifies the relationship between the organizationally distinct

25. Indiana Labor Commissioner, *Second Biennial Report for the Years 1899–1900* (Indianapolis: Wm. B. Buford, 1901), p. 118. Information on individual committee members taken from 1900 Census data for Evansville. See appendix 2.

26. Lahne, *Cotton Mill Worker*, pp. 187–88.

27. United Textile Workers' Union, *Proceedings, 1902*, "American Labor Unions Constitutions and Proceedings," microform edition (Ann Arbor: University Microforms, 1980s–) [hereafter cited as "Constitutions and Proceedings"], pp. 34, 19–20.

28. United Textile Workers' Union, *Proceedings, 1903*, "Constitutions and Proceedings," p. 30.

29. Unless otherwise noted, the story of this strike comes from coverage in the *Pawtucket Evening Times*. This strike was also discussed in chapter 3.

mule spinners and the rest of the UTW membership. During the course of this brief strike, the mule spinners, already granted a 10 percent wage hike, supported the efforts of female twister-tenders to resist both the effective wage cut accompanying Rhode Island's new fifty-hour-week act and the alleged speed-up of production that ensued. As the women's strike spread to other workers in the J & P Coats mills, mule spinners helped them organize meetings and form a local of the United Textile Workers. This strike thus embodies the mule spinners' vision of how the United Textile Workers would operate: the level-headed and experienced mule spinners would assist co-workers in moving toward a new sort of coordinated unionism. The newly organized co-workers would then demonstrate their appreciation through both praise and appropriately responsible union behavior.

Perhaps the Coats mill strike in Pawtucket demonstrated such collegiality of action precisely because it was a thread mill. In the cloth mills of Lowell the following year, very different possibilities appeared for the UTW form of unionism.[30] Following models established by textile unions in Fall River and New Bedford, Lowell textile workers coordinated their actions through the Lowell Textile Council. As an umbrella organization of the various craft union locals, the council did better than that in New Bedford in 1898, when individual occupational groups disagreed on the strike's demands. In 1902, when New England mule spinners decided to ask for a 10 percent wage hike, the Lowell Textile Council demanded the increase for all the city's mill workers. Though Lowell did not see a strike in 1902, the council voted unanimously to request the 10 percent wage increase once again in 1903.

Throughout the days leading up to the strike of 1903, as well as during the strike itself, the Lowell Textile Council demonstrated considerable flexibility in its organizational tactics. Though the preexisting union locals within the Textile Council took the form of occupationally based craft unions, council delegates understood that solidarity was more important than craft union purity. When they began to organize into unions workers who had not belonged to unions before the strike, they were willing to experiment with organizational forms. Most of the new unions took the craft union form; the one hundred or so male slasher tenders in the city formed a union along occupational lines, as did the female ring spinners. These occupational divisions often created single-sex unions, but no one ever suggested forming a union just for women operatives. The Textile Council did encourage some ethnic groups to form just that sort of cross-occupational union, though. Polish operatives held an organizational meeting the day after the strike

30. Unless otherwise noted, the story of this strike comes from coverage in the *Boston Globe*; the *Lowell Courier*; the Massachusetts State Board of Conciliation and Arbitration, *Sixteenth Annual Report for 1902* (Boston: Wright & Potter, 1902), and *Seventeenth Annual Report for 1903* (Boston: Wright & Potter, 1903); and the *American Wool and Cotton Reporter*. See also the narrative of this strike in chapter 1.

Secretaries of textile craft unions at Lowell Textile Council headquarters addressing circulars, 1903 (*Boston Globe,* April 10, 1903, p. 3).

began; Portuguese and Greek textile workers also met, organized, and sent delegates to the council separately.

With its roots in the finely honed craft unionism of the mule spinners' and loom fixers' unions, the United Textile Workers undertook this type of organizational experimentation only under the duress of a strike such as that in Lowell. Beyond such emergency situations, the individual unions making up the UTW hesitated to move beyond the amalgamation of craft unions in its traditional center of power in New England. Only in the industrial periphery would the union organize all textile workers into single union locals, ignoring occupational divisions. Even as the continuing mechanization and de-skilling of jobs made solidarity across occupational lines ever more important, the UTW moved only hesitantly toward a wider organizational structure. After the formation of the Industrial Workers of the World (IWW) in 1905, the UTW would confront an explicitly industrial union competitor in strikes like that in Lawrence, Massachusetts, in 1912.[31] Even before the IWW appeared on the scene, however, the UTW faced a broader alternative organizational model. What would the gendered implications of such a

---

31. See Ardis Cameron, *Radicals of the Worst Sort: Laboring Women in Lawrence, Massachusetts, 1860–1912* (Urbana: University of Illinois Press, 1993); see also Clifford M. Kuhn, *Contesting the New South Order: The 1914–1915 Strike at Atlanta's Fulton Mills* (Chapel Hill: University of North Carolina Press, 2001), on the IWW in the South.

model be? The example of the Philadelphia textile strike of 1903 suggests one set of possibilities.[32]

In Philadelphia, textile workers faced an industry far more divided than that in most New England or southern textile towns. The textile industry in that city was made up of many small specialty manufacturers,[33] and in this context Philadelphia's Central Union of Textile Workers (CUTW) took its own eclectic approach to organizing in its 1903 strike for the fifty-five-hour workweek. Often employed in workplaces that had only a few dozen workers, Philadelphia workers found that occupational distinctions could make "local" craft unions useless. Instead, the city's textile workers organized in a number of different ways. Though some organized into occupationally based craft unions, such as the "beamers' and twisters' " or the "dyers' and mercerizers'" unions, others organized by industry subsector. Ingrain carpet weavers had their own union distinct from those of other weavers, such as the cloth weavers', blanket weavers', and upholstery weavers' unions. Other textile workers involved in the 1903 strike organized by geographical location (the "Manayunk —— union") or, for those employed in some of the larger firms in the city, by firm. Except to the extent that these various distinctions were reinforced by an ethnic or sexual division of labor, the resulting unions did not reflect these particular subgroups.

Philadelphia's textile unions, in other words, reflected the fragmented and dissimilar experiences workers had in their myriad workplaces. While Lowell's textile workers, on strike in the same year, could draw on similarities of experiences among workers employed in different firms, Philadelphia's workers had few such similarities. Their varied workplace experiences informed their modes of organization and infused their strike and their unions with a kind of collective individualism.[34]

Philadelphia's Central Union of Textile Workers also came closer to approximating the industrial unionism of the mid-twentieth century than did most other unions at the time. Ultimately, "shop committees" made decisions about the 1903 strike's actions. In this type of organization, the individual worker's employer became more important than his or her occupation in providing organizational definition. This fact had several results. Unlike under the more strict occupational divisions of the UTW version of craft-based unionism, no female strike leaders appeared in the Philadelphia strike, despite the strike's alleged attention to child labor and other such family issues.

---

32. Unless otherwise noted, the story of this strike comes from coverage in the *Philadelphia Inquirer* [hereafter cited as *Inquirer*] and the *Philadelphia Public Ledger* [hereafter cited as *Ledger*].

33. See chapter 5, as well as Melvin Thomas Copeland, *The Cotton Manufacturing Industry of the United States* (New York: A. M. Kelley, 1966), p. 51, and Philip Scranton, *Figured Tapestry: Production, Markets, and Power in Philadelphia Textiles, 1885–1941* (Cambridge: Cambridge University Press, 1989), pp. 260–65.

34. See chapter 1 for discussion of similarities among Lowell workers.

Women workers rarely stepped (or step!) forward to leadership roles in mixed-sex unions; to the extent that this was true, the occupational distinctions made by craft unions held greater potential for women's leadership and activism. If the sexual division of labor created single-sex occupations, then, once the unions of the AFL began to organize all workers, women would join and lead their own occupationally based unions. The more "true" industrial unions of Philadelphia could maintain an all-male public presentation, even though more than half the city's textile workers were female. No renegade Harriett Pickerings appeared, and Mother Jones paid little attention to the female strikers.

Some forty-three separate unions belonged to the Central Union of Textile Workers. A handful of locals belonging to the AFL's United Textile Workers joined them in the 1903 strike. In the midst of all the other chaos of the strike, this issue of affiliation created even more dissension. Discord flared not only among the Philadelphia unions but also within the UTW itself. Less than a week after the strike began, Edward McNulty of the Philadelphia branch of the UTW wrote to AFL President Samuel Gompers:

> The situation in Philadelphia is becoming serious, there are great [sic] many unorganized textile workers on strike and the fear is that if the struggle continues they will go back; of course we are not responsible for this except for the fact that it may set the labor movement back, also there is a backwardness upon the part of the national officers of the United Textile Workers of America. I have asked them to come to Philadelphia so as to help in nationalizing the movement, but so far there has been no response. Also several hundred of our members were forced out on account of the strike and they will not get any strike benefits. Also I think that they at least should allow me something for general expenses. The organization running the strike have [sic] funds and a corp [sic] of organizers whose expenses are paid which handicaps me.[35]

McNulty continued to correspond with Gompers, telling him a week later: "I have every reason to believe there will be an increasing membership in the U.T.W. of A. if they will identify themselves with the movement."[36]

Despite continued encouragement from Gompers, McNulty and other AFL boosters in Philadelphia faced more problems during the strike. The AFL executive council sent out circulars on behalf of the strikers, and money poured in to strike headquarters from AFL unions. The ways and means committee of the strike reported in late August that the United Mine Workers alone sent in almost one-third of the total donations.[37] The United Textile

35. Excerpt from letter from Edward McNulty to Gompers, June 10, 1903, quoted in letter from Gompers to Albert Hibbert, SG Letterbooks, June 12, 1903, 73:666. See also Gompers to McNulty, SG Letterbooks, June 12, 1903, 73:665.
36. Letter from McNulty to Gompers quoted in full in Gompers to A. Hibbert, SG Letterbooks, June 12, 1903, 73:666.
37. *Ledger*, August 24, 1903, p. 2; *Inquirer*, October 25, 1903, p. 9.

Workers, oriented toward the plight of New England workers and facing their own financial problems after the defeat of the Lowell strike, paid little attention to the Philadelphia strikers. Because only a few of the strikers belonged to UTW-affiliated locals, the national union provided little in the way of support. Its executive council refused to authorize the strike for the union's locals, so no strike benefits were paid. While the union did contribute two hundred dollars to the strike fund and excuse the affiliated locals from the usual per-capita tax, they otherwise offered nothing beyond moral support. When the UTW held its 1903 convention in Philadelphia in October, they adopted a resolution, offered by McNulty, that called for the Central Union of Textile Workers to affiliate with the national union.[38] This call, however, was truly too little, too late. At the beginning of September, as the strike crumbled, the *Public Ledger* put it this way: "The dolorous wail has been, 'We stood united, but we fell divided.' "[39] The grand Philadelphia strike ultimately failed for all textile workers, male and female.

Textile workers were not alone in their organizational experimentation in these years. In the fall and winter of 1898/99, striking shoe workers in Marlboro, Massachusetts, demonstrated the attempts of shoe workers to broaden their amalgamation of unions.[40] The ten local unions of shoe workers in Marlboro followed closely the general style of the state's textile councils; a "joint council" coordinated actions by occupationally defined craft unions. Locals of stitchers, heelers, sole-leather workers, bottom finishers, cutters, sole-fasteners, lasters, treers, dressers, and packers, and a "mixed" union of seventy-seven members made up the joint council. For more than a decade the town's manufacturers had recognized these ten unions, and most difficulties had been solved through formal or informal arbitration.[41] In late summer of 1898, however, seventy-five of the female stitchers in the Rice & Hutchins Company Middlesex factory quit work, complaining of mistreatment by their forewoman and demanding that she be discharged. Rice & Hutchins later pointed to this incident as "unjustifiable, premature, and ill-timed" and argued that it gave them reason to take action the following November.[42]

On Thursday, November 10, the three largest shoe manufacturers in Marlboro posted notices stating that after November 23 they would no longer deal with the shoe workers' unions. The agreed-on price list would

38. *Ledger*, October 23, 1903, p. 2; *Inquirer*, October 23, 1903, p. 2, and October 24, 1903, p. 5.

39. *Ledger*, September 2, 1903, p. 3.

40. Unless otherwise noted, the story of this strike comes from coverage in the Boston Globe.

41. Fay Spencer Baldwin et al., *The Strike of the Shoe Workers in Marlboro, Mass., Nov. 14, 1898–May 5, 1899: A Report Prepared for the Civic Department of the Twentieth Century Club of Boston* (Boston: Boston Co-operative, [1899?]), microfiche edition, *Pamphlets in American History: Labor*, L815 (Sanford, N.C.: Microfilming Corporation of America 1979), p. 4.

42. Baldwin et al., *Strike of the Shoe Workers*, p. 8.

expire that day, and the manufacturers would impose their own list of prices. All workers would have to sign an "iron-clad" agreement, promising: "I will not . . . either by myself or by joining with others, take any action, secretly or otherwise, with the intent to interfere with the continuous running of the factory; and . . . I will not recognize any authority which makes requests or gives orders contrary to the letter and spirit of this agreement."[43] The immediate response of the shoe unions was to provide a listing of the many times that they had responded to the manufacturers' unreasonable demands with dignity and in a responsible way, thereby avoiding strikes. This time, however, the Marlboro unions met and agreed to strike. Though John Tobin, president of the boot and shoe workers' union, attempted to effect a compromise, no agreement was reached. The town's ten years of amicable labor relations came to an abrupt end the following Monday, when some 3,000 to 3,500 shoe workers in seven of the town's ten shoe factories quit work at noon.

The story of the strike itself should sound familiar by now. Though only approximately half the strikers belonged to unions, virtually the entire shoe-working population of the town joined the strike. In a town reputed to have 80 percent of its workforce employed in shoe factories, the strike of thousands created what one observer characterized as "a whole community [in] industrial disorder."[44] After seeing considerable solidarity early in the strike, shoe workers watched as the factories reopened in late December. Many of the workers chose to leave town as strikebreakers arrived; others began to return to work as the strike wore on. Pickets gathered around the factories; scabs were assaulted. As they had in New Bedford, Gompers, DeLeon, and Debs all trooped through town to bolster strikers' morale. But in the end, strikers came to believe that continuing the strike would destroy union power just as surely as signing the manufacturers' iron-clad agreements would. On May 5, 1899, the joint council of the unions voted that strikers could return to work without facing union punishment as scabs. Despite the union's hopes that this move would save the union from total destruction, the ignominious end to the strike effectively ended unionization in Marlboro.

Despite the noted strength of socialists among Massachusetts' shoe workers, they had only a minimal presence in Marlboro in 1898. The town of Haverhill, similarly dominated by the shoe industry, had recently elected the first openly socialist candidates, both shoe workers, to the state legislature.[45] One of these men, James Carey, introduced legislation to investigate the Marlboro strike immediately after his inauguration in January 1899. Despite this, the Socialist Labor Party had to send its paid lecturer, Martha Moore

43. *American Federationist* 6 (April 1899): 42. Also quoted in Baldwin et al., *Strike of the Shoe Workers*, pp. 6–7; Massachusetts State Board of Arbitration and Conciliation, *Thirteenth Annual Report* (Boston: Wright & Potter, 1899), p. 74.

44. Baldwin et al., *Strike of the Shoe Workers*, p. 15.

45. Henry F. Bedford, *Socialism and the Workers in Massachusetts, 1886–1912* (Amherst: University of Massachusetts Press, 1966), p. 87.

Avery, from Boston to "agitate for socialism" among the strikers. When Avery arrived in Marlboro, she reported back to SLP headquarters: "There is *not* one man whom we know there."[46] Few among socialists, and even fewer among Marlboro's shoe workers, fully trusted Avery, who was seen, even by many socialists, as a self-serving troublemaker.[47] DeLeon's eventual speech to the strikers gained neither members for the Socialist Trades and Labor Alliance nor voters in later elections. The Massachusetts state section of the SLP repeatedly made efforts to proselytize among the Marlboro strikers, but to no avail. Without some more organic connection to the strikers and their issues, socialists made no progress in the Marlboro strike. Neither the amalgamated shoe workers nor the various socialist groups could overcome the united employers.

Socialists in Massachusetts all too often played the role of spoilers in strike and union situations in the late nineteenth century. In New York City, the role of socialists in the union movement was simultaneously even more complicated and less so. The unions that would ultimately form the International Ladies' Garment Workers' Union (ILGWU) grew out of the garment districts of the Lower East Side and so had at their core eastern European Jewish radicals. Virtually no historian has ever written about the development of garment unionism in the United States without noting the integral role of Jewish radicalism. No one could argue that socialists or trade unionists represented groups foreign to the workers' own lives and communities. Socialism, Zionism, and a range of other left-wing sympathies ran rampant throughout Jewish communities based economically in the garment trades.[48] Ethnic, occupational, and broad political identities reinforced rather than undercutting one another in such communities.

This type of overdetermination of union sympathy is apparent in virtually every strike of garment workers in the major garment districts of the turn of the century. But what do these strikes tell us about gender and its role in the new, more industrial unions of the early twentieth century?

During the first two and a half months of 1890, a series of rolling strikes spread among the cloak makers of New York City, ultimately involving almost five thousand workers and 142 separate cloak-making shops.[49] Women

---

46. Martha Moore Avery to H. Kuhn, November 22, 1898, *SLP Records*, reel 22, frame 353.

47. Bedford, *Socialism and the Workers*, pp. 143–45.

48. Susan A. Glenn, *Daughters of the Shtetl: Life and Labor in the Immigrant Generation* (Ithaca: Cornell University Press, 1990); Annelise Orleck, *Common Sense and a Little Fire: Women and Working-Class Politics in the United States, 1900–1965* (Chapel Hill: North Carolina University Press, 1995); Carolyn D. McCreesh, *Women in the Campaign to Organize Garment Workers, 1880–1917* (New York: Garland, 1985); Louis Levine, *The Women's Garment Workers: A History of the International Ladies' Garment Workers' Union* (New York: B. W. Huebsch, 1924).

49. Unless otherwise noted, the story of these strikes comes from coverage in the *New York Tribune* [hereafter cited as *Tribune*] and the *New York World* [hereafter cited as *World*].

made up almost one-quarter of the strikers. The strikes began when the shop of A. Friedlander & Company announced cuts in their piecework wages at the end of January. While the shop did not close down completely during the strike, strikers remained steadfast. The New York State Bureau of Labor Statistics opined: "There is not a worse paid set of artisans than the cloak-makers. Distress is chronic, and no one enters upon cloakmaking unless constrained by dire necessity."[50] Under such dire conditions, cloak makers did not take long to react to the threatened wage reduction. The strikers held solidly to their cause. By February 5, Friedlander had given up, rescinded the wage cut, and even offered wage increases of twenty-five to seventy-five cents per garment.

The success of cloak makers working for Friedlander provided other cloak makers with the encouragement they needed to strike against their own employers, demanding wage increases. When Meyer Jonasson, purportedly "then the largest cloak manufacturer in the world,"[51] granted his employees' demands, cloak makers flooded into what became known as the United Brotherhood of Cloak Makers. By May the union boasted more than seven thousand members.[52] The state bureau would note both the "enthusiasm . . . displayed in defending [organization]" and make the supposition that "the foreign element in this trade is very excitable and gets into fights on small provocation."[53] Later strikes in February and March all began as offensive strikes for wage increases; further outbreaks in May, June, and July began when employers locked out the new union members.

The two clusters of strikes in 1890 provide but one example of early attempts at a more inclusive form of unionism in the garment industry. Carried out under the auspices of the New York City cloak makers' union and the United Hebrew Trades, these strikes provide insight into the unions that eventually congealed into the International Ladies' Garment Workers' Union in the early twentieth century. These strikes, like those of the textile and shoe workers, illustrate both the possibilities and the limits inherent in such early attempts to expand unionism beyond the strictly craft-bounded designations of the early AFL.

The 1890 cloak makers' strikes demonstrate both the potential that new types of unions held for expanding roles for women workers as well as the

50. New York Bureau of Statistics of Labor, *Eighth Annual Report for the Year 1890*, part 2: *Strikes and Boycotts* (Albany: James B. Lyon, 1891) [hereafter cited as N.Y. BLS, *8th AR*], p. 1032.

51. Abraham Rosenberg, "How Our Unions Were Built Up," manuscript in International Ladies' Garment Workers' Union Records [hereafter cited as ILGWU Records], Unpublished Union Histories, 1911–71, 5780/167, box 1, Kheel Center for Labor-Management Documentation and Archives, Cornell University Library.

52. Abraham Rosenberg, "Brief History of the Cloakmakers' Union of New York," in *Fifth Annual Convention of the International Ladies' Garment Workers' Union, Boston, Mass., June 6, 1904*, n.p., ILGWU Records, Publications, 5780/PUBS, box 12, file 229.

53. N.Y. BLS, *8th AR*, pp. 1034 and 1035.

ways in which those unions would still hold women closely in check. In garment strikes in particular, where individual shops tended to be small and workers—even skilled ones—easily replaced by recent immigrants, solidarity binding all workers together became crucial. This solidarity had to extend to women and girls as well as to men. Just as mule spinners operated simultaneously as independent lone wolves and educators of others in the textile industry, so the skilled male garment cutters functioned in the garment industry. The Gotham Knife Cutters' Assembly of the Knights of Labor, made up of New York City Irish and "Americanized" Germans, illustrates this. In the summer of 1890 this assembly set out to organize "the girls" in the trade. By August, the organizing committee reported that "the girls were organized as the Lady Gotham."[54] Later that same month, the assembly passed a resolution "that all Bro[ther]s be instructed to do the utmost to organize the girls in their shop."[55] It also made financial contributions to the striking cloak makers.[56] When the ILGWU was founded in 1900, the cloak cutters of New York City remained aloof, but in 1901 they reconstituted themselves as the United Cloak and Suit Cutters, writing out any vestiges of the Knights of Labor from their constitution. In 1902 they finally affiliated with the ILGWU as Local 6, but, again like the mule spinners, they moved in and out of the union several times in the early twentieth century. At the same time, they also contributed several of their members as leaders of the early ILGWU.[57]

Though union leaders at times complained that women workers did not demonstrate long-term organizational loyalty, joining nascent unions at the inception of strikes and leaving them when the strikes ended, the same leaders also commented on the tenacity of female strikers. Cross-gender strikes in the late nineteenth-century garment industry make it clear that both men and women had difficulties with organizational loyalty simultaneous with acting as strike militants. When strikes involved entire communities, as the ones in 1890 did, women could display even greater ferociousness than male strikers. While male unionists, such as those of the United Hebrew Trades in 1890, might not recognize females who worked at home as even possibilities for organization, such workers took to the streets in support of better wages and conditions for all cloak makers. A decade later, the cloak makers' hero, Joseph Barondess, remembering the later May and June strikes, recalled the despair of strike leaders when it looked like the strikes might drag on for months. Realizing the crucial role of public sympathy, Barondess recounted:

54. Knights of Labor, Sanctuary Local Assembly 3038, "Minutes," August 1, 1890, p. 177, ILGWU Records, Predecessor Records and Local Records, 1884–1948, 5780/45, box 1 [hereafter cited as "KoL LA 3038, Minutes"].

55. KoL LA 3038, Minutes, August 29, 1890, p. 184.

56. Ibid., June 6, 1890, p. 162; July 11, 1890, p. 171.

57. See "Fiftieth Anniversary Celebration, 1902–1952, Amalgamated Ladies' Garment Cutters' Union, Local 10, ILGWU," in Archives Union File, 6046, box 192, file 4, Kheel Center for Labor-Management Documentation and Archives, Cornell University Library.

"Having thus seen clearly into the situation, we called meetings of the women—the wives of the strikers and their children; arranged for a monster hunger demonstration and in that way, we compelled the New York Press to take up the cause of our strike."[58] In this description, Barondess "forgot" that many of the strikers themselves were women; they were not just strikers' wives, though many of the female strikers were probably family members of strikers as well as workers. Barondess saw women and thought "wives," but many of the women who "compelled" public opinion in the cloak makers' strike were themselves workers and strikers in the industry. The 1890 strikes not only involved some one thousand female workers but also saw some of those women form their own unions within the trade. The male-dominated United Hebrew Trades, however, gave women little assistance or encouragement.

The situation for garment unions was complex in the 1890s. Workers faced increased mechanization and further de-skilling of their work, accompanied throughout much of the decade by chaotic economic conditions. The garment industry, riven by sweatshop production and seasonal fluctuations, was particularly volatile. Socialists and Bundists competed for workers' loyalty, especially in the Jewish garment districts of major cities. In this setting, unions confronted a difficult task. Though the immigrant workers could be provoked easily to battle against their abysmal working conditions and wages, union leaders had a harder time convincing them to commit to the long-term business of union membership. Despite the complaints unionists had against women workers in this regard, male garment workers were just as difficult to enlist in the cause. Even the famed proclivity of Jewish workers for organization and action did not guarantee stable union membership.

Accordingly, during the 1890s, myriad unions rose up in response to specific complaints, only to collapse again soon after. Only a few individuals, such as the cloak makers' Barondess, managed to sustain a thread of organizational memory through the decade. By 1900 the remnants of Barondess's cloak makers' union sought to bring about a larger and more inclusive organization. In the spring of that year, the United Brotherhood of Cloak Makers of New York "took the initiative and issued a call for a convention to the various organizations throughout the country of [the women's garment industry]." New Yorker Bernard Braff later recalled that this call was in itself "an admission compelled by experience, that unsupported individual action on the field of labor was useless where permanent results were desired."[59] Delegates from Baltimore, Philadelphia, and Newark joined their New York

58. J. Barondess to A. Maroscheck, May 1, 1900, in Letterbooks, Barondess Papers, Manuscripts and Archives Division, New York Public Library, Astor, Lenox, and Tilden Foundations, microfilm, reel 1, frame 184.

59. Braff, "The International Ladies' Garment Workers' Union," in International Ladies' Garment Workers' Union, *Convention Souvenir*, 1902, n.p., in ILGWU Records, Publications, 5780/PUBS, box 42, file 927.

comrades at the ensuing meeting on June 3. Joseph Barondess addressed the eleven delegates, reminding them that at this meeting "a corner-stone would be laid for the sacred edifice of unity in the Cloakmaking trade." Early in the following discussion, the group voted to allow "all unions in the ladies' garment trades" to join the new International Ladies' Garment Workers' Union.[60] This new union did not see itself as a rival to the older United Garment Workers, which organized workers in the ready-made men's clothing industry.

In the decade between the cloak makers' strikes and the founding of the ILGWU, Barondess apparently forgot that women were anything more than passive victims. His amnesia is particularly intriguing given his involvement in other women's strikes at the time he wrote the letter quoted above. For example, in early August 1900 some five hundred employees of Floersheimer & Roman, manufacturers of silk shirtwaists in Manhattan, struck against a proposed reduction in wages of as much as 50 percent.[61] About four hundred of the strikers were "women and girls."[62] The day after the strike began, the *New York Tribune* reported that the women were "running the strike," and a later report in the *New York World* described the strike committee as consisting of "six young women and three young men."[63] Organized first into the United Hebrew Trades and then into the brand-new Ladies' Garment Workers' Union, the workers hoped that other shops would join their struggle and that "the strike [would] become general."[64] While their hope for a general strike never materialized, the young strikers maintained a vigilant picket line throughout their six-day-long strike. Early in the strike, police arrested one of the male picketers for allegedly accosting a strikebreaker. His female co-workers proceeded to collect 350 pennies to pay his three-dollar fine, and the recipient then spent the remaining fifty cents buying ice-cream sodas for his fellow picketers.

Within a few days, a committee from the Central Federated Union, including Joseph Barondess, negotiated an end to the strike. Mr. Floersheimer readily agreed to the equal distribution of work and the employment of none but union members in his shop. He further offered to fire an assistant forewoman charged with having "exacted presents from" the workers and restored part, but not all, of the wage reduction. "The girls were almost unanimously in favor of accepting the compromise, but some of the men wished to hold out." When Barondess urged the men to accept the offer, one striker "rushed at him, declaring that he was a traitor. He would have assaulted

60. "Minutes of the Meeting of June 3, 1900 . . . ," p. 2, in ILGWU Records, 5780/Perm, box 2 [hereafter cited as ILGWU Minutes], pp. 2, 3, 5.

61. Unless otherwise noted, the story of this strike come from coverage in *World*.

62. New York State Board of Mediation and Arbitration, *Fourteenth Annual Report* (Albany: James B. Lyon, State Printer, 1901) [hereafter cited as, NYM&A *14th AR*], p. 208.

63. *Tribune*, August 2, 1900, p. 12; *World*, August 6, 1900, p. 4.

64. *World*, August 5, 1900, p. 11.

Barondess had not a dozen girls pounced on him and borne him to the floor." Another striker who spoke against the settlement later was also "pulled down by half a dozen girls."[65] The strikers finally voted to accept Floersheimer's offer, following which their employer "ordered a keg of beer for the men and soda for the girls."[66]

The young women in this strike were militant strikers, despite the heat of a New York City August and what some might see as their frivolous attention to ice cream sodas. The strikers enjoyed their sodas and then joined the appropriate labor organizations—both the relatively long-standing United Hebrew Trades and the scarcely two-month-old ILGWU. Perhaps the influence of these organizations encouraged the strikers to come up with the idea of attempting to make their strike a more general one, or perhaps it was simply the influence of years of examples of rolling strikes, such as those of 1890. The young women of 1900 also left most leadership roles to men, whether it be the role of president of the local or that of negotiator with the boss. At the same time, the young women knew what they wanted and they fought for it. In 1900 the Floersheimer & Roman workers physically attacked the men who disagreed with their settlement of the strike, foreshadowing the militance of women in the famous shirtwaist strike of 1909.

The 1909 shirtwaist strike has served as the seminal [sic] event in the standard labor-history view of the Ladies' Garment Workers' Union as the epitome of voice and opportunity for women workers. Both the strike and the ILGWU in general stand as symbols of the emergence of the "new woman" in the union movement. Here at last, the story goes, women begin to emerge from decades of quiescence to take their place in the pantheon of labor.[67] This perspective both ignores the controlling role of men in the ILGWU and tends to discount the actions of other garment unions and workers before 1909 in expanding the role of union women.[68] Looked at from the viewpoint of cross-gender strikes, with all their possibilities and

65. *World*, August 7, 1900, p. 12.

66. *New York Times*, August 7, 1900, p. 2.

67. See, for example, Françoise Basch, "The Shirtwaist Strike in History and Myth," in Theresa Serber Malkiel, *The Diary of a Shirtwaist Striker* (Ithaca: ILR Press, 1990), pp. 1–77; Annelise Orleck, *Common Sense and a Little Fire: Women and Working-Class Politics in the United States, 1900–1965* (Chapel Hill: North Carolina University Press, 1995); Alice Kessler-Harris, "Where Are the Organized Women Workers?" *Feminist Studies* 3 (1975): 92–110; Ann Schofield, "The Uprising of the 20,000: The Making of a Labor Legend," in *A Needle, a Bobbin, a Strike: Women Needleworkers in America*, ed. Joan M. Jensen and Sue Davidson (Philadelphia: Temple University Press, 1984), pp. 167–82; Meredith Tax, "The Uprising of the Thirty Thousand," in *The Rising of the Women: Feminist Solidarity and Class Conflict, 1880–1917* (New York: Monthly Review Press, 1980), pp. 205–40.

68. Nan Enstad, *Ladies of Labor, Girls of Adventure: Working Women, Popular Culture, and Labor Politics at the Turn of the Twentieth Century* (New York: Columbia University Press, 1999), begins to critique the role of the ILGWU in the 1909 strike, but because she does so entirely within the context of the strike itself, the usefulness of her analysis is limited. McCreesh, *Women in the Campaign to Organize Garment Workers*, does better exploring the antecedents of the ILGWU (see below).

lost opportunities, women garment workers' experiences in enlarging the terms of unionism look quite different.

The Journeymen Tailors' Union of America rightfully stands as an example of "pure" craft unionism (see chapter 3). The union organized a specific occupation, that of "tailor," and defined that occupation in a way that ensured its continued domination by male workers. From the 1880s on, though, the tailors' union faced a number of recurrent problems. Part of the union's definition of "tailor" entailed the person (read *man*) involved in the total production of custom-made men's clothing, and some tailors stretched this definition to include members of the tailor's family as well as the male tailor himself. As retailers of men's clothing pushed the tailors they employed to higher and higher productivity levels, some tailors began to argue that not only male apprentices but also female "helpers" should be included in the union ranks, albeit at a lower level of benefits. These changes all forced the tailors' union to confront the meaning and significance of the labor of women workers. Not unlike the situation faced by the cigar makers' union when it attempted to decide how to deal with tenement and machine production of cigars, the boogeyman in all these cases might be an immigrant but was also often a woman.

The introduction of mass-produced men's clothing then began to whittle away further at the traditional image of the tailor. Workers in the developing garment districts of New York, Philadelphia, Boston, Baltimore, Chicago, and elsewhere soon found themselves working on only a small portion of any garment. Whether these workers toiled in factory-like settings or in the small sweatshops like those in Baltimore, it became increasingly difficult for them to argue that their work sewing a single seam on one hundred individual garments constituted the "skilled" work of a "tailor."

The United Garment Workers of America (UGW) developed in response to this situation. In early 1891, the "Clothing Operatives' Protective Union" of Boston, AFL federal labor union number 5233, issued a call for

> members of all bona fide "ready-made" or operative tailors' unions to send delegates to a conference to be held in New York City on Sunday April 12, 1891, the purpose of the conference to be the formation of an independent and sound international union on lines that will make it impossible for the members of other trades to interfere with the condition of our affairs [a reference to the Knights of Labor], that will enable us to issue a label that will be unqualifiedly endorsed by organized labor, and that will enable the members of this craft to command the support of each other in times of trouble.[69]

69. "Clothing Operatives' Protective Union, A.F. of L. 5233," *The Tailor* 2 (March 1891): 1.

New York City area garment unions soon joined in this effort, encouraging "every organized body of Clothing Operatives, Cutters and Trimmers to send delegates" to the convention.[70]

When the new general secretary of the United Garment Workers of America, Charles Reichers, sent out his first statement to the labor movement, he noted that the new union "represent[ed] sixteen thousand people in the ready made clothing trade, comprised of cutters, trimmers, liners, basters, operators, finishers, pressers, buttonhole makers, etc., male and female."[71] This initial explicit reference to the presence of women in the new union signals one of the key differences between the garment workers' and tailors' unions. While the garment workers' union established separate unions for skilled garment cutters in many locations, it was just as likely to divide workers into separate locals along product lines, ethnicity, or gender. At the same time, these divisions never represented efforts to exclude particular groups of workers. The union remained focused on its goal of organizing all workers in the ready-made clothing industry. In 1891 the union's first constitution stated simply that members had to "be employed in the manufacture of garments and working at the trade, male of female."[72] First discussed favorably in 1898, by 1901 the union's constitution further limited membership to those "employed in the manufacture of garments for men, boys and children."[73]

The United Garment Workers has often been dismissed as a conservative union interested only in representing American-born, skilled, workers. While this characterization may be apt for the later UGW, little evidence of these qualities appears in the time period covered here. Throughout these years, conventions of the UGW would vote to appoint "Hebrew" organizers and print copies of its constitution and other important notices in various languages.[74] In fact, the conservatism of this union appears to have existed more in the form of electoral conservatism than in that of organizational conservatism. While the union's first constitution began with a preamble calling on workers to "become economically free by organizing politically," by 1903 General Secretary White argued that "politics in unions have never got one more penny in wages nor an hour less on the workday," helping to defeat a resolution calling for "political discussions in all locals" by a vote of 83–46.[75]

---

70. "Call for a Convention," *The Tailor* 2 (March 1891): 1.

71. "Garment Workers, Attention!" *The Tailor* 2 (June 1891): 6.

72. *Constitution of the UGWA*, 1891, "Constitutions and Proceedings," p. 9.

73. *Constitution of the UGWA*, 1901, "Constitutions and Proceedings," p. 33; *Proceedings of the Seventh Annual Convention of the UGWA, held at Cincinnati, Ohio, August 8–13, 1898*, "Constitutions and Proceedings," p. 15.

74. *Ninth Annual Convention of UGWA*, 1900, "Constitutions and Proceedings," p. 12; *Fifth Annual Convention*, 1895, "Constitutions and Proceedings," p. 9; *Tenth Annual Convention*, 1901, "Constitutions and Proceedings," p. 18.

75. *Constitution of the UGWA*, 1891, "Constitutions and Proceedings," p. 3; *Weekly Bulletin of the Clothing Trades*, August 19, 1903 (2:42), pp. 1–2.

Following well-established AFL principles, the United Garment Workers came to eschew partisan politics of any sort. In contrast, the ILGWU would state plainly in its constitution's preamble that one of its goals was "to organize industrially into a class-conscious labor union politically represented . . . by representatives of a political party whose aim is the abolition of the capitalist system."[76] If electoral politics varied between the United Garment Workers and the Ladies' Garment Workers, methods of organization for the two unions remained markedly similar. In fact, in the early months of the ILGWU's existence, its new executive board "resolved to conduct business until the next convention according to the constitution of the Garment Workers."[77]

The final characteristic by which the United Garment Workers is often defined as more conservative than the ILGWU is the UGW's reliance on the union label as a key organizing tool. Here, the argument is that such a focus kept union leadership from recognizing their members' economic strength and militance and instead fostered closer relationships with employers, the bosses of the garment sweatshops. Yet the ILGWU spent as much time as the UGW did worrying about the union label in the organization's early years. The ILGWU's very first executive board meeting approved a design for the union label and discussed the exact location in which the label would be sewn. At the next meeting of the board, in February 1901, the board spent time making sure that a new union local would receive a copy of the label.[78]

The organizational flexibility of the United Garment Workers was evident in the Baltimore strike of 1892, when immigrant Jewish workers organized into separate male and female locals of the UGW and fought against the worst abuses of the sweatshop system of labor in which they found themselves. At the 1892 convention of the UGW, the organization as a whole supported both immigrant workers and women workers, giving a charter to a Boston local of "Lithuanian" tailors and circulating a questionnaire asking how many copies of the English and Hebrew versions of the union's journal were needed. Furthermore, out of almost fifty locals reporting to the convention that year, at least three were specifically women's locals.[79] Rather than a conservative block in the path of the later, more progressive garment unions of the early twentieth century, the UGW served as a forerunner of those unions' methods of organizing workers along the lines of ethnicity and gender as well as occupation.

76. International Ladies' Garment Workers' Union, *Constitution*, 1918, p. 1, cited in *Experience with Trade Union Agreements—Clothing Industries*, Research Report no. 38 by the National Industrial Conference Board, June 1921 (New York: Century Company, 1921), p. 62.

77. ILGWU Minutes, Executive Board Meeting, February 5, 1901, p. 12.

78. ILGWU Minutes, Executive Board Meeting, July 1, 1900, p. 9, and February 5, 1901, p. 12.

79. *Official Proceedings of the Third Annual Convention of the United Garment Workers of America*, Philadelphia, Pennsylvania, November 21, 22, and 23, 1892, "Constitutions and Proceedings," pp. 9, 15, 7–8, 14.

DISCRIMINATE

AGAINST

INFERIOR
UNCLEAN
SWEAT-SHOP
CLOTHING.

INSIST UPON
THIS LABEL

ENDORSED BY ALL TRADES UNIONS
AND LEADING REFORM SOCIETIES.

Advertisement for United Garment Workers' Union label in the ILGWU *Convention Souvenir* of 1902 (courtesy of UNITE Archives, Kheel Center for Labor-Management Documentation and Archives, Cornell University Library).

The 1896 Baltimore garment workers' strike demonstrates this.[80] In true UGW style, at least ten separate local unions became involved in this strike of approximately five thousand workers. Some of these locals defined themselves by occupation, such as Local 6, made up of four hundred male cutters and trimmers, while others defined themselves by the product they produced (Local 26, of seven hundred coat tailors; or Local 38, of eight hundred trouser makers), their ethnicity (Local 69, of Bohemians; Local 96, of Lithuanian tailors; or Local 44, of German American tailors), or their gender (Local 33, the "ladies' branch of finishers"). Some of these locals combined more than one category, such as Local 90, of Lithuanian women, or the "cloak makers' union of women."[81]

Demanding 15 to 20 percent wage increases, the four to five thousand workers involved in the strike remained out for more than a month. The strike began against Schloss Brothers, one of the largest wholesale manufacturers in Baltimore, but quickly spread to the twenty-four other firms belonging to the Clothiers' Board of Trade as well as to ten smaller firms. Just as

80. Unless otherwise noted, the story of this strike comes from coverage in the *Baltimore Sun* [hereafter cited as *Sun*].
81. *Sun*, February 27, 1896, p. 8; Maryland Bureau of Industrial Statistics, *Fifth Annual Report for 1896* (Baltimore: King Brothers, 1897), p. 150.

Remember ! !

Rally about the label, boys.

Your label is your most valuable asset. At all times its value is par —100 cents to the $.

Your home is protected from the contagion of sweat shop and tenement house when you buy label goods.

"A man of words and not of deeds is like a garden full of seeds." Talk about the label only when you can show one in your own clothes.

See that your wife, daughter or sweetheart wear only such clothes as bear our label, or else boycott them.

Always bear in mind that genuine labels are pink in color, the printing black and that labels are consecutively numbered. To be genuine it must be sewn into the garment by machine.

It's a Guarantee of Honest Labor, If attached to a Lady's Garment.

The union label message of the ILGWU, from 1902 *Convention Souvenir* (courtesy of UNITE Archives, Kheel Center for Labor-Management Documentation and Archives, Cornell University Library).

they had in the 1892 strike, the employers attempted both to divide workers along gender lines and to foment clashes between the garment workers' union and the remnants of the Knights of Labor in the city. As in the earlier strike, women workers in 1896 refused to bargain separately or to give up their union membership. Unlike the strike of four years before, the Knights-AFL issue turned out to create more smoke than fire.

The 1896 strike foundered on the dual rocks of the "unfavorable state of trade" and the national union's previous involvement in two other major strikes, in Chicago and Cincinnati. Just a few days after the beginning of the

Jewish holiday of Passover at the end of March, the United Garment Workers officially called off the strike. Henry White, now national secretary of the union, bemoaned the fact that strikers had not been able to arbitrate an end to the strike, pointing out that the weak ending to the struggle simply postponed a confrontation over the issues of wages and hours.

When Samuel Gompers arrived in Baltimore a few weeks after the strike ended, he addressed the Baltimore Federation of Labor, stating that the economy was so messed up that "it may be characterized as employers' anarchism."[82] Employers' anarchism or not, the confused response of the garment workers' union to the militance in Baltimore speaks of the growing conservatism of the five-year-old organization. Over the following years, the UGW came to look more and more conservative as it clung to all aspects of the AFL's "business unionism." High dues and benefits, as well as a requirement for official strike authorization, existed alongside political conservatism in the union even as it strove more than any other union of the 1890s to include women workers in its membership ranks. Carolyn McCreesh puts it this way: "The UGW became one of the few national trade unions to include women in their total program, even though they played only a peripheral [leadership] role in the early years."[83] Rank-and-file women found new opportunities for unionization in the UGW, even as their sisters in the women's clothing industry began to join the more explicitly socialist International Ladies' Garment Workers' Union.

The contrasts and similarities between the ILGWU and the UGW can be seen in a comparison of two strikes of garment workers that were well beyond the influence of New York City's United Hebrew Trades. Both the Los Angeles strike of garment workers in January 1901 and the San Francisco cloak makers' strike of 1903 and early 1904 arose out of differences over union agreements with employers. The Los Angeles strike was carried out under the auspices of the United Garment Workers.[84] Almost two hundred workers, all but nineteen of them women, struck over a "difference of opinion" about the terms of an agreement between UGW Local 125 and two employers in the city. The strike lasted only five days, ending in a success for the union. (During 1901, the state Bureau of Labor Statistics counted less than 8 percent of all strikes in Los Angeles as union "successes.")

A strike of San Francisco cloak makers under the auspices of the International Ladies' Garment Workers' Union two years later lasted longer and had a less satisfactory conclusion.[85] The strike of members of ILGWU Local 8 began in late November 1903, when the cloak makers' union asked em-

82. *Sun*, April 9, 1896, p. 8.
83. McCreesh, *Women in the Campaign to Organize Garment Workers*, p. 51.
84. Unless otherwise noted, the story of this strike comes from California Bureau of Labor Statistics, *Tenth Biennial Report for the Years 1901–1902* (Sacramento: State Printer, 1902).
85. Unless otherwise noted, the story of this strike comes from coverage in the *San Francisco Chronicle* [hereafter cited as *SFChron*].

ployers to cut two hours off Saturday hours without reducing wages at all. The union quickly backed down from this initial demand, saying it would accept a one-hour pay cut instead, "expecting that the bosses would meet them half way."[86] Several firms signed agreements with the union right away, and many in the city expected the struggle to be a short one. Six small manufacturers refused to give in, though, leaving fewer than one hundred strikers out initially.

Striking cloak makers received assistance from the San Francisco Labor Council as well as from various fund-raising "entertainments." Women from the cloak shops were just as active as men in these activities; out of twelve individuals listed as involved in the first fund-raising effort, five were women. In the long run, though, the efforts of the local labor council proved more useful than the thespian efforts of the cloak workers. Local cloak manufacturers soon attempted to coordinate their efforts, leading some who had already signed the union agreement to renege and lock out their employees. In this setting, the labor council moved to arbitrate the differences between the two sides. It soon met with its own frustrations, however, as members of the union refused to give their arbitration committee power to reach a final agreement. Accordingly, the strike dragged on, as labor council leaders attempted to bring the two sides together. By the end of January, the council voted to send one hundred dollars to the cloak makers, but it also "adopted a resolution to cease activity on behalf of the cloakmakers until that union shall appoint a committee with full power to arbitrate existing differences."[87]

The cloak makers did cede power to the council's arbitrators then, who in turn arbitrated several ends to the strike. The first "successful" agreement came on January 30, 1904, when strikers agreed to return to work under the old hours and wages, and workers now working in the shops would join the union. This first agreement fell apart over the second issue. Previously nonunion workers had shown up at union headquarters on February 2 with their five-dollar initiation fees in hand, only to find that the union was adding strikebreaking fines to the fees, increasing the amount due to anywhere from twenty-five to seventy-five dollars. After refusing to pay these fees, the nonunion workers showed up for work the next day. The union workers refused to work alongside them, and the strike was on again. A few weeks later, union members relented and announced they would allow the nonunion workers to join Local 8 after paying only the regular initiation fee. Manufacturers agreed to open their shops to union members once again, "as needed," but it was several weeks before all the strikers could return to work.

Throughout this San Francisco strike, many noted the militance of the strikers. Early in December, the union set up pickets in front of the major retail cloak stores in the city, asking patrons to boycott the struck products.

---

86. *SFChron*, November 24, 1903, p. 13.
87. *SFChron*, January 23, 1904, p. 8.

Two weeks after the picket lines went up, eight men were arrested in front of the Pacific Cloak House. One group of men had gathered in front of the store, allegedly yelling, "Unfair!" while another group yelled back, "Fair!" The *San Francisco Chronicle* reported further: "A large crowd gathered, and as the sidewalks were being blockaded, Sergeant Mahoney, without making any distinction between the rival factions, arrested eight of the principal offenders."[88] That such sidewalk uproars continued can be deduced from the comment by one San Francisco journalist writing on the possible settlement of the strike: "The yells of the pickets along Market street will no longer try to drown the noise of traffic on the city's busiest thoroughfare."[89]

In its strike militance, then, as well as in its inclusion of the entire workforce of the cloak shops, this strike shows characteristics that make it identical both to Ladies' Garment Workers' strikes in New York City and to United Garment Workers' strikes elsewhere around the nation. Wherever they were located, and whatever their institutional affiliation, garment workers, both male and female, would fight against the conditions of their work lives. In carrying out these struggles, they battled as one, largely undivided by occupational distinctions.

Both textile workers and garment workers then attempted to broaden their organizations in the 1890s and early 1900s. Both continued to make some occupational distinctions, even while separate occupationally defined "locals" would work together, in virtual lockstep. During strikes and in the more mundane days of union-building that surrounded such strikes, skilled male workers sat at the core of the United Garment Workers and the International Ladies' Garment Workers' Union, just as the mule spinners formed the core of the United Textile Workers. While women workers may not have been encouraged to strive for leadership roles in the unions themselves, they did play vital roles in strike situations. Militance knew no gender in either industry. Both industries and their unions also experienced protracted battles over socialism in these decades. While the Socialist Trades and Labor Alliance of the Socialist Labor Party rarely provided viable structural alternatives for rank-and-file workers, it often kept the AFL-affiliated unions off balance.

Samuel Gompers's own union, the Cigar Makers' International Union (CMIU), displayed virtually all the same characteristics. This is seen most clearly in the great strike and lockout of cigar makers in New York City in 1900.[90] In this strike, the cigar makers' union battled against a combination of the city's largest cigar manufacturers. The strike that began the controversy "[swept] under its influence every hand cigar maker, cigar packer, machine girl and tenement-house worker employed in the three factories [of Kerbs,

88. *SFChron*, December 18, 1903, p. 12.
89. *SFChron*, January 31, 1904, p. 48.
90. Unless otherwise noted, the story of this strike comes from coverage in *World* and *Tribune*. See chapter 1.

Wertheim & Schiffer]."[91] The inclusive nature of the strike was apparent from the start, as the original demands presented to the manufacturer included wage increases for all types of workers employed by the firm.[92] In this way, the union demonstrated its desire to expand membership beyond the ranks of the most-skilled and all-male hand cigar rollers. The union not only accepted into its ranks the "machine girls and tenement-house workers," but also agreed to pay strike benefits to all strikers, even those who previously had not belonged to the union. Union members in good standing received five dollars a week in benefits, while nonunion strikers received three dollars.

As in many of the other strikes discussed in this chapter, this strike was marked by the efforts of adherents of the Socialist Labor Party to enlist strikers and/or strikebreakers into the ranks of the Socialist Trades and Labor Alliance. As in the Massachusetts strikes of textile and shoe workers, accusations flew against both the "pure and simple labor fakir[s]" of the AFL and the "snakes"[93] of the SLP. Just as in the garment strikes, the cigar makers made good use of ethnic community ties among the affected workers. The ranks of those on strike or locked out during the spring and summer of 1900 were overwhelmingly dominated by Bohemian workers, many of them recent immigrants. Strikers regularly held their meetings at Bohemian National Hall. Even the manufacturers must have recognized the strength of the Bohemian community in the strike, for the editor of the *United States Tobacco Journal* published, and then responded to, the letter of "a high school boy, seventeen years of age":

> My father and mother, who came from Bohemia, were married in this country, and I was born in this city. Both of my parents are cigarmakers. My father is a member of the union, my mother is not. Both are just now out of employment. They say they will not go back to work until the Kerbs, Wertheim & Schiffer strike is won by the workpeople. . . . During the enforced idleness of my parents the past month—the first time in my life, I believe, that they have been out of work for so long a time, they have both taken, but my father particularly, a very great interest in my school history of the United States. They have had me read it to them in the evenings. . . . The declaration of Thomas Jefferson that "eternal vigilance is the price of liberty," has struck my father with great force. He asks me to explain its application to his own case. He puts the matter in this way: "At the shop, I am not free, because I have to obey the shop rules; so much work for so much pay. If I obey my union implicitity [*sic*] I am not free, because I am its bondman[.] Since each condition is a manifestation of tyranny, how am I to act? Of what avail to my case is vigilance?"[94]

91. *Cigar Makers' Official Journal* 25 (April 1900): 14.
92. See NYM&A, *14th AR*, pp. 126–27.
93. *The People*, April 1, 1900 (10:1), p. 3; *Cigar Makers' Official Journal* 25 (April 1900): 4.
94. *United States Tobacco Journal*, April 14, 1900 (44:12), p. 10.

The *Journal* responded with a diatribe against the union's "odious form of tyranny," excusing shop conditions by reference to "Necessity." Manufacturers as well as union leaders understood the necessity of recognizing the desire of immigrant Bohemian strikers to conform to an "American" way of life and freedom. The only disagreement was whether that "American" way included union dues and loyalties.

Finally, the 1900 cigar makers' strike reveals women strikers in very much the same light as seen in strikes in other industries. During the strike itself, women played a large role, serving as enthusiastic pickets for the strike. This often got them the attention of their erstwhile employers, who attempted to gain injunctions on this basis. Jacob Wertheim, for example, accused four young women, formerly in his employment, of "loitering and walking slowly and continually up and down in front of the factory, jostling against employees coming in and going out, sneering, hooting and laughing at employees, calling them by vile names and urging them to leave our employment, and persuading would-be employees, by means of argument, threat and fear of bodily harm, not to enter our employment, also to take the names of our employees."[95]

Though the ultimate collapse of the strike makes it impossible to judge whether such women would have become stalwart union members for the long run, they appear as enthusiastic as any of their sister garment workers. The gutsy Rosie Golden, who took it on herself to extend the strike to former co-workers in Philadelphia, received in return a position on the Strike Committee.[96] Though women made up approximately half the strikers, one of the first major strike meetings at Bohemian National Hall saw strikers represented by 150 delegates, ten of them women, while another forty to sixty women watched the proceedings. However, none of these women remained in union leadership positions after the strike and the end of the lockout.

All the unions under examination here attempted to broaden their jurisdictional definitions in response to changing industrial conditions at the turn of the century. These alterations often had contradictory effects for women workers within their industries. Women continued to play active roles during strikes, serving as pickets, spearheading fund-raising efforts, and serving on strike and negotiating committees. As unions broadened membership definitions, these women became more likely to receive union benefits, including strike benefits, while carrying on their activities. Male craft unionists in the new, broader unions could use their greater experience to assist female co-workers in enlisting in the long-term project of union membership. At the same time, this very experience held by skilled male members of dominant

---

95. See, for example, the affidavit of Jacob Wertheim before the New York State Supreme Court, cited in *United States Tobacco Journal*, April 28, 1900 (44:14), p. 6.

96. See chapter 1 for more information about Rosie Golden and her strike activities.

crafts within the new amalgamated unions could also work in the opposite direction.

Male craft unionists could become impatient with the slow process of educating ever-changing cohorts of female co-workers in the necessity for steady and "responsible" union membership. The male cutters moved in and out of the International Ladies' Garment Workers' Union, while the mule spinners retained their independent status separate from the United Textile Workers even while ostensibly belonging to the union. Even Samuel Gompers's beloved cigar rollers, while supporting the less-skilled Bohemian workers in the New York strike, must have questioned their union's support of these recent adherents to the union cause.

The long-term process by which gendered definitions of skill and union membership had become encoded into the national unions ensured that there would continue to be problems in the relationships among women and men workers, even within the new amalgamated unions. Male leadership of these unions at the national level stood unchallenged, though women at times participated in running local unions, especially in the industrial periphery. Given the seemingly unchanging and rigid sexual division of labor, the model of coordinating the activities of individual craft unions could at times allow female leadership to surface. Ring spinners, shoe stitchers, cigar mold operators, buttonhole makers—if these occupations organized their own craft unions, those unions would be all female and so would be their leadership. Sue Cobble makes this argument for the case of craft unionism in her study of waitresses, and Eric Arnesen makes a similar argument in favor of segregated unions in the early twentieth century for their ability to promote the voice and leadership of black workers.[97] In many of these situations, though, when these unions "amalgamated" with their male craft union counterparts, those men could use their "superior" knowledge of unionism and their longer relationships with bosses, journalists, and politicians to manipulate strikes to their own purposes.

Would ignoring gendered craft distinctions improve women's situations in strikes and unions? The examples of cross-gender strikes seen here suggest an ambiguous answer to that question. In the strikes taking place in the industrial periphery, women often acted as strike leaders, and men in these situations, perhaps less influenced by decades of distinctions along lines of gendered skill, seem to have had little difficulty following such leaders. The one example that comes closest to being an "industrial" union, that of the Philadelphia textile strike of 1903, finds women obliterated as strikers. At

97. See Dorothy Sue Cobble, "Organizing the Postindustrial Work Force: Lessons from the History of Waitress Unionism," *Industrial and Labor Relations Review* 44 (April 1991): 419–36. Eric Arnesen makes a similar argument about biracial unionism in "Following the Color Line of Labor: Black Workers and the Labor Movement before 1930," *Radical History Review* 55 (Winter 1993): 53–87.

least up to that time, an equitable solution to the quandary of how to provide women with representation in unions had not been found.

In fact, the question of women workers' "participation" in all aspects of the union movement remained crucial. Even while looking askance at what they often deemed to be the "irresponsible" behavior of women, the most stalwart craft unionists could be grateful for the decisions women made to strike alongside men. In a strike situation, a "Joan of Arc" might play a crucial role in inspiring women workers to take action, while a "Salome" might go too far in delivering (male) heads to the masses. The realities of Harriet's or Rosie's lives would still remain inaccessible to most male union-ists. Female and male union members remained united, yet apart.

8 Conclusion

Taking your measure to a T
—"[Notes by LO'R]," in Leonora O'Reilly Papers

The first meeting of what would become the Women's Trade Union League took place on November 14, 1903, at the office of the Boston Civic League. At this gathering were Mary Kenney O'Sullivan, widow of Boston labor journalist Jack O'Sullivan and a good friend of Samuel Gompers; William English Walling, New York settlement house worker; John R. O'Brien, president of the Retail Clerks' International Protective Association; "others interested in the settlement work in Boston"; and a small group of delegates from the annual convention of the American Federation of Labor, which had opened that week in Boston.[1] Over the course of the week, in two subsequent formal meetings and probably countless informal ones, this small group of activists set out the basic outline for the structure and functioning of the league.[2]

Almost twenty years later, one of the league's members said that "the establishment of the National Women's Trade Union League marked an altogether fresh start in the labor history of women" and added:

> The fact of its being a federation of trade unions with women members meant that it gave expression within the labor movement itself to the urgent necessity for the organization of women, and brought home this necessity most impressively to labor men. Trade union women of different trades came together, closely and constantly, as they had rarely done before. This increased their knowledge of one another's problems, and has resulted in practical co-operation among all.[3]

---

1. "Reports of Meetings Held for the Purpose of Organizing the Women's Trade Union League," in National Women's Trade Union League, Records (Library of Congress, 1976), microfilm edition [hereafter cited as NWTUL Records], series 1, Headquarters Records: 1903–50, reel 1, frame 74.

2. Ibid., frames 74–80. For informal meetings, see Mary Kenny O'Sullivan's recollection of her long lunch with William Walling at the Revere House, in "Mary Kenney O'Sullivan Autobiography" (p. 201), Schlesinger Library, Radcliffe College, microfilm edition of Papers of the Women's Trade Union League [hereafter cited as Papers of the WTUL], Collection 8, Smaller Collections, frame 201.

3. "National Women's Trade Union League of America [1903–22]," in NWTUL Records, series 2, reel 17, frame 20.

While this optimistic and hagiographic summary is borne out in the historical record in many ways, the stories of attempts at collaboration among female and male strikers recounted in this book suggest that a certain amount of skepticism might be necessary.

The Women's Trade Union League has come down in women's history to us most popularly as a crucial participant in the 1909–10 strike of New York City shirtwaist strikers. In its best-known versions, this story tells how the city's fur-clad "society ladies," its rabble-rousing socialists, and Lower East Side female Jewish garment workers came together on the picket lines and in the city's jails to discover both their mutual interests and some of the limits to that interest.[4] The Women's Trade Union League itself often pointed to this strike as a germinal event during which the league came into its own as an actor on the stage of the labor movement.

The path by which the Women's Trade Union League came into its own in 1909 had already been established six years earlier, by the end of November 1903. When the league's first constitution was drawn up, those in attendance at the group's second meeting, on November 17, passed two amendments. First, before assisting in any organizing, the league vowed to "communicate" with the appropriate union of the given trade, and second, the league agreed to affiliate with any existing central labor bodies in a given location.[5] In her notes taken during the first meeting of the New York City league, Leonora O'Reilly had scribbled down a continuation of these concerns, such as: "Keep at it until we get the best Trade Unionists believing in us," "Take suggestions given by union delegates and build up from their suggestions," and "Where there is an organization in existance [sic] have first meeting for women called by existing T.U. organization and let League furnish speakers."[6] In other words, both in organizational structure and in the more private thoughts of those setting up such a structure, the Women's Trade Union League promised from its start to follow the direction and guidance of the AFL. Given the personal closeness of early league activists

4. See, for example, Françoise Basch, "The Shirtwaist Strike in History and Myth," in Theresa Serber Malkiel, *The Diary of a Shirtwaist Striker* (Ithaca: ILR Press, 1990), pp. 1–77; Nan Enstad, *Ladies of Labor, Girls of Adventure: Working Women, Popular Culture, and Labor Politics at the Turn of the Twentieth Century* (New York: Columbia University Press, 1999); Annelise Orleck, *Common Sense and a Little Fire: Women and Working-Class Politics in the United States, 1900–1965* (Chapel Hill: North Carolina University Press, 1995); Ann Schofield, "The Uprising of the 20,000: The Making of a Labor Legend," in *A Needle, a Bobbin, a Strike: Women Needleworkers in America*, ed. Joan M. Jensen and Sue Davidson (Philadelphia: Temple University Press, 1984), pp. 167–82; Nancy Schrom Dye, *As Equals and as Sisters: Feminism, the Labor Movement, and the Women's Trade Union League of New York* (Columbia: University of Missouri Press, 1980); Meredith Tax, chapter 8, "The Uprising of the Thirty Thousand," in *The Rising of the Women: Feminist Solidarity and Class Conflict, 1880–1917* (New York: Monthly Review Press, 1980), pp. 205–40.

5. "Reports of Meetings," NWTUL Records, series 1, reel 1, p. 3, frame 76.

6. "[Notes by L O'R]," in Leonora O'Reilly Papers, Schlesinger Library, Radcliffe College, Papers of the WTUL, reel 4, frame 653.

like O'Sullivan to Gompers and other AFL leaders, and given the obvious domination of the labor field by the AFL unions in the first decades of the twentieth century, the choice by league founders to follow the AFL's lead in organizing women workers was an obvious one.

Ultimately, though, this decision limited and hampered the successes of the league. The AFL unions to which the league pledged allegiance had deep-seated gender biases at their very cores and utilized gendered constructions in their operations on a daily basis. Some of the league's members came to realize this. When Gompers's friend Mary O'Sullivan visited the 1912 textile strikers in Lawrence, Massachusetts, she noted: "Nothing was so conducive to organization by the Industrial Workers of the World as the high-handed methods used by the three branches of the American Federation of Labor. These divisions were the Lawrence Central Labor Union, the Boston Women's Trade Union League, and the Textile Workers of America."[7] Not even the Women's Trade Union League could overcome completely the established organizational biases of the AFL.

The cross-gender strikes examined in this book expose many of the roots of these organizational biases. The Knights of Labor might have begun with a broad vision of women's interconnected roles in households and workplaces, but by the time the Order began its descent to oblivion in the late 1880s and 1890s, its tightening grip on the activities of all members constrained women even more than it did men. Faced with the new and energetic unions of the AFL, the male leadership of the Knights abandoned many of the organization's high ideals. All too quickly, the Knights became an organization that was more interested in pumping up its own ties to powerful men than in providing a vehicle for the self-expression and aspirations of working women—or working men.

For the unions that came together in the new American Federation of Labor in 1886, the situation was quite different. Whether these craft unions were brand-new themselves or holdovers from before the depression of the 1870s, their main focus through the 1890s was on binding together their far-flung national memberships. Seeking out definitional boundaries led the AFL unions to depend on a series of trade-specific definitions of skill and economic power that ultimately relied on gender as a key element. By doing this, even those unions that should have been most concerned with organizing women too often drew lines for membership that excluded female co-workers. Neither race nor ethnicity provided reliable means of uniting union members, but those factors could operate as powerful lines of division between members and nonmembers, or between workers and employers. In either case, the racial or ethnic line that proved crucial in one case might operate in exactly the opposite way in another circumstance. If workers in different locations ex-

---

7. O'Sullivan Autobiography, in Papers of the WTUL, Collection 8, Smaller Collections, p. 252, frame 226.

perienced race and ethnicity in different ways, their experience of gender rarely saw dramatic differences.

Comparing strike events in different locations provides more than racial and ethnic variation. Strikes that took place in what I call here the industrial periphery of the nation involved workers rarely assumed—then and now—to be active union members. While we may all know stories of and reasons for the militance of metal miners in the West,[8] historians have rarely acknowledged such workers as the Wisconsin tobacco sorters or the Denver textile-mill operatives seen here. These workers in their "peripheral" situations often begin to demonstrate even more clearly than "core" strikers the influences of gendered thinking on the unions of the time. Usually far from the influence of the national union movement, and often integrally connected to local developments, these strikes bring home the gendered nature of the national unions precisely because of their absence.

It may not be an accident that strikes in the industrial periphery also often highlight strikers' family roles. Both local and national union leaders proved to be capable of manipulating a rhetoric of strikers' families to their advantage. However, strikers themselves often relied on familial and household networks that were very different from union-promulgated images. For both women and men, strike families extended far beyond the solidarity implied in union "brotherhood."

As unions began to attempt to extend solidarity beyond the narrowest craft boundaries, they experimented with a number of structural variations. Ranging from a simple amalgamation of craft unions, through a widening of that form to encompass ethnic or gendered groups, to tentative experiments with organizing all workers in a factory or industry into a single industrial-type union, the hardening assumptions about gender from which AFL leaders operated expose the mixed opportunities involved in all. Because of the strict sexual division of labor, amalgamating occupationally based craft unions often provided the greatest opportunities for women workers to achieve a level of leadership in unions. At the same time, such an amalgamation necessarily had to deal with (or ignore) the craft unionists' gendered sense of skill and "appropriate" manly behavior. Not even the Women's Trade Union League could completely overcome the resulting barricades among potential allies.

In December 1903, Leonora O'Reilly reminded herself that "women are inately [sic] political[,] workingwomen especially," and added: "They won't hurt you to your face, but they do a heap of thinking behind your back, yes

---

8. David Brundage, *The Making of Western Labor Radicalism: Denver's Organized Workers, 1878–1905* (Urbana: University of Illinois Press, 1994); Elizabeth Jameson, *All That Glitters: Class, Conflict, and Community in Cripple Creek* (Urbana: University of Illinois Press, 1998); Melvyn Dubofsky, *We Shall Be All: A History of the Industrial Workers of the World* (Chicago: Quadrangle Books, 1969).

and while your [*sic*] with them they are taking your measure to a T."[9] O'Reilly jotted this down as a reminder to herself of the possible chasm between the experiences of upper-class and working-class women, but I do not think she would mind that I borrow it here to similarly summarize the potential gap between the experiences of working-class women and men at their workplaces and in their unions. When working women "took the measure" of their male counterparts, they could often refer back to experiences on the picket lines, in the union halls, and behind the closed doors of negotiating employers.

On many different levels, male and female co-workers "measured" one another constantly. Across lines of occupation and skill, family roles and union membership, nationality and race, women and men all operated from their common store of societally accepted gender definitions. As Jean-Paul Sartre's concept of seriality reminds us, each individual holds within herself or himself the capacity to draw on the resources or limitations of any of these categories at any moment. The use of cross-gender strikes as the fundamental basis for this book privileges two of these categories of identity over the many other possibilities: gender is privileged because the constant appearance of both male and female strikers brings it to our attention repeatedly, and class is privileged because a strike is fundamentally a moment of crisis in the relationship between workers and their employers, a moment highlighting the distinctions between the two classes. The organization of work and of the workplace clearly reinforces these two categories. But at the same time, other categories can also be reinforced and emerge as crucial during the unfolding of any given strike. Ethnicity, race, religion, age, family status, industry, neighborhood, the relationship of either the individual or the group to the labor movement both locally and nationally—this is only a partial list of the various identities possible at any given time.

The examination of cross-gender strikes provides us with a starting point for understanding many things: how men and women might have gotten along on a daily basis in their workplaces; how both unions and employers attempted to use gender as a means of manipulating workers; how the labor movement might have ended up still operating largely as a "boys' club" after more than one hundred years of existence.

At the end of the strikes recounted here, workers, both male and female, walked away from the picket lines and parades and meetings and returned home to contemplate their experiences. Whether they returned to work the next day or faced unemployment, the strike had taught them important lessons. Some of the lessons dealt with the futility of striking out against those more powerful. Other lessons dealt with the possibilities of action by the downtrodden when they join together. No single strike provided a single

---

9. "[Notes by L O'R]," in O'Reilly Papers, Papers of the WTUL, reel 4, frames 653–54.

lesson; no single lesson was learned by every individual striker. Nonetheless, some common themes appear from the strikes presented here.

The leaders of the American Federation of Labor, nationally but often at the local level as well, felt that they learned from these types of situations that women and other less-skilled groups of workers rarely wielded the workplace power necessary for successful completion of strikes, or ended strikes with the commitment necessary for stable union membership. However, rarely did they learn that women's wages still were not high enough to enable them to afford union dues, and they did not, on the whole, gain insight into the household and family duties of women that kept them away from meetings. Indeed, AFL activists most often learned that the union and even the workplace itself were best left to the select group of men who made up their primary target membership.

Some of the rank-and-file workers who followed these leaders took away similar lessons. Skilled male workers like mule spinners, shoe lasters, garment cutters, and hand cigar-rollers could reach the end of strikes with the same levels of scorn for their female co-workers with which they had begun the strikes. Such workers all too often faced employers' threats of mechanization and de-skilling not with a determination to organize the workers who would operate the new machines and perform the subdivided work, but rather with the grim—and losing—proposition of fighting against workplace reorganization. These workers sought to maintain solidarity first and foremost within the narrowest of Perlman and Taft's "concentric circles," "the craft group—which looks upon the jobs in the craft as its common property."[10]

Other male workers left strikes having learned a wide range of lessons, only some of which led them to dismiss their female co-workers' concerns. Less skilled, and therefore less concerned with enshrining their skill as crucial, they might learn to appreciate the obstinacy and creativity of their female counterparts, on the picket lines or on the production floor. Others might come to appreciate the lessons offered by female strikers like Galveston's Mrs. Ormond, who had spelled out for her community exactly which family tasks stood threatened by overtime work. Certainly the married weavers of New Bedford and elsewhere ended their strike with the same understanding of the workplace achievements and discontents of their spouses with which they had begun.

And female strikers? They learned a new form of freedom as women as they marched publicly in parades for the first time or walked picket lines and taunted scabs. They used their creativity and organizational skills to organize both unions and strike benefit events, and a few of them became union activists and leaders like Cilea Grott and Rose Golden. Having already moved from their homes to the workplace, such women now learned that

10. Selig Perlman and Philip Taft, *History of Labor in the United States*, vol. 4: *Labor Movements, 1896–1932* (1935; reprint, New York: A. M. Kelley, 1966), p. 9.

an even wider world awaited them. These were the women who were now ready for the organized activism offered by the new Women's Trade Union League in the early twentieth century.

But even these women learned other lessons simultaneously. Despite women's strike activism and militance, the male leaders of strikes and unions often preferred to portray them as weak and helpless, the downtrodden victims of evil bosses. For many women, the end of strikes left them contemplating their depleted savings and wondering whether the effort had been worth the isolated moments of empowerment and excitement. Especially after strikes in which the workers had been defeated, women might see little reason—or have little ability—to continue or begin paying union dues. Returning to their pre-strike lives of the same old routines of household work and their jobs, women displayed impeccable logic either in searching out different employment or in seeking to escape paid employment through marriage. Either way, they would prove the dire predictions of union leaders about the "inability" of women to maintain union commitments.

These varied strike lessons learned by men and women, both leaders and the led, ultimately encouraged the AFL's acceptance of arguments that viewed women as unfit for stable union membership. While this book suggests ways in which this view varied from industry to industry and location to location, gendered definitions of "appropriate" union membership ultimately functioned to unite female and male strikers at times, and yet simultaneously kept them apart. Perhaps a better understanding of the historical roots of these gendered definitions will enable today's women and men to do better at working together for changes that will benefit all.

Strike Case Studies and Selected Bibliography

Forty case studies of cross-gender strikes form the core of this book's research base. The strikes are listed in table A1.1 by starting date, location, and industry. That table also notes the chapters of this book in which the strikes are discussed.

My initial idea for this project arose from research I conducted in 1985–86 as an associate editor for the Samuel Gompers Papers. One of my many assignments was to provide a footnote for the 1890 strike of Kearney, New Jersey, thread workers; another was to proofread Grace Pallidino's footnote for the Columbus, Ohio, tailors' strike in the same year.[1] With all my tendencies toward analysis thwarted by the requirements of documentary editing, I decided I wanted to write an article comparing these two strikes and the 1893 strike of hatters in Danbury, Connecticut, examined by Dana Frank.[2] My vision at this point was that this would be an update of Alice Kessler-Harris's 1975 article "Where Are the Organized Women Workers?"[3] I would bring more recent work on gender identities to bear on this project, illustrating how much we could learn about the militance of working women by examining strikes that involved both men and women.

With that in mind, and still caught up in revising my dissertation for publication,[4] I began to look around to see if I could find a few more strikes that involved both women and men. Thanks to support for junior faculty provided by Cornell University's School of Industrial and Labor Relations, I could send a research assistant off to the school's Catherwood Library with the general instruction: look for strikes involving men and women. In just two weeks, he was back, saying that he had found some nine hundred such

1. See *The Samuel Gompers Papers*, ed. Stuart Kaufman et al., vol. 3: *Unrest and Depression, 1891–94* (Urbana: University of Illinois Press, 1989), p. 56 n. 19, and vol. 2: *The Early Years of the American Federation of Labor, 1887–90* (Urbana: University of Illinois Press, 1987), p. 343 n. 7, respectively.

2. Dana Frank, "Hard Times in Hat Town: The Danbury Lockout of 1893–1894," *Essays in History* (1981–1982): 263–88.

3. Alice Kessler-Harris, "Where Are the Organized Women Workers?" *Feminist Studies* 3 (1975): 92–110.

4. *Sons and Daughters of Labor: Class and Clerical Work in Turn-of-the-Century Pittsburgh* (Ithaca: Cornell University Press, 1990).

strikes—and what should he do now? All of a sudden, my project had become considerably larger.

Table A1.1. Forty cross-gender strike cases

Starting date	City/location	Industry	Chapters in this book
January 26, 1887	Worcester Co., Mass.	Boots & shoes	2
March 2, 1892	Chicago, Ill.	Boots & shoes	1, 3
August 18, 1893	Auburn, Me.	Boots & shoes	4
October 12, 1897	Charleston, S.C.	Boots & shoes	4
November 15, 1898	Marlboro, Mass.	Boots & shoes	6, 7
October 17, 1887	San Francisco, Calif.	Clothing	2
February 16, 1889	Omaha, Neb.	Clothing	3, 6
January 30, 1890	New York, N.Y.	Clothing	7
April 14, 1890	Columbus, Ohio	Clothing	3
May 5, 1892	Baltimore, Md.	Clothing	1, 2, 4
October 5, 1892	Boston, Mass.	Clothing	2
February 18, 1896	Baltimore, Md.	Clothing	4, 7
August 2, 1900	New York, N.Y.	Clothing	7
August 27, 1900	New York, N.Y.	Clothing	7
January 21, 1901	Los Angeles, Calif.	Clothing	7
November 23, 1903	San Francisco, Calif.	Clothing	7
July 1, 1887	Cohoes, N.Y.	Textiles	2
December 12, 1890	Newark, N.J.	Textiles	3, 4, 6
May 28, 1893	Overland/Denver, Colo.	Textiles	5, 6
September 19, 1893	Natchez, Miss.	Textiles	2
July 13, 1894	New Orleans, La.	Textiles	5
March 15, 1895	Galveston, Tex.	Textiles	5
August 4, 1897	Atlanta, Ga.	Textiles	4
January 17, 1898	New Bedford, Mass.	Textiles	6, 7
July 3, 1900	Evansville, Ind.	Textiles	5, 6, 7
October 3, 1900	Alamance Co., N.C.	Textiles	6
April 21, 1902	Oregon City, Ore.	Textiles	4, 5, 6
May 20, 1902	Pawtucket, R.I.	Textiles	3, 7
June 18, 1902	Wilkes-Barre, Pa.	Textiles	4, 6
March 30, 1903	Lowell, Mass.	Textiles	1, 4, 7
May 29, 1903	Philadelphia, Pa.	Textiles	6, 7
January 20, 1888	New York, N.Y.	Tobacco	3, 6
January 31, 1888	Davenport, Iowa	Tobacco	3
October 12, 1889	Key West, Fla.	Tobacco	5, 6
May 5, 1890	Petersburg, Va.	Tobacco	4
February 17, 1891	Stoughton, Wisc.	Tobacco	5
June 5, 1895	Detroit, Mich.	Tobacco	3, 6
January 24, 1898	Winston, N.C.	Tobacco	4, 5, 6
March 12, 1900	New York, N.Y.	Tobacco	1, 7
December 28, 1900	Louisville, Ky.	Tobacco	4, 5

Source: Strike case studies

What he had found was the 1894 U.S. Bureau of Labor report on strikes and lockouts. This report, produced under the direction of Carroll D. Wright, listed every strike and lockout found by labor bureau investigators between

1887 and July 1894.[5] Though apparently no manuscript materials exist for the reports, the published tables for volume 10 give considerable detail on each individual strike. No unions or businesses are listed by name, but other details make it possible to track down the individual strikes in other sources. Twenty-two of my strike case studies were first identified through this source.

In selecting these twenty-two strikes for further case-study construction, I initially chose strikes that were the only cross-gender strikes in their states, such as those of tailors in Omaha, Nebraska, or textile workers in Natchez, Mississippi. My hope was that by using this simple method of selection I could gain a wider selection of ethnicities involved in strikes than I could by simply choosing well-known centers of strike activities such as Massachusetts and New York City. I then began an examination of state-level reports by labor statistics bureaus and mediation boards, in order to discover which strikes I might be able to find information about. This in turn helped me weed through the many strikes in Massachusetts and New York—the two most strike-prone states in the late nineteenth century—as well as elsewhere. I also examined the extant American Federation of Labor records for references to strikes in what had now become "my" four industries.[6] Finally, I also added several strikes to my list while spending a sabbatical year in 1993/94 poring over industry journals in the annex of the New York Public Library.

When I selected a strike as one of my case studies, I almost always began research on that strike by consulting at least one local newspaper. From newspaper accounts, I attempted to construct at least a skeletal outline of the events of the strike. While newspapers differed in the quality of their strike coverage from place to place, the reliance of late nineteenth-century journalism on what was often ludicrously detailed reporting (such as verbatim reports of speeches delivered) meant that even when a newspaper's political bias was obvious its coverage of a local strike could provide basic details. When possible, I used more than one paper from the strike location or nearby. (For example, for many Massachusetts strikes the *Boston Globe* provided more detailed coverage than local papers did.)

5. U.S. Bureau of Labor, *Tenth Annual Report: Strikes and Lockouts* (Washington, D.C.: Government Printing Office, 1896). See also Gary L. Bailey, "The Commissioner of Labor's Strikes and Lockouts: A Cautionary Note," *Labor History* 32 (Summer 1991): 423–40. An earlier labor bureau report covers strikes from 1881 to the end of 1886: U.S. Bureau of Labor, *Third Annual Report: Strikes and Lockouts* (Washington, D.C.: Government Printing Office, 1888). Two later volumes cover strikes to 1900 and 1905, respectively, but these merely report strikes by states, making it impossible to identify individual strikes. U.S. Bureau of Labor, *Sixteenth Annual Report: Strikes and Lockouts* (Washington, D.C.: Government Printing Office, 1901), and *Twenty-first Annual Report: Strikes and Lockouts* (Washington, D.C.: Government Printing Office, 1907).

6. *The American Federation of Labor Records: The Samuel Gompers Era,* microfilm edition (Madison: State Historical Society of Wisconsin, 1981), and *The American Federation of Labor and the Unions: National and International Union Records from the Samuel Gompers Era,* microfilm edition (Sanford, N.C.: Microfilming Corporation of America, 1983).

For each case study, I also examined the relevant state reports, as discussed above, as well as AFL records, and searched for references to individual strikes and their participants in the Samuel Gompers Letterbooks.[7] I also went through the AFL's official journal, the *American Federationist*, from its inception in 1894 through 1904, as well as the newspaper of the Knights of Labor, variously titled *Journal of United Labor* (1887–1889) and *Journal of the Knights of Labor* (1889–1891). For Knights of Labor strikes, I also searched the John W. Hayes Papers, though I was rarely successful in finding material there. I also read any historical works on the strike cities in order to cull whatever I could about the general tenor of life for workers in their local settings. Similarly, I read anything I could find on the industries, companies, and unions involved in the strikes.

Toward the end of the process of constructing the case studies, I contacted archives in virtually every case-study location, as well as other possibly relevant collections. Most of these queries about archival materials turned up no additional sources, although I had many extended exchanges with archivists who tried their best to find material for me. What labor archivist Richard Strassberg has called "the black hole of the late nineteenth century" largely proved itself to be such for me as well. All too often I became quite excited upon finding records in an archive for the specific company against which "my" workers had struck, only to discover that the records omitted the exact time of the strike or that they consisted only of uninformative bills and receipts.

The exception to this archival black hole was the case of the Lowell strike of 1903. As one of the most-studied factory locations in the United States, the richness of the Lowell textile mills records allowed me to gain further insight into both that strike and others. I spent a wonderful week divided between Cambridge and Lowell, examining the records at the Baker Library and the many sources available at the Center for Lowell History, as well as strolling along the mill town's canals, which wind between the old brick mill buildings, many now preserved in the Lowell National Historical Park.

Finally, even though I had sworn early on not to turn this project into a statistical one, I have done enough quantitative historical research to realize that small quantitative projects could add yet another dimension to my case studies. These quantitative pieces of research are described in appendix 2.

The information on the forty strikes presented in this book is the result of all my research. About some strikes, such as that in Lowell, I had piles of materials; about others, I still have only the sketchiest newspaper coverage of strike events. For some strikes, the lack of information forced me to abandon using them at all.[8]

---

7. American Federation of Labor Letterpress Copybooks of Samuel Gompers and William Green, 1883–1925, microfilm of originals at Library of Congress.

8. The most painful example of this is the 1902 Danbury Hatters' strike, famous in labor history for the Supreme Court case (*Loewe v. Lawlor*, 208 U.S. 274 [1908]) that arose from it.

Table A1.1 indicates that some strikes provide examples in several different chapters of this book, while others barely appear at all in the text. I can do nothing other than hope that my readers will trust my judgment that some strikes provide the best examples of a number of different points, while others, though not disproving any of my arguments, do not add anything to them either.

Ironically, short, successful strikes left much less information behind for historians to investigate.[9] My forty strikes, then, overstate the failure rate for turn-of-the-century strikes. They also tend to be longer strikes. Long strikes, of course, are ideal for my uses. They not only left much more information but also allowed time and pressure to expose the fracture lines between various groups of workers. Nonetheless, my "sample" of strikes is technically representative of virtually nothing, but that does not mean those strikes cannot reveal many things to us.

I would like to extend special thanks here to three Cornell School of Industrial and Labor Relations undergraduates who began the case studies of particular strikes. Linda Bresson-Allard began research on the 1897 Atlanta strike at the Fulton Mills and the strike of Charleston, South Carolina, shoe workers that same year. Annie Hsu attempted to follow the Marlboro, Massachusetts, shoe strike of 1898, and Rebecca Michaels similarly worked on the New Bedford textile strike of that year. I am extremely grateful to all three of these students for their hard work and perseverance. At the same time, I take full responsibility for the accuracy of the ultimate recounting of these strikes in this book.

The selected bibliography below cites just a few of the most interesting and/or useful sources I used in this study.

SELECTED BIBLIOGRAPHY

Archival Collections

Barondess Papers. Manuscripts and Archives Division. The New York Public Library. Astor, Lenox, and Tilden Foundations, New York, New York.
Boott/Flather Collection. Center for Lowell History. University of Massachusetts at Lowell, Lowell, Massachusetts.

Before *Loewe* and the Anti Boycott League began its legal attacks on the United Hatters, the strike was just one of several small labor skirmishes in Danbury. Accordingly, there is no newspaper coverage of the actual strike itself until the legal actions began almost a year after the company's workers walked off their jobs.

9. In this category, I was quite excited about tracking down the story of a short, successful strike of shoe workers working on a military shoe contract at Chicago's J. E. Tilt Company in 1898. However, all I could find on the strike were the two brief original references from the *Shoe and Leather Reporter*, July 28, 1898 (66:4), p. 200, and August 4, 1898 (66:5), p. 261, and a brief article in the *Chicago Tribune*, July 28, 1898, p. 7, noting the start of the strike.

Fulton Bag & Cotton Mill Collection. Georgia Institute of Technology Library, Atlanta, Georgia.

International Ladies' Garment Workers' Union Records. Kheel Center for Labor-Management Documentation and Archives. Cornell University Library, Ithaca, New York.

Lawrence Manufacturing Company Records. Baker Library. Harvard University Graduate School of Business Administration, Cambridge, Massachusetts.

Pierce Manufacturing Corporation Records. Old Dartmouth Historical Society. New Bedford Whaling Museum, New Bedford, Massachusetts.

Microfilm Collections

The American Federation of Labor and the Unions: National and International Union Records from the Samuel Gompers Era. Sanford, N.C.: Microfilming Corporation of America, 1983.

American Federation of Labor Letterpress Copybooks of Samuel Gompers and William Green, 1883–1925. Microfilm; originals at Library of Congress.

The American Federation of Labor Records: The Samuel Gompers Era. Madison: State Historical Society of Wisconsin, 1981.

American Labor Unions' Constitutions and Proceedings. Ann Arbor: University Microforms, 1980s–.

John William Hayes Papers. Sanford, N.C.: Microfilming Corporation of America, 1975.

National Women's Trade Union League. Records. Library of Congress, 1976.

Pamphlets in American History: Labor. Sanford, N.C.: Microfilming Corporation of America, 1979.

Papers of the Women's Trade Union League. Woodbridge, Conn.: Published for the Schlesinger Library, Radcliffe College by Research Publications, 1981.

Records of the Socialist Labor Party [1877–1907]. State Historical Society of Wisconsin, 1970.

Industry Journals

American Wool and Cotton Reporter, 1887–1903
Shoe and Leather Reporter, 1887–1903
Southern Tobacconist and Manufacturers' Record, 1897–1904
Tobacco (London), 1887–91
Tobacco (New York), 1887–1903
Tobacco Leaf, May 14, 1902–December 30, 1903
The Tradesman, May 1, 1892–December 15, 1903
United States Tobacco Journal, 1897–1903

Labor Union Journals

American Federationist, March 1894–December 1903
Cigar Makers' Official Journal, 1887–1903
Journal of the Knights of Labor, December 19, 1889–December 31, 1891
Journal of United Labor, January 8, 1887–December 17, 1889
The Tailor, October 1887–June 1894
The Union Boot and Shoe Worker, December 1900–February 1904

Government Documents

United States. Bureau of Labor. *Third Annual Report: Strikes and Lockouts*. Washington, D.C.: Government Printing Office, 1888.

United States. Bureau of Labor. *Tenth Annual Report: Strikes and Lockouts*. Washington, D.C.: Government Printing Office, 1896.

United States. Bureau of Labor. *Sixteenth Annual Report: Strikes and Lockouts*. Washington, D.C.: Government Printing Office, 1901.

United States. Bureau of Labor. *Twenty-first Annual Report: Strikes and Lockouts*. Washington, D.C.: Government Printing Office, 1907.

United States. Bureau of Labor. *Index of All Reports Issued by Bureaus of Labor Statistics in the United States, Prior to March 1, 1902*. Washington, D.C.: Government Printing Office, 1902.

1900 Census Projects

As mentioned in appendix 1, I did not intend to carry out any quantitative research for this project, but as I put together the case studies, the lure of the 1900 census became irresistible. I began with two of the smallest strike locations, Oregon City, Oregon, and Wilkes-Barre, Pennsylvania, both of which experienced textile strikes in 1902. For each town, I chose every person listed in the census as a woolen-mill or lace-factory worker, respectively, and then took down information on the households in which they lived. In these two cases, I also made special note of the presence in the textile workers' households both of other textile workers and of paper mill workers or coal miners, respectively.[1]

After completing these first two data sets, I decided to select several other locations for similar data collection. I determined that the strikes would have to have occurred within two years of 1900—or between 1898 and 1902—in order to ensure some level of correspondence between the data collected and the participants in the strikes. While the data from 1900 may not reflect the strike participants exactly, especially those from earlier years, I believe that it gives a good idea of the variations in family structure and ethnic backgrounds of the strikers. My only other rule was that I would not attempt data sets for large urban areas, because it would be far too difficult to gather information on a single company's employees, and too time-consuming to locate every person working in a particular industry. Ultimately, I ended up using the strike locations represented in table A2.1. Because several of the locations were single-industry towns, the data sets quickly became larger than was manageable, even with the veritable horde of graduate students I now had working on the projects.[2] For these, I ended up coding only one-tenth or one-fifth of the individuals in the particular industry in each city.

Finally, the one exception to this description is a small New York City data set. This data set became possible only when I discovered that the New York Public Library's Local History room contained a detailed map of that city's 1900 census enumeration districts. This map allowed me to pinpoint the census reel containing the tenement houses owned by the Harburger &

1. Hye-Young Kang assisted with these first data sets.
2. "Census workers" included Elizabeth Chimienti, Joshua Fowler, Hye-Young Kang, Chang-Kil Lee, and Hyea-Sook Ryoo.

Homan cigar company. I then collected information on all thirty-nine households in the three buildings (a total of 179 residents).

Data tables referred to in the text appear below. All of the tables are based on the data sets I constructed from the 1900 Federal Manuscript Census for the specific locations.

Table A2.1. Quantitative sample sizes

Year	City	State	Industry	Sample?	Data set size
1898	Winston	N.C.	Tobacco	All	N = 739
1898	New Bedford	Mass.	Textiles	1/10	N = 991
1898	Marlboro	Mass.	Boots & shoes	1/5	N = 342
1900	Evansville	Ind.	Textiles	All	N = 575
1900	Alamance County	N.C.	Textiles	1/5	N = 647
1902	Oregon City	Ore.	Textiles	All	N = 163
1902	Wilkes-Barre	Pa.	Textiles	All	N = 405

Table A2.2. Ethnicity of workers in five locations (%)

	Evansville, Ind.	Marlboro, Mass.	New Bedford, Mass.	Oregon City, Ore.	Wilkes-Barre, Pa.
U.S.	33.2	14.5	2.3	53.4	12.6
English	3.0	1.8	26.4	3.1	17.3
French Canadian	NA	41.5	29.8	NA	0.2
German	42.8	0.2	3.0	17.2	18.8
Irish	5.9	34.8	8.1	6.7	37.0
"New" immigrant	0.4	2.2	16.0	4.3	2.5
Southern U.S.	11.8	NA	NA	NA	NA
Welsh	0.5	—	0.1	4.3	4.4
Other	2.4	7.3[a]	20.1[b]	11.0[c]	6.7

NA = not applicable
[a] Includes 4.4% Canadian, not French Canadian.
[b] Includes 13.2% Canadian, not French Canadian.
[c] Includes 2.5% Canadian, not French Canadian.

Table A2.3. Family size and gender, cotton mill workers of Alamance County, North Carolina

Number of members in family	Gender of cotton mill workers (%)		
	Female	Male	Total
1	1.1	7.2	4.7
2	12.4	10.2	11.1
3	21.7	15.6	18.0
4	25.8	20.1	22.4
5	21.5	17.9	19.4
6	10.2	15.6	13.4
7	3.2	6.9	5.4
8	1.8	4.9	3.6
9+	2.4	1.6	1.9
Total	100.1	100	99.9

N = 647 sample

Table A2.4. Percentage of workers by age and sex, for six locations (%)

Location	Under 15 years		15–19 years		20–29 years		30–39 years		40–49 years		Over 50 years	
	Female	Male	Female	Male	Female	Male	Female	Male	Female	Male	Female	Male
Alamance Co, N.C., textile workers (N = 647 sample)	23.4	13.8	39.7	25.1	25.9	33.8	6.9	15.5	2.0	6.8	1.6	4.8
Evansville, Ind., textile workers (N = 575)	4.0	16.9	37.3	26.6	41.7	28.2	11.1	12.9	3.5	6.5	1.1	8.1
Marlboro, Mass., shoe workers (N = 342 sample)	—	—	27.5	17.2	55.0	33.4	13.8	20.3	1.8	18.0	0.9	11.2
New Bedford, Mass., textile workers (N = 991 sample)	5.8	4.3	33.3	20.7	34.3	31.7	18.2	21.7	6.1	12.3	2.3	9.1
Oregon City, Ore., textile workers (N = 163)	1.8	1.9	30.4	23.4	48.2	32.7	17.9	15.0	1.8	10.3	0.0	15.9
Winston-Salem, N.C., African American tobacco workers (N = 739)	10.5	10.4	20.1	19.8	39.8	35.5	22.3	19.8	4.5	7.3	2.5	6.3

Table A2.5. Presence of other selected workers in households of selected workers, for six locations

Presence of other selected workers in household	Alamance Co, N.C., textile workers			Evansville, Ind., textile workers			Marlboro, Mass., shoe workers			New Bedford, Mass., textile workers			Oregon City, Ore., textile workers			Winston Salem, N.C., African American tobacco workers		
	Female	Male	Total	Female	Male	Total	Female	Male	Total	Female	Male	Total	Female	Male	Total	Female	Male	Total
No	4.0	23.6	16.1	36.4	42.0	37.7	16.5	40.8	33.0	13.3	24.2	19.5	46.4	50.5	49.1	20.4	28.7	25.2
Yes	96.0	76.4	83.9	63.6	58.0	62.3	83.5	59.2	67.8	86.7	75.8	80.5	53.6	49.5	50.9	79.6	71.3	74.8
Total	100.0	100.0	100.0	100.0	100.0	100.0	100.0	100.0	100.0	100.0	100.0	100.0	100.0	100.0	100.0	100.0	100.0	100.0

Table A2.6. Relationship of other selected workers in household to selected worker

Relationship of other selected workers in household	Alamance Co., N.C., textile workers (N = 647 sample)	Evansville, Ind., textile workers (N = 575)	Marlboro, Mass., shoe workers (N = 342)	New Bedford, Mass., textile workers (N = 991 sample)	Oregon City, Ore., textile workers (N = 163)	Winston - Salem, N.C., African American tobacco workers (N = 553)
Siblings	54.2	65.7	55.4	44.7	48.2	30.0
Spouse	7.1	2.3	3.1	15.4	4.8	19.9
Parent	21.3	2.0	25.3	24.4	14.5	19.3
Children	7.8	1.4	12.2	11.5	12.0	13.0
Extended family	11.7	0.6	0.4	0.4	3.6	6.0
Unrelated	14.8	29.1	1.8	24.4	21.7	28.6
Total (may add up to >100)	116.9	101.1	98.2	120.8	104.8	116.8

Table A2.7. Marital status and age of men and women among New Bedford textile workers and Marlboro shoe workers (%)

	Marital status	New Bedford textile workers		Marlboro shoe workers	
		Female	Male	Female	Male
	Married	25.4	52.7	11.0	55.4
	Single	69.2	45.5	86.2	43.8
	Widowed	5.1	1.6	2.8	0.9
Women	Age	Marital status		Marital status	
		Married	Single	Married	Single
	15–19	3.5	96.5	0.0	100.0
	20–24	17.4	81.4	8.3	91.7
	25–29	48.3	48.3	16.7	83.3
	30–34	50.0	43.5	0.0	91.7
	35–39	62.5	21.9	66.7	0.0
	40–49	50.0	30.8	50.0	0.0
Men	Age	Marital status		Marital status	
		Married	Single	Married	Single
	15–19	0.9	99.1	5.0	95.0
	20–24	26.1	73.9	15.6	84.4
	25–29	66.7	33.3	50.0	50.0
	30–34	89.7	8.6	60.0	40.0
	35–39	84.1	15.9	77.3	13.6
	40–49	92.7	5.8	97.6	2.4

Table A2.8. Presence of other selected types of workers in households of selected worker, for two locations

Other workers in household	Oregon City, Ore., textile workers (%) (N = 163)		
	Female	Male	All
Paper mill workers in household	16.1	20.6	19.0
No paper mill workers in household	83.9	79.4	81.0
	Wilkes-Barre, Pa., lace workers (%) (N = 405)		
	Female	Male	All
Miners in household	41.0	17.9	32.1
No miners in household	59.0	82.1	67.9

Index